Patterns of Decision Making in State Legislatures

Eric M. Uslaner
Ronald E. Weber

The Praeger Special Studies program—utilizing the most modern and efficient book production techniques and a selective worldwide distribution network—makes available to the academic, government, and business communities significant, timely research in U.S. and international economic, social, and political development.

Patterns of Decision Making in State Legislatures

PRAEGER SPECIAL STUDIES IN U.S. ECONOMIC, SOCIAL, AND POLITICAL ISSUES

Praeger Publishers   New York   London

Library of Congress Cataloging in Publication Data

Uslaner, Eric M
    Patterns of decision making in State legislatures.

    (Praeger special studies in U. S. economic, social, and political issues)
    Bibliography: p.
    Includes index.
    1.   Legislative bodies—United States—States.
2. Legislators—United States—States. I.   Weber, Ronald E., 1938-   joint author.   II.   Title.
JK2495.U84   1977   328'.30973   76-12884
ISBN 0-275-23230-1

PRAEGER PUBLISHERS
200 Park Avenue, New York, N.Y. 10017, U.S.A.

Published in the United States of America in 1977
by Praeger Publishers, Inc.

789   038   987654321

Printed in the United States of America

This book is the first report in published form of the results of a three-part survey of elites involved in the policy-making and political processes in the American states. The other parts of the survey involve county party chairmen and state bureaucrats and are discussed in Chapters 1 and 6. Ultimately our goal is to develop a linkage model of the process of policy formation in the American states, an ambitious task. But in the present study our intention is much more modest. We are presenting a first report of findings of our survey of legislators in the 50 states, only the second such study ever conducted. In the chapters that follow, we are dealing with legislators as respondents to a survey, but we attempt to also keep in mind the institutional context in which they serve. Future writing projects call for aggregating the data to the state level for more detailed analyses. The present book is based upon some of the main themes we had in mind when we designed the survey, together with James Thurber of American University. We have not made any attempt to cover all of the important topics in state politics. This would be clearly impossible—but even if it were not, such an approach would obscure the underlying focal points of at least this first investigation. Here we test hypotheses that have interested us for quite some time and provided the basis for many of the items on our questionnaire.

Portions of this book have made the rounds before. An earlier version of Chapter 2 (with some overlap with Chapter 4) was presented at the 1975 Annual Meeting of the Midwest Political Science Association. We presented a version of Chapter 5 at the 1976 Annual Meeting of the American Political Science Association and Chapter 4 at the 1976 Annual Meeting of the Southern Political Science Association.

Our greatest debts are to our collaborator in preparing the survey, James Thurber, and to our predecessor, Wayne L. Francis, who conducted the first 50-state survey of American state legislators, worked with us in the preparation of our questionnaire, and was consistently helpful in making "judgment calls" throughout the preparation of this manuscript. We have also benefited from the comments of panelists and members of the audience at the various professional meetings and those of our colleagues which helped us improve the manuscript. Listed alphabetically, they are: Aage R. Clausen, Malcolm Jewell, Wendell Lawther, Arthur Levy, Michael Mezey, Susan Gluck Mezey, Mavis Mann Reeves, David Rohde, Alan Rosenthal, and Donna Shalala. None of these people is responsible for what we have written, of course. As for our own responsibility, we are reasonably confident that we have reached agreement between ourselves on most aspects of the research strategy—until such time as further criticism is received.

The survey and the writing were both conducted without outside financial assistance, although such funding would have indeed been desirable. Thus, we are particularly grateful for the institutional support we have received. This book could not have been written without the support of the Office of Research and Advanced Studies, Indiana University, and the Department of Political Science, University of Florida. These institutions provided assistance during the data-gathering and analysis stage of the preparation of the book. The General Research Board of the University of Maryland—College Park and the Sabbatical Leaves Fund of Indiana University were generous in their support during the period in which the manuscript was completed. We also wish to thank Leonard J. Clark, Kenneth M. Hays, and David J. Webber for their assistance with the data analysis for this book and the staff of the Political Science Laboratory and Data Archive at Indiana University for its help with the execution of the legislator survey. Computations for this book were performed at the Indiana University Wrubel Computing Center with support from the Research Computing Fund of Indiana University.

A final word about style is in order. Throughout the book, we refer to the single legislator by masculine pronouns. We do not want this to be construed as in any way being sexist, but simply as a short-hand device to maintain consistent style. While the choice of gender may appear unfortunate, it is nevertheless the case that the overwhelming majority of state legislators are males (white males, to be sure). As representation becomes more equal, perhaps we can reach a point at which "she" and "her" can be consistently used without belying the actual membership of state legislatures.

CONTENTS

Page

PREFACE   v

LIST OF TABLES   x

LIST OF ACRONYMS   xviii

Chapter

1   THE STUDY OF STATE LEGISLATURES   1

        Introduction   1
        The State Legislator Sample   4
        Theoretical Perspectives   7
        Measurement of State Legislator Orientations   11
        Analysis of the Data   16
        Plan of the Study   19

2   DECISION-MAKING SOURCES WITHIN STATE LEGIS-
    LATURES: PARTIES AND CUES   21

        Introduction   21
        Cues in Congress and State Legislatures   24
        Variable Measurement and Hypotheses   27
        The Sources of Legislators' Cues   33
        Arenas of Power in State Legislatures   41
        Sources of Variation in Partisan Cues   46
        Partisan Cues, Party Support, and the District   51
        Friends and Neighbors in the Legislature   64
        Decision Loci and Orientations toward the Parties   69

3   DECISION-MAKING SOURCES WITHIN STATE LEGIS-
    LATURES: THE COMMITTEE PERSPECTIVE   74

        Introduction   74
        Variations in Committee Systems: Comparisons
            across Time and Space   77
        Hypotheses and Operationalizations   82

Chapter   Page

    Sources of Cues and Decisions and Committee
        Orientations   85
    Determinants of Committee Power   92
    Parties and Committees in State Legislatures   98
    Conclusion   103

4   PATTERNS OF GUBERNATORIAL POWER AND
    INFLUENCE IN THE STATES   106

    Introduction   106
    Operationalization of the Variables   112
    Legislative Cue Seeking, Perception of Decision
        Loci, and Orientations toward the Executive   113
    Cues, Decision Loci, and the Legislator-Governor
        Party-Match   118
    Gubernatorial Activity on Policy Areas in the
        States   128

5   LEGISLATIVE PROFESSIONALISM AND LEGISLATIVE
    REFORM: A RECONSIDERATION   136

    Introduction   136
    Proposals for Legislative Reform   139
    Measurement of Variables   147
    Hypotheses   149
    Legislative Professionalism and Policy Liberalism   150
    The Professionalism-Policy Linkage and Party
        Competition   169
    The Professionalism-Policy Linkage and District
        Typicality   174
    Conclusion   177

6   CONCLUSIONS AND DIRECTIONS FOR FUTURE
    RESEARCH   179

    Where We Have Gone   179
    Summary of Findings   181
    The Research Agenda   185

APPENDIX: STATE LEGISLATOR OPINION STUDY   189

REFERENCES   195

Chapter	Page
INDEX	207
ABOUT THE AUTHORS	211

LIST OF TABLES

Table		Page
1.1	Sample Characteristics of States, 1973-74	6
1.2	Distributions of Responses to State Legislator Orientation Items Included in Survey	12
1.3	Factor Analysis of Four Political Party System Items	13
1.4	Factor Analysis of Nine Legislative System Items	14
1.5	Factor Analysis of Three Role-in-Policy-Making Items	16
1.6	Distribution of State Legislator Orientation Scale Scores	17
2.1	Sources of Cues Attributed by State Legislators	34
2.2	Comparison of State Legislator Responses on Cue Taking with Kingdon's Sample of Congressmen	36
2.3	Decision Loci Attributed by State Legislators	42
2.4	Decision Locus by Cues from Legislative Party Leaders	44
2.5	Source of Cues by GPO Scale, Party Cue Givers Compared with Others	46
2.6	Source of Cues by LPO Scale, Party Cue Givers Compared with Others	47
2.7	Source of Cues by GPO Scale, Party Leaders Compared with Others	48
2.8	Source of Cues by LPO Scale, Party Leaders Compared with Others	48
2.9	Number of Party Cues Taken by GPO Scale	49
2.10	Number of Party Cues Taken by LPO Scale	49

2.11   Rank Order of Cue Taking from Party Leaders
        in Legislature by GPO Scale   50

2.12   Rank Order of Cue Taking from Party Leaders
        in Legislature by LPO Scale   51

2.13   All Party Cue Givers as Source of Cues by GPO
        Scale, Controlling for District Competitiveness   52

2.14   All Party Cue Givers as Source of Cues by LPO
        Scale, Controlling for District Competitiveness   53

2.15   All Party Cue Givers as Source of Cues by GPO
        Scale, Controlling for District Typicality   54

2.16   All Party Cue Givers as Source of Cues by LPO
        Scale, Controlling for District Typicality   55

2.17   Party Leaders in Legislature as Source of Cues
        by GPO Scale, Controlling for District Competitiveness   56

2.18   Party Leaders in Legislature as Source of Cues
        by LPO Scale, Controlling for District Competitiveness   57

2.19   Party Leaders in Legislature as Source of Cues
        by GPO Scale, Controlling for District Typicality   58

2.20   Party Leaders in Legislature as Source of Cues
        by LPO Scale, Controlling for District Typicality   59

2.21   Number of Party Cues Taken by GPO Scale,
        Controlling for District Competitiveness   60

2.22   Number of Party Cues Taken by LPO Scale,
        Controlling for District Competitiveness   60

2.23   Number of Party Cues Taken by GPO Scale,
        Controlling for District Typicality   61

2.24   Number of Party Cues Taken by LPO Scale,
        Controlling for District Typicality   62

2.25   Rank Order of Cue Taking from Party Leaders in
        Legislature by GPO Scale, Controlling for District
        Competitiveness   62

2.26   Rank Order of Cue Taking from Party Leaders in
        Legislature by LPO Scale, Controlling for
        District Competitiveness   63

2.27   Rank Order of Cue Taking from Party Leaders in
        Legislature by GPO Scale, Controlling for
        District Typicality   63

2.28   Rank Order of Cue Taking from Party Leaders in
        Legislature by LPO Scale, Controlling for
        District Typicality   64

2.29   Cue Sources from Legislators of Own Party
        from Same or Adjacent District by GPO Scale   65

2.30   Cue Sources from Legislators of Own Party
        from Same or Adjacent District by LPO Scale   66

2.31   Cue Sources from Personal Friends and Legislators
        from Same or Neighboring Districts by GPO Scale   66

2.32   Cue Sources from Personal Friends and Legislators
        from Same or Neighboring Districts by LPO Scale   67

2.33   Cues from Personal Friends by GPO Scale   68

2.34   Cues from Personal Friends by LPO Scale   69

2.35   Source of Decision Locus by GPO Scale   70

2.36   Source of Decision Locus by LPO Scale   71

2.37   Source of Decision Locus by GPO Scale,
        Controlling for District Competitiveness   71

2.38   Source of Decision Locus by LPO Scale,
        Controlling for District Competitiveness   72

2.39   Source of Decision Locus by GPO Scale,
        Controlling for District Typicality   72

2.40   Source of Decision Locus by LPO Scale,
        Controlling for District Typicality   73

3.1   Decision Locus by Cues from Committee Leaders   85

3.2	Source of Cues by LSO Scale	86
3.3	Rank Order of Cue Taking from Committee Leaders in Legislature by LSO Scale	87
3.4	Committee Primary Cue Givers by LSO Scale: By Competitiveness of District	88
3.5	Rank Order of Committee Leader Cues by LSO Scale: By Competitiveness of District	89
3.6	Committee Primary Cue Givers by LSO Scale: By Typicality of District	90
3.7	Rank Order of Committee Leader Cues by LSO Scale: By Typicality of District	90
3.8	Source of Primary Cues by District Competitiveness	91
3.9	Source of Primary Cues by District Typicality	91
3.10	Source of Decision Locus by LSO Scale	92
3.11	Source of Decision Locus by LSO Scale, Controlling for District Competitiveness	93
3.12	Source of Decision Locus by LSO Scale, Controlling for District Typicality	94
3.13	Source of Decision Locus by District Competitiveness	95
3.14	Source of Decision Locus by District Typicality	96
3.15	Legislator's Position on the LSO Scale by the GPO Scale	98
3.16	Legislator's Position on the LSO Scale by the LPO Scale	99
3.17	Source of Cues by GPO Scale	100
3.18	Source of Cues by LPO Scale	100
3.19	Source of Decision Locus by GPO Scale	101

3.20   Source of Decision Locus by LPO Scale   102

3.21   Rank Order of Cue Taking from Committee
        Leaders in Legislature by Rank Order of Cue
        Taking from Party Leaders in Legislature   104

4.1   Source of Cues by Perception of Decision Locus   114

4.2   Source of Cues by GO Scale   115

4.3   Rank Order of Cue Taking from Executive
        Branch by GO Scale   116

4.4   Perception of Decision Locus by GO Scale   117

4.5   Source of Cues by Governor-Legislator
        Party-Match   118

4.6   Perception of Decision Locus by Governor-
        Legislator Party-Match   119

4.7   Sources of Cues by GO Scale: Members of
        Governor's Party   120

4.8   Sources of Cues by GO Scale: Members of
        Opposition Party   121

4.9   Rank Order of Cue Taking from Executive
        Branch by GO Scale: Members of Governor's Party   122

4.10   Rank Order of Cue Taking from Executive
        Branch by GO Scale: Members of Opposition Party   123

4.11   Perceptions of Decision Locus by GO Scale:
        Members of Governor's Party   124

4.12   Perceptions of Decision Locus by GO Scale:
        Members of Opposition Party   125

4.13   Source of Cues by Perception of Decision
        Locus: Members of Governor's Party   126

4.14   Source of Cues by Perception of Decision Locus:
        Members of Opposition Party   127

4.15   Source of Rank-Ordered Cues by Perception of
        Decision Locus: Summary Measures for Full
        Sample and Subgroups   128

4.16   Distribution of Issue Mentions by Policy Area:
        1963 and 1973-74   131

4.17   Distribution of Gubernatorial Activity by
        Policy Area: 1963 and 1973-74   132

5.1   Legislators' Position on the Capital-Punishment
        Issue by the FTLO Scale   152

5.2   Legislators' Position on the Capital-Punishment
        Issue by the LSO Scale   153

5.3   Legislators' Position on the Abortion Issue
        by the FTLO Scale   154

5.4   Legislators' Position on the Abortion Issue
        by the LSO Scale   155

5.5   Legislators' Position on the Antipollution-
        Device Issue by the FTLO Scale   156

5.6   Legislators' Position on the Antipollution-
        Device Issue by the LSO Scale   156

5.7   Legislators' Position on the Gun-Permit
        Issue by the FTLO Scale   157

5.8   Legislators' Position on the Gun-Permit
        Issue by the LSO Scale   157

5.9   Legislators' Position on the Teacher-
        Unionization Issue by the FTLO Scale   158

5.10   Legislators' Position on the Teacher-
        Unionization Issue by the LSO Scale   158

5.11   Legislators' Position on the Teachers' Strike
        Issue by the FTLO Scale   159

5.12   Legislators' Position on the Teachers' Strike
        Issue by the LSO Scale   159

5.13   Legislators' Position on the Policemen- and
       Firemen-Unionization Issue by the FTLO Scale   160

5.14   Legislators' Position on the Policemen- and
       Firemen-Unionization Issue by the LSO Scale   161

5.15   Legislators' Position on Policemen- and
       Firemen-Strike Issue by the FTLO Scale   162

5.16   Legislators' Position on the Policemen- and
       Firemen-Strike Issue by the LSO Scale   162

5.17   Legislators' Position on the Marijuana-
       Legalization Issue by the FTLO Scale   163

5.18   Legislators' Position on the Marijuana-
       Legalization Issue by the LSO Scale   163

5.19   Legislators' Position on the Breath-Test
       Issue by the FTLO Scale   164

5.20   Legislators' Position on the Breath-Test
       Issue by the LSO Scale   164

5.21   Legislators' Position on the No-Fault
       Insurance Issue by the FTLO Scale   165

5.22   Legislators' Position on the No-Fault
       Insurance Issue by the LSO Scale   165

5.23   Legislators' Position on the School-Aid
       Issue by the FTLO Scale   166

5.24   Legislators' Position on the School-Aid
       Issue by the LSO Scale   167

5.25   Legislators' Position on the Birth-Control
       Information Issue by the FTLO Scale   168

5.26   Legislators' Position on the Birth-Control
       Information Issue by the LSO Scale   169

5.27   Summary Table of Measures of Association
       between Professionalism Scale and Policy-
       Support Variables   170

5.28   Legislators' Policy Positions with the FTLO
Scale by Perceived Competitiveness of the
Legislative District   171

5.29   Legislators' Policy Positions with the LSO
Scale by Perceived Competitiveness of the
Legislative District   172

5.30   Legislators' Policy Positions with the FTLO
Scale by Typicality of the Legislative District   175

5.31   Legislators' Policy Positions with the LSO
Scale by Typicality of the Legislative District   176

LIST OF ACRONYMS

CO	Committee Orientation
FAIIR	Functional, Accountable, Informed, Independent, Representative
FTLO	Full-Time-Legislator Orientation
GO	Gubernatorial Orientation
GPO	General Party Orientation
LEO	Legislative-Expertise Orientation
LPO	Legislative Party Orientation
LSO	Legislator Staff Orientation
PRE	Proportionate Reduction in Error

Patterns of
Decision Making in
State Legislatures

1

THE STUDY OF
STATE LEGISLATURES

INTRODUCTION

The state legislature is once again emerging as a major area
of research among students of American politics. As the subfield of
comparative state politics has grown over the past two decades, there
has also been a surge of interest in the comparative study of legislative institutions. In the American context, however, the study of state
legislative institutions has generally not been as fully comparative as
has been the research on state policy outputs and outcomes. Except
for the report of the Committee on American Legislatures of the
American Political Science Association (Zeller 1954), the early studies of state legislatures, like every aspect of state politics, were primarily concerned with the chambers in a single state.

Major breakthroughs in the comparative study of American state
legislative institutions came in the late 1940s and 1950s with the work
of V. O. Key, Jr. (1949; 1956) and Duane Lockard (1959). While the
focus in each of these studies was often upon particular states, an attempt was made to compare states within regions (Key 1949; Lockard
1959) or selectively examine legislative institutional characteristics
across several states (Key 1956). While this initial comparative work
was under way, a plethora of studies of individual state legislatures
were executed drawing upon intellectual stimulation from the Committee on Political Behavior of the Social Science Research Council (see
Garceau 1966) and financial support from the Carnegie Foundation
and the Citizenship Clearing House.

Employing newly available quantitative methods of research,
party voting in state legislatures became the object of much study
(see Jewell 1969; pp. 106-21). Some of this research on party voting

in state legislatures has become comparative, most notably the work of Jewell (1955), Keefe (1956), Derge (1958), LeBlanc (1969), Chaffey (1970), Broach (1972), and LeLoup (1976a). With the new emphasis upon studying the roll-call behavior of state legislators also came methodological criticisms (Crane 1960; Greenstein and Jackson 1963). At the same time that the study of roll-call voting in the states was being criticized, the emphasis in the study of state politics began to shift noticeably and quite rapidly. Comparative roll-call data were difficult to obtain, even putting aside the direct question of comparability of voting alignments across several states. Even single-state studies were limited in what they could reveal. Here the question was also one of data availability as much as anything else. Only Charles S. Hyneman had compiled readily accessible roll-call data across time for a particular state—Indiana—and other scholars' attempts to replicate his painstaking work were frustrated by the difficulties of reconstructing the data from sources that were at best difficult to read and at worst incomplete or even misleading.

There was, however, another development that shifted the bulk of the research in the area of state politics—the "discovery" of public policy as a field of inquiry across the states. The first comprehensive analysis was performed by Dawson and Robinson (1963) for the 46 contiguous states with partisan legislatures (Nebraska is still non-partisan—and unicameral—whereas Minnesota has recently instituted partisan elections for the two houses of its legislature). The literature that has emerged from this new mode of analysis is summarized in Hofferbert (1972) and Jones (1973) and has centered around the question of whether political or socioeconomic factors best "explain" aggregate policy formation in the American states. The general consensus has been that economics, not politics, is the primary determinant of policy formation in the states, although the evidence cannot be said to be conclusive. Some of the most recent studies, employing time-series analysis of aggregate policy outcomes, reinforce this bias in favor of "economic determinism" (Gray 1976; Winters 1976). Indeed, some observers have gone so far as to concentrate on the budgetary process as the major component of policy making in the states, thus further removing policy from politics. Aggregate analyses of gross measures of policy, such as expenditures, do not, we maintain, tell us much about the policy-making process in the states. Hence, they cannot be satisfactory explanations of anything other than trends.

While we believe that the most fruitful way of examining state politics—or any other aspect of politics—is over time, we do take exception to much of the work in aggregate policy analysis that has dominated the literature in the past decade and a half. Our objections are twofold: first, we believe that the question of politics versus econom-

ics is bogus, based at least in part upon a misreading of the pioneer-
ing work of Key and Lockard (see Uslaner forthcoming) and inadequate
theorizing about the proper role of political factors in the policy-making process (Uslaner and Weber 1973, 1975a); and second, the longitudinal models selected for analysis, by virtue of the pattern of covariation between similar economic trends between expenditure levels
and "economic" determinants of such policy measures, cannot sort
out the actual impact of "political" versus "economic" causes of policy formation (see Peroff and Uslaner 1976).

    We are concerned with the political determinants of policy mak-
ing and therefore believe that patterns of interaction of such political
actors as state legislators are clearly important, if not decisive, in
understanding the state policy-making process. Yet we know very
little about the men and women who serve in the legislatures of the
50 states. While it is possible to obtain some demographic data on
the membership from published sources, we still need to know what
the values of these state legislators are and how those values affect
behavior in order to consider the political factors in any policy-making process. To get such information, we have only one research
strategy available: interviewing the members of these chambers, as
was done in the studies of Wahlke et al. (1962); Francis (1967); and
Patterson, Hedlund, and Boynton (1975).

    We are not alone either in criticizing the comparative policy
research or in attempting to get information directly from the legislators themselves. There has been a resurgence of interest in the
internal politics of the state legislature, including extensive use of
the techniques of participant-observation and interviewing (see Rosenthal 1974a; Hedlund and Hamm 1976; Wissel, O'Connor, and King
1976). These studies are working to restore the concern for politics
as a process that was seemingly lost in the aggregate policy analyses.
With a single exception, however, they have done so at a price. That
price has been a comprehensive comparative focus across the 50
states, their institutions, and time.

    The single exception was the study by Wayne Francis (1967)
based upon a survey of legislators in all 50 states. We shall discuss
the Francis work in detail below, but we should note at the outset that
it forms the basis for much of our own research design. In particular,
our study is based upon a survey of legislators in all 50 states. Since
much of our design was based directly upon the work of Francis (ad-
justing for some changes in the most salient factors of American
state politics as well as our own theoretical concerns), we have the
basis for comparisons over time as well. Even though we have a
cross-sectional study, the availability of the Francis design, aided
by very helpful cooperation from Francis himself, provides us with
a unique longitudinal data base, which will be briefly examined in

Chapter 4. The primary limitation of the other studies has been a re-
striction to a single state or set of states, with no direct method of
establishing representatives for comparative purposes. We are not
faced with this problem since our survey is based upon all 50 states
and both houses of the 49 states with bicameral legislatures. We turn
now to a discussion of the survey, our sampling techniques, and the
responses to our survey.

THE STATE LEGISLATOR SAMPLE

The sample for this book consists of 1,256 legislators from the
50 American states. A stratified random sample of legislators was
drawn for each state using an address list of legislators published by
the Council of State Governments (1973). The sample was stratified
by state and legislative chamber to ensure that enough responses were
obtained to permit intrastate and intrachamber analyses, as well as
analyses of the full sample. Each state sample was also augmented
to include legislators with important formal positions in the chamber
(president pro tem of senate, speaker of the house, majority and minority leaders, and so on) if they were not already included in the
random sample. Altogether a total of 3,316 legislators was selected
for the sample. Thus, the overall response rate was 37.9 percent.
    The data were collected by means of a six-page mail question-
naire (see Appendix) during the latter half of 1974. In all but three
of the states the legislators surveyed were those who were serving
in the 1973-74 biennium, and their responses reflect their experiences from the legislative sessions held during that two-year period.
In Kentucky, New Jersey, and Virginia the legislators surveyed were
serving in the first half of the 1974-75 biennium used in those states,
and their responses were based upon their experiences from only one
session of their legislatures. The questionnaire was administered
in three waves, with the first and second waves employing bulk-rate
mailing and the third wave using first-class mailing.
    The total of 1,256 usable questionnaire responses had 44.7 per-
cent coming from senators and 55.3 percent from house members.
These percentages compare with an actual distribution in the 1973-
74 biennium of 26.2 percent serving in state senates and 73.8 percent
serving in lower houses. The larger percentage of senators in the
sample than in the population occurred because the sample was stratified to achieve approximately equally sized subsamples for each
chamber.
    Democrats compose 52.5 percent of the sample, with Republi-
cans forming 46.2 percent and Independents 1.4 percent (all of the
Independents came from Nebraska where the legislators compete in

elections devoid of party labels). In the actual total population of state
legislators serving in the 1973-74 biennium, the distribution of members by party was as follows: Democrats 59.2 percent; Republicans
39.8 percent; and Independents 1.0 percent. This comparison clearly
demonstrates that from the total sample Republicans responded at a
higher rate than Democrats, yielding a sample that overrepresents
Republicans.

Data are provided in Table 1.1 by state to permit the evaluation
of the sample on the basis of three criteria: (1) the absolute number
of returns; (2) the number of returns in relation to the number of legislators elected to the legislature; and (3) the party affiliation of the
respondents. According to column two of the table, the lowest number
of respondents came from Alabama (12), while the largest number
came from Montana (41). Based upon the absolute-number-of-returns
criterion, the results should be the least reliable for Alabama, Alaska,
California, Massachusetts, Michigan, Nebraska, and Texas.

Column three of Table 1.1 presents the information needed to
employ the second criterion suggested above. On a percentage basis,
our sample represents as few as 5 percent of the legislators in Massachusetts and as many as 37 percent of the members in Hawaii. Overall the 1,256 legislators in our sample represent 17 percent of all
state legislators serving in the 1973-74 biennium. The use of the second criterion suggests that results will be the least reliable for Alabama, Illinois, Massachusetts, Michigan, New Hampshire, and Texas.

The last three columns of Table 1.1 list by state the data needed
to evaluate the sample in accordance with the party-affiliation criterion. In most of the states the proportion of questionnaire returns
coming from Democrats (column five) is less than the proportion of
Democrats serving in the legislature (column four). Column six reports the difference in percentage points between the two columns.
Democrats are underrepresented in 35 states, while Republicans are
underrepresented in only 10 states (both parties are appropriately
represented in four states). Column six also indicates that the degree
of Democratic underrepresentation was on the average much greater
than the degree of Republican underrepresentation.

Because the original sample of 1,256 legislator respondents
overrepresented one political party (the Republicans) vis-à-vis the
other party (the Democrats), we decided that the sample would need
to be weighted to overcome this problem. In addition, our examination of Table 1.1 indicated that the variation in the raw number of
responses by state was fairly large (a range from 12 to 41), and that
this problem probably deserved attention in any weighting scheme.
Hence, we developed a set of weights for the respondents from each
state which served to weight each state's group of legislators in relation to its true percentage in the total population of all state legisla-

TABLE 1.1

Sample Characteristics of States, 1973-74

	All Legislators			Percent Democrat		
	Total	Returns	Percent	Total	Returns	Difference
Alabama	135	12	9	99	92	7
Alaska	60	16	27	48	38	10
Arizona	90	21	23	38	38	0
Arkansas	135	19	14	99	95	4
California	117	13	11	59	54	5
Colorado	100	21	21	41	38	3
Connecticut	187	26	14	38	35	3
Delaware	62	23	37	48	35	13
Florida	160	31	19	64	65	1
Georgia	236	27	11	84	78	6
Hawaii	76	28	37	68	61	7
Idaho	105	34	32	30	24	6
Illinois	236	21	9	50	48	2
Indiana	150	30	20	32	33	1
Iowa	150	30	20	44	33	11
Kansas	165	26	16	35	35	0
Kentucky	138	26	19	79	65	14
Louisiana	144	19	13	97	95	2
Maine	184	33	18	45	30	15
Maryland	185	33	12	83	61	22
Massachusetts	280	15	5	78	60	18
Michigan	148	13	9	53	31	22
Minnesota	201	26	13	57	54	3
Mississippi	174	22	13	97	91	6
Missouri	197	27	14	60	56	4
Montana	150	41	27	54	61	7
Nebraska	49	15	31	—	—	—
Nevada	60	21	35	65	67	2
New Hampshire	423	32	8	35	19	16
New Mexico	112	30	27	72	73	1
New York	210	22	11	43	32	11
North Carolina	170	22	13	71	68	3
North Dakota	153	22	14	22	26	4
Ohio	131	25	19	56	44	12
Oklahoma	149	24	16	76	67	9
Oregon	90	31	34	57	58	1
Pennsylvania	251	28	11	48	36	12
Rhode Island	150	24	16	73	71	2
South Carolina	170	27	16	86	100	14
South Dakota	105	32	31	50	44	6
Tennessee	132	23	17	53	48	5
Texas	181	16	9	89	81	8
Utah	104	36	35	42	42	0
Vermont	180	28	16	38	36	2
Virginia	140	24	17	71	71	0
Washington	147	34	23	59	62	3
West Virginia	134	28	21	60	57	3
Wisconsin	132	34	26	58	62	4
Wyoming	92	32	35	33	28	5
Total	7550	1256	17	59	52	7

Source: The source for this and all succeeding tables in this study is the data gathered for this study.

6

tors and to weight each legislator within a state on the basis of the
actual proportions of legislators by party. After the weights were
applied to each respondent, the sample was no longer unrepresentative by political party and each state's group of legislators was prop-
erly represented in the sample in relation to the legislators from
every other state. A recalculation of the responses by party after
the weighting reveals the following distribution: Democrats 60.3 percent; Republicans 38.6 percent; and Independents 1.0 percent. The
weighting scheme produced a party distribution with about one percentage point difference between the Democrats in the sample and the
Democrats in the total population of legislators.

THEORETICAL PERSPECTIVES

In this study we focus on how the subjective orientations of state
legislators toward governmental institutions affect the ways they go
about making decisions on the issues before them; color their perceptions concerning where the major decisions are actually made; and
relate to their opinions on a number of matters of state policy. We
are not concerned with delineating an overall picture of the decision-
making process in American state legislatures—or in any particular
state legislature. Rather, we interest ourselves in the individual legislator as the unit of analysis, and the correspondence between his
attitudes toward a particular institution (for example, the governorship) and his propensity to rely upon that office for information. Furthermore, we pose the question of whether members who are supportive of a stronger role for the governor are more likely to see the
state's chief executive as the major source of power in the deliberations of the legislature. The first question deals with preferred
sources of information or cues, a subject that has been considered
in some detail by students of the Congress (Kingdon 1973; Matthews
and Stimson 1975) in recent years. The second is called the "perceived decision locus" in the state legislature, a factor not generally
considered in its own right but often confused with the broader concept of information seeking. In Chapter 2, we shall consider the differences between these concepts in greater detail and examine the
literature on legislative decision making to highlight the distinction
even further.

Our emphasis overall is on the extent to which subjective orientations toward the institutions of the political party, the committee
system, and the governorship are reflected in the behavior of members and in their perceptions of how decisions are made, rather than
on the process of how legislators interact in a larger framework or
on how a particular bill or set of bills is passed, defeated, or stalled

in committee or party caucus. These latter questions are important, and, as the research agenda set out in Chapter 6 indicates, we intend to pursue them. The aim of the present study is more modest, however. First and foremost, we want to move away from the analysis of gross aggregate concepts such as expenditures (as a dependent variable) and social, political, and economic traits such as income, party competition, apportionment, and occupation as predictors of such expenditure levels. This literature has, we believe, grossly oversimplified the policy-making process in the American states. Furthermore, it is filled with what we see as conceptual problems stemming not only from insufficient theorizing but also from a misinterpretation of what sound theory we find in the literature (see Uslaner forthcoming). We do not see how such analyses will tell us much about the policy-making process as a political process. While we do not deny that socioeconomic factors may play a major role in some aspects of the state policy-making process, our principal concern is how, not if, political factors interact and how they influence questions of public policy.

We thus begin our analysis with an investigation of the values of actors in the process (here, state legislators) and how these values affect patterns of behavior and preceptions of patterns of influence. These are the building blocks of a more extensive model of the policy-making process as we perceive our enterprise. Again, we use the individual respondent as the unit of analysis in this study. Aggregate analyses based upon these orientations and self-attributed perceptions of power and influence in a legislative body are the next step in building a model of the policy-making process in the American states. Examining the relation between these orientations and perceptions and policy preferences is the third step. In the fifth chapter, we begin such an analysis by examining the relation between individuals' attitudes toward legislative "professionalism" and their preferences on 13 nonfiscal policy alternatives in a preliminary effort to indicate the type of linkage process we intend to examine in greater detail in future studies. The next step is to compare the behavior of legislators and other potentially relevant actors in the state policy-making system. Similar surveys of county party chairmen and bureaucrats in the 50 states of our legislative sample will permit such direct comparisons. Then, of course, we must pursue the relation between policy preferences and policy decisions reached in the states, clearly a task for aggregate analysis of our survey data. This study should be viewed as a first report on a much larger project—and an evaluation of the ways in which alternative value systems affect members' behavior and perceptions of power and influence, subject to some institutional constraints (including the perceived level of interparty competition in a member's district, among other factors).

Which institutions have we chosen and why? Our analysis centers on the political parties, the committees, and the executive branch (primarily the governor). We have not considered in detail the many other important factors in state legislative politics—indeed, the most important source of information, according to our findings in Chapter 2, is friendship groups. Nor do we consider bureaucratic politics extensively, preferring to examine the impact of bureaucrats on state legislative politics when our sample of such actors can be more directly compared with our legislative respondents than this study permits. We have chosen the party and committee systems and the executive branch because they loom so large in traditional thought about legislative politics, if not state legislative politics. We have relatively explicit expectations from this literature, both normative and empirical, on the relation between the valuation members place on these institutions and their propensity to look toward them as major sources of information and/or power in a decision-making system. Furthermore, with respect to the party and committee systems, we have a long tradition of theory on legislatures (including some work on state legislatures) which posits such institutions to be fundamentally incompatible as major centers of power. To what extent does this long-standing hypothesis receive support based upon the perceptions and values of the members of state legislatures themselves?

Executive power is another critical question in the study of legislative behavior and in the analysis of state politics. The dominant theme in American politics is executive dominance and legislative submission. This is considered true particularly at the national level (the president versus Congress), but also in state politics. To what extent is this the case? And do the patterns of support for the institution of the governorship lead members either to rely heavily upon the chief executive as a source of information, or, particularly, to perceive the governor as the major power center in the policy-making process?

In examining these linkages between the values of our legislative respondents and their propensity to seek information from and to perceive power in the institutions we have discussed, we are not establishing a model of the decision-making process in the American states. Instead, we are concerned with certain identifiable patterns of decision making in state legislatures—hence the title of this book. These patterns, the sources of information a member chooses to employ and where he perceives the power relationship to be, are two key elements in a larger context which would constitute a model of the decision-making process. But before we can begin to work toward the development of such a model, we must first examine the major components of the process. We do so here with respect to the theoretical literature about each institution.

We examine the relation between members' values and their perceptions of power and behavior with respect to information resources in Chapters 2, 3, and 4. We begin our search for the components of a decision-making model by employing measures of attitudes, perceptions, and behavior that are as consistent as possible with respect to each institution of state politics. Thus, the measurement of our independent and dependent variables is identical throughout the study regardless of the particular institution under consideration. Where we have different expectations, they are reflected in our hypotheses about the relative effects of the members' values on their perceptions and behavior, and, in the case of the governorship, in one control variable rather than in measurement techniques. In the case of the governors, we examine the behavior both of the respondents who belong to the same party as the governor and the opposition party, because we have no a priori reason to expect that all legislators will view the governor as either a source of power or information in the same way. In fact, our initial expectation is the opposite. We also examine in each case the impact legislator value systems have upon perceptions of power and the sources of information for: (1) legislators from the least to the most competitive districts, according to our respondents' perceptions of the political composition of their districts; and (2) the extent to which the representation each legislator is providing is "typical" of the district's partisan orientations. Both controls will be discussed in detail in the next chapter.

We depart from this research strategy only twice. First, in Chapter 4, we consider not only the relationship between the orientations of members toward the governorship and the attribution of power and influence to the chief executive but also the specific issues that appear to be the most salient to the members and their relative status as areas of gubernatorial concern. Thus, we not only seek to determine the overall pattern of attributed gubernatorial power and reported executive influence but also the perceptions of members concerning the issues in which the chief executive of a state is most involved. Here, we consider the changes that have occurred over the past decade, by examining the responses to our survey in comparison with those of the Francis (1967) study of members who served ten years ago. Second, our final substantive chapter examines the relation between members' values with respect to legislative professionalism and their attitudes on questions of nonfiscal policies, generally considered to be reformist or innovative (see Walker 1969). In this chapter, we present a preliminary analysis of the effects of subjective orientations about the structure of the legislature (our concern in the previous three chapters) with attitudes on questions of public policy. This is the first attempt we are making to link attitudes toward institutions with attitudes toward policy questions. Clearly, this view oversimplifies the policy-making process in the states considerably, but we believe that it is an important attempt to establish an attitude-policy linkage, addressing in a straightforward manner some traditional questions in the study of legislative reform. We do not make any specific suggestions for reform, but, as we note in Chapter 5, our results do provide support for the overall hypothesis that the structure of legislative institutions does in fact affect the policies that one would expect from a representative institution (given the attitudes of the members).

We have discussed the importance of members' subjective orientations toward the various institutions of state government at some length above. We turn now to a discussion of the measurement of such orientations: the cue-seeking and decision-locus variables will be discussed in the next chapter and compared to studies of information resources in the Congress. After our description of the techniques of scale construction, we shall turn to an examination of the measures of association employed in our data analysis and then to an outline of the study to follow.

MEASUREMENT OF STATE LEGISLATOR ORIENTATIONS

We included a total of 16 Likert-type attitude items in our questionnaire to tap legislator orientations toward the executive and legislative branches of state government and toward the political party system. The items arrayed in Table 1.2, along with the percentage distribution for each item, were either selected for inclusion because they had previously been used successfully by other researchers or were developed by us particularly for this sample survey. These 16 items became the raw data used to construct scales measuring state legislator orientations toward various state institutions.

Factor analysis was employed in two steps to define which attitude items should go into each scale. A factor analysis of all 16 items was first used to determine which items might possibly go together into scales. The results of the first factor analysis were then used to define smaller groupings of items for a second factor analysis. The second factor analysis made the final determination as to which items to include in a specific scale. The scales were then constructed using the summated ratings method originally devised by Likert (see Edwards 1957, pp. 149-71; Maranell 1974, pp. 231-71).

Our factor analysis of all 16 items suggested that four political-party system items could be used to form two scales. A separate factor analysis of the four items defined two factors (see Table 1.3) and we then created two party-orientation scales from the data. The first

TABLE 1.2

Distributions of Responses to State Legislator Orientation
Items Included in Survey
(in percent)

Item	Strongly Agree	Agree	Disagree	Strongly Disagree	No Opinion No Answer
Political party system					
The leadership in my party in the legislature makes a concerted effort to hold the party together on roll-call votes.	11.8	39.4	30.4	7.2	11.2
If a bill is important for his party's record, a member should vote with his party, even if it costs him some support in his district.	2.4	19.1	47.1	20.2	11.2
The party helped him to get elected to the legislature. Even if he disagrees with its stand, he has an obligation to vote with his party.	0.8	10.1	57.5	22.1	9.6
A legislator's first loyalty should be to his party's legislative leaders rather than to the governor, if they are in disagreement.	7.1	35.6	25.0	5.9	26.4
Legislative system					
Legislators should be paid enough so that they do not need to work at any other job.	24.9	20.9	34.8	12.2	7.2
The business of state government is simple enough that legislators can afford to spend a lot of time consulting with their constituents.	2.7	21.5	51.0	16.3	8.6
The legislature should be in session all year long to conduct the state's business.	6.3	13.5	40.5	32.6	7.0
Every legislator should be provided a sum of money with which to establish a district office to handle constituent matters.	16.0	31.4	32.2	11.4	8.9
The business of state government is so complex that legislators must spend a lot of time in the state capital developing expertise on various policy matters.	15.7	56.4	18.2	2.6	7.0
Every legislator should have an individual office for personal and staff use.	23.6	43.7	19.9	4.0	8.8
Legislators should never be paid so much that they might begin to feel like professional legislators.	17.2	40.4	24.8	8.0	9.6
No legislator except those in leadership positions should be provided with full-time staff aides.	4.6	26.6	39.2	20.0	9.6
Standing committees of the legislature should be staffed on a permanent year-round basis.	26.1	48.2	14.8	2.4	8.4
Role in policy making					
The legislature should play the major role in the making of public policy in this state.	46.1	37.9	8.0	0.0	7.9
The legislature and the governor should be equal partners in the making of public policy in this state.	12.5	47.7	27.0	4.9	7.9
The governor should play the major role in the making of policy in this state.	4.9	23.4	47.2	13.1	11.4

Note: Weighted N = 1,252.

scale, which we named the General Party Orientation (GPO) Scale, measures the extent to which the respondent thinks that a legislator should vote with his party even if he disagrees with the party's position or if the vote will cost him support in his district. A high position on the scale reflects this proparty orientation, and a low position indicates an antiparty orientation. The second scale, the Legislative Party Orientation (LPO) Scale, measures a legislator's feeling that he should look to the party's leadership in the legislature. A high orientation on this scale is proparty leadership, while a low orientation suggests that the respondent is antiparty leadership.

The results of our factor analysis of affective orientations toward the party system, presented in Table 1.3, are not as clear-cut as those of Jack Dennis (1966; 1975) in "separating" diffuse support from specific legislative party orientations. Indeed, the two items in our survey which load on the GPO scale refer to voting with one's legislative party if: (1) a bill is important for the party record; or (2) even when a member disagrees with his party's position. We chose to call this a "general" party orientation scale even though it does contain some of the key elements of the doctrine of responsible party government because we expect that elites would have higher levels of support for the party system in general, and these questions appear to tap a more general orientation toward the party system in the legislature than toward the party leadership in the chamber.

The legislative party may mean many things to different legislators, as Fred I. Greenstein and Elton F. Jackson (1963) have argued. And they also argue that a specific affective response to questions about party leadership would better measure "principled agree-

TABLE 1.3

Factor Analysis of Four Political Party System Items

Item	Rotated Factor Loadings	
	I	II
Party leadership makes concerted effort to hold party together on roll calls	.132	.451
If bill is important for party record, member should vote with party	.631	.216
Member obligated to vote with party, even if he disagrees with party stand	.648	.217
Legislator's first loyalty should be to his party's legislative leaders	.185	.464
Percent of total variance explained	28.7	5.8

ment with party" (p. 161). The items loading on our LPO scale tap just such an orientation: whether the leadership of the party makes a concerted effort to achieve party cohesion; and whether a member's first loyalty should be to his party's legislative leaders. We thus consider the LPO scale to be a more similar dimension to Dennis's party responsibility factor, while the General-Party Orientation Scale is closer to his "diffuse support" measure.

The factor analysis of all 16 attitudinal items also indicated that nine legislative system items could be employed to create three different scales (see Table 1.4). The first scale produced from the raw data, the Full-Time-Legislator Orientation (FTLO) Scale, measures the extent to which the respondents think that the legislator's job

TABLE 1.4

Factor Analysis of Nine Legislative System Items

Item	Rotated Factor Loadings		
	I	II	III
Legislators should be paid enough so no need to work at any other job	.762	.302	.403
Business of state government is simple enough so time can be spent consulting constituents	.006	-.065	-.322
Legislature should be in session all year long	.624	.196	.188
Legislators should be provided money to set up district offices	.360	.591	.150
Business of state government is so complex that a lot of time must be spent developing expertise	.277	.302	.535
Legislators should have an individual office for personal and staff use	.211	.708	.242
Legislators should never be paid so much that they feel like professionals	-.658	-.240	.023
No legislator except those in leadership positions should have full-time staff aides	-.236	-.621	-.090
Standing committees of legislature should be staffed on permanent year-round basis	.186	.491	.243
Percent of total variance explained	35.7	6.8	3.0

should be full-time and that the legislature should meet all year long. A high position on the scale indicates that orientation, while a low position reflects an anti-full-time legislator view. We named the second scale created from these items the Legislator Staff Orientation (LSO) Scale. It measures an orientation toward having the legislature staffed well and having staffed personal offices in the capital and the legislative district. A high position on the scale reflects that attitude, and a low position indicates opposition to such staffing innovations. The third dimension seems to tap some measure of the complexity of the decision-making process in the legislature, but it does not have a clear enough interpretation (nor does it account for much of the total variance) to include it in the analysis. We shall thus concentrate on the first two scales derived from our questions on the legislative system.

The first two dimensions we have generated to measure legislative professionalism do not differ drastically from the objective measures developed by Grumm (1971) and the Citizens' Conference (1971). Our factor-analytic solution does differ from that of Grumm in that we have found that support for the legislator's personal needs (such as income and the ability to serve as a full-time member of the chamber) is not part of the same subjective dimension as support for staff, despite the aggregate findings' contrary results. Our full-time-legislator scale seems to be most similar to the Citizens' Conference concept of a "functional" legislature, while our LSO scale seems most to resemble the Conference's concept of an "informed" legislator. Three of the latter group's criteria are absent in our analysis—the accountable legislature, the independent legislature, and the representative chamber. They seem difficult to measure according to the types of questions we posed to our sample of legislators, although we do not deny their importance.

The third dimension produced by the factor analysis of the legislative system items does not compare with any indices used previously in aggregate analyses of legislative professionalism. For this reason and because the concept of legislative expertise did not relate theoretically to the focus upon cue seeking and decision loci in this book, we decided to exclude this third scale from any further use in the book.

Finally, the first factor analysis of all 16 attitude items indicated that three role in policy-making items should go together to form a composite scale. A second factor analysis of only the three items confirmed this conclusion (see Table 1.5). These three items were adapted from three used by Roger Davidson, David Kovenock, and Michael O'Leary (1966, pp. 69-73). A composite scale was constructed from the three items reflecting degree of orientation toward having the governor play the major role in state policy making. A

TABLE 1.5

Factor Analysis of Three Role-in-Policy-Making Items

Items	Factor Loadings I
Legislature should play major role	-.292
Legislature and governor should be equal partners	.555
Governor should play major role	.480
Percent of total variance explained	46.3

high position on the scale indicates strong agreement with this position, while a low position reflects strong agreement with having the legislature play the major role instead of the governor. We name this scale the Gubernatorial Orientation (GO) Scale.

For the purposes of the analyses to be presented in this book, we then grouped each respondent into either a high, medium, or low category on the basis of their scale scores on each of the orientation scales. The results of this grouping are presented in Table 1.6. For every scale the medium category is the modal category. Most legislators are like the mass public in their tendency to define their orientations away from either extreme position. Even with this tendency toward the middle position, the legislators seem to be leaning in the direction of a full-time legislature and away from a strong role for legislative parties.

Now that we have completed a presentation of how the raw state-legislator orientation items were used to construct the five scales to be employed in this book, we turn to a discussion of how we will conduct and present the data analyses for this book.

ANALYSIS OF THE DATA

In our data analyses, we shall depend without exception upon nominal and ordinal measures of association, and we shall restrict our analysis to simple measures. We are not concerned with levels of statistical significance for the measures of association because our large sample size will generally reveal even the smallest measures of association to be "statistically significant," and because there is, among data analysts, a strong debate about the validity of these tests (see Morrison and Henkel 1970; Henkel 1976). Based upon our reading of this debate, we lean toward the view that such tests are not very useful.

Our reliance upon zero-order measures of association, rather than partial measures, permits us to examine the overall patterns within control groups as we have delineated them. As we shall see in the data analysis to follow, it is not always the case that the most extreme control variable (such as perceived party competition) will yield the strongest (weakest) relationship between members' subjective orientations and their perceptions and behavior. However, the partial measures of association are based upon this assumption (see Hildebrand, Laing, and Rosenthal 1977). Precision in analysis may be sacrificed, rather than enhanced, by incorrect specification of the overall relationship among several variables. Thus, we chose the most direct method of making comparisons, not the most statistically "sophisticated." This is also our justification for relying upon basically bivariate relationships and not extending our analysis to several predictor variables for each dependent variable. The world is in fact multivariate, but rushing in with every conceivable predictor of members' perceptions of power and behavior with respect to cue seeking does not seem as rewarding as testing simpler hypotheses based upon attitudes that we posit to be most directly related to these patterns of decision making.

The measures of association we shall employ can be divided into two categories: situations in which we have dichotomous row and column variables; and situations in which we have two or more values for the column variable and three or more values for the row variable—but not an equal number of values for both. In the first case, we shall use the traditional measures of association for dichotomous variables—the linear measure phi (o) and the curvilinear Yule's Q. We have two reasons for examining both measures. First, the hypoth-

TABLE 1.6

Distribution of State Legislator Orientation Scale Scores
(in percent)

Scale Name	High	Medium	Low	N
General-Party Orientation Scale	25.1	60.0	14.9	1,167
Legislative-Party Orientation Scale	13.0	55.4	31.7	1,157
Full-Time-Legislator Orientation Scale	37.8	45.4	16.9	1,187
Legislator-Staff Orientation Scale	22.5	52.8	24.7	1,183
Gubernatorial Orientation Scale	30.0	61.3	8.7	1,189

eses we offer are consistent with either measure: we hypothesize an
overall directional relationship, but the exact form of the relationship is difficult to assess a priori. Second, this problem is further
compounded by the fact that our subjective orientation measures are
based upon cumulative scaling techniques, whereas our independent
variables are not measured in such an ordered and cumulative way.
Thus, the hypotheses we propose can be consistent with results of a
data analysis which either demonstrate a strict monotonic (linear) relationship or which allow departures from strong monotonicity. Therefore, we could rely exclusively on curvilinear measures. However,
such measures tend to be strongly affected by skewed marginals—that
is, a situation in which either the dependent or independent variable
has very few cases in one category. This problem will be discussed
in the context of the data analysis below. The linear coefficient, therefore, is a more conservative measure than the curvilenear coefficient.
In the case of tables marked by skewed marginals, it is particularly
useful to compare the results of each analysis to determine whether
there appears to be any pattern in the cross-tabulation.

    The linear measure, phi, is for tables with two rows and two
columns, a direct analogue of the traditional Pearson correlation coefficient. Yule's Q is a measure of association based upon the concept of "proportionate reduction in error" (see Hildebrand, Laing,
and Rosenthal 1977), or PRE. A PRE measure is an estimate of the
increase in predictive power one gains from knowing the values of the
independent variable in comparison to the expected predictions that
would be made under the assumption that a null model holds (the coefficient being employed would equal zero). The PRE interpretation
is a standard against which many measures of association for nominal and ordinal data are judged. In the second case of a table which
is larger than two by two, we shall examine the linear measure tau-c
and the curvilinear coefficient, gamma. Gamma is a direct extension
of Yule's Q for larger tables and thus has a PRE interpretation.
Tau-b, a measure of association for tables which have more than two
rows and columns but have equal numbers of rows and columns, is
the traditional PRE measure employed when we have more than two
categories on either variable. However, if the table does not have
the same number of rows and columns, then tau-b will not be an appropriate measure. Instead, we employ tau-c, similar to tau-b but
including a correction factor for nonsquare tables. This factor makes
tau-c unsuitable as a PRE measure (Hildebrand, Laing, and Rosenthal 1977). However, the values of tau-c and a computed tau-b are
so close that we lose little generality in assuming that a value of the
former of virtually zero is almost equivalent to support for a null
model (the independent variable does not improve predictive power
over a set of random factors). When comparing tau-c with gamma,

we must be conscious of the fact that the curvilinear measure can attain spuriously high values (or low ones, but the real danger is in overinterpreting strong coefficients) when the marginals are badly skewed. On the other hand, tau-c generally underestimates the extent of a statistical relationship between two variables. Therefore, we shall treat as "reasonable" values for this latter measure numbers which may appear to be somewhat small when viewed from the overall interval of [0, ±1] that the coefficient can possible take. Finally, note that all of the measures of association we employ are symmetric in that they do not take on different values if the dependent and independent variables exchange places. In some cases, an asymmetric measure such as Somer's d may appear to be somewhat more appropriate. However, changing the coefficients would not affect the conclusions we draw for any table in the study. For ease of exposition, we decided to be as parsimonious as possible in the presentation of measures of association. In all cases, we shall compute measures of association only for the cases for which we have values for the dependent, independent, and (when applicable) control variables. Thus, the sample size will vary across the tables throughout the book, although the pattern of variations is hardly disturbing.

PLAN OF THE STUDY

In the next chapter, we first consider the overall distribution of information sources and perceptions of decision loci within the legislative body, as our respondents have ordered them. Wherever possible, we shall make comparisons with data on similar questions from studies of the Congress and speculate on the reasons for the similarities and the differences we find. We then move to a consideration of the role of the party system in the legislative process. One obvious reason for doing so is that the importance of the party system in state legislatures appears to be considerable in contrast with that of the Congress, the only major discrepancy we observe. Our major reason for treating the parties first is that they have played such a large role in the study of both state politics and American politics in general. The typical variable representing "politics" in aggregate analyses of state policy formation is some measure of partisanship or party competition—and the general answer we obtain is that political parties do not matter very much in the policy-formation process. We thus examine the relation between subjective orientations toward the party system among our respondents and their cue-seeking behavior and attribution of power to the party caucus in the legislature.

In Chapter 3, we consider the committee system as a referent for our respondents. Since the literature on committees and parties (reviewed in that chapter) views these two arenas as conflicting sources of power in legislatures, it seems appropriate to move directly from a consideration of the party system to an analysis of committees. In this chapter, we test this claim to the extent that our data permit. We then examine, in the fourth chapter, gubernatorial power and influence in the states. Finally, we assess in a preliminary way the possible policy implications of a reformist orientation among state legislators in the fifth chapter. The concluding chapter attempts to put the findings of the preceding chapters into an overall perspective, as well as discussing the research agenda for the future which this and the companion studies we have conducted will allow us to conduct.

2

DECISION-MAKING
SOURCES WITHIN STATE
LEGISLATURES: PARTIES
AND CUES

INTRODUCTION

Recent studies of legislative decision making at the national level in the United States have suggested the need to go beyond the analysis of roll-call voting to determine why legislators behave as they do. As John W. Kingdon has argued:

> . . . nearly all roll call studies have discovered the cen-
> tral importance of political party in the explanation of leg-
> islative cleavage. Yet we know little about the process
> by which the party influences its congressmen. Party
> voting may be a function of some constituency factor, co-
> alition support of different kinds, sanctions employed by
> legislative leaders, administration pressure, cue-giving
> within the Congress, ideological similarity among fellow
> party members, and other possible factors, or various
> combinations of them. (1973, p. 11)

The approach taken by Kingdon, as well as by many other students of the Congress (Matthews and Stimson 1975; Matthews and Stimson 1970; Stimson 1975; Cherryholmes and Shapiro 1969; Mishler, Lee, and Thorpe 1973; Asher 1973; Kovenock 1973), is to attempt to deter- mine (either by survey techniques or simulation) what factors in a legislator's environment appear to be the most salient in determining his behavior on roll-call votes. The critical factor in such studies is the provision of information to a member of Congress by key ac- tors who are in positions to persuade the member to vote either yea or nay on a given roll call. Thus, these studies begin with the assumption that the legislator has only a limited amount of information about the consequences of a particular vote and relies on other people he can trust to provide him with cues as to what are the likely costs and benefits of voting a particular way. Indeed, Matthews and Stimson (1975; p. 60) consider cue giving and cue taking to represent "normal decision-making" in the United States House of Representatives and report that only 4 percent of the members they interviewed never rely upon such sources of information.

The importance of cues in the legislative process is undeniable; we shall consider below some of the reasons why this is so. In this chapter, we shall be primarily concerned with cues from party-related sources. Here, even before we have discussed the roles of cues in legislative decision making, we find that the very concept of a cue is somewhat ambiguous. The simulation studies merely indicate that a cue giver and a cue taker have common patterns of voting across a set of roll calls. They do not make any attempts to determine how important the alternative cue givers are from the perspective of the cue taker. Any such inferences that do emerge from these studies (see Matthews and Stimson 1975; Matthews and Stimson 1970; Cherryholmes and Shapiro 1969; Grant 1973) are either based upon patterns of covariation in voting behavior or on a priori assumptions about the probability of voting with a particular member or bloc (if not both). Such models may represent oversimplifications of the dynamics of legislative decision making; for Herbert F. Weisberg (1976) has argued that the very high predictive accuracy of some of these models may be attributable to phenomena much simpler than the conscious search for information by a legislator.

The key difference in the work of Kingdon, on the one hand, and Matthews and Stimson, on the other, is in the treatment of the way legislators receive cues. Both studies assume that the member of the U. S. House is seeking information about the probable consequences of his voting decision. Because he is only one among 435, he cannot be expected to know the consequences of his voting decision for a wide range of issues. To reduce his level of uncertainty, he seeks out cues on how to vote from party and committee leaders, administration figures, outside interest groups, constituents, and so on. Thus, cue taking is perceived as a rational way to reduce information costs in the voting decision, particularly in a legislative arena that places a high value on specialization and reciprocity (see Matthews 1960; Matthews and Stimson 1975).

Both the Kingdon (1973; p. 287) and Matthews-Stimson (1975; p. 171) studies employ survey techniques and both at least initially begin their analyses with questions about how legislators "make up their minds." And the potential cue givers each considers are very similar. The studies diverge on the question of the use of the cues

received by the member. Kingdon (1973; pp. 18ff.) seeks to determine the impact of cues on roll-call decisions of legislators. Following his initial probes on whether members received cues from alternative sources, he inquires whether this information was "determinative," of "major importance," of "minor importance," or "not important" in the congressman's voting decision. He selected roll calls
in advance and then sought to postdict the actual determinants of members' votes.

In contrast, the Matthews-Stimson approach is not concerned
with behavior on specific legislation as a starting point in their investigation. Rather, they pose a "hypothetical question": "Suppose you
had to cast a roll-call vote and could only know the position of three
of the people or groups on this list. Which three would you want to
know?" (1975, p. 172). Nine potential sources of information were
given and the respondent was asked to rank order his three most preferred cue givers. In comparison to kingdon's analysis, Matthews,
and Stimson state: "We define a cue as any communication—verbal or
non-verbal—intended or unintended—that is employed by the cue-taker
as a prescription for his vote. By definition then, cues are influential
although not necessarily decisive. Cue-taking is a 'power' relationship in a limited sense" (p. 31).

Our approach to the general question of cues was developed in-
dependently of either the Kingdon or Matthews-Stimson design. As
we shall see, it is similar to both designs in that we ask respondents
to rank order their cue givers. But we also inquire about who they
actually consult rather than whose position they would most like to
know. In comparing our study with the previous two, however, our
question on cues is much more similar to that of Matthews and Stimson than it is to that of Kingdon. We do not argue that the former approach is better (or worse) than the latter, but only that they are different. We cannot compare our results with those of Kingdon as directly as we can with the findings of Matthews and Stimson, since we
have no information on the extent to which the cues received are determinative.

We do, however, want to know which actors in state legislative
systems are indeed determinative. Although our analysis is not identical to Kingdon's, we did ask our respondents where they thought the
most significant decisions are made in the legislature. Thus, we have
two distinct questions, both of which we shall consider in this book:
which actors do state legislators depend upon for information (cues)
when making up their minds on roll calls?; and where is the "center
of power" in the legislative arena? A legislator who believes that the
party caucus is the most significant factor in the decision-making
process may nevertheless not seek out cues from party leaders or
other party members. Some members may resent the power of the

most significant decisional centers and rely upon other sources. Alternatively, others may see the process of voting on roll calls to be fundamentally different from that of "making the most significant decisions." There are many other scenarios we could cite, but it should be clear that the two questions are at least conceptually distinct. This study will attempt to answer both in at least a limited way.

CUES IN CONGRESS AND STATE LEGISLATURES

Given that most members of Congress take cues most of the time, what do we expect of our respondents who are members of state legislative bodies? The state legislator, in comparison with the congressman, is in a situation calling for even greater reliance upon the views of "relevant others." The Congress of the United States, with its well-developed committee system and patterns of informal rules (see Polsby 1968), its provision of up to 18 full-time staff members and office space for each member of the House (with even more generous provisions in the Senate), and its status as a full-time legislative body meeting throughout the entire year, offers members considerable opportunities to keep up with the business of the legislature. In the states, on the other hand, service in the legislature is often only a part-time occupation, with individual office space and staff more the exception than the rule, and information about the probable consequences of the outcome of a voting decision limited to at best a select few individuals (see Grumm 1971; Burns 1971; Citizens' Conference on State Legislatures 1971). If the president is viewed as markedly advantaged over the typical member of Congress in the information he possesses, then the governor of a state should be put on an even higher pedestal when compared to state legislatures (see Sharkansky 1968; McCally 1966). The typical state legislator is almost totally dependent upon others for information (voting cues) on complex issues during the normally short legislative session in his state (see Porter 1974). To whom, then, does he look most frequently? And under what conditions will certain cue givers be more prominent than others?

In this chapter, the central focus of our analysis will be the political party as cue giver and source of the most significant decisions in the legislature. While the parties and chief executives may not be the most important cue givers or the major centers of power in various state legislatures, we concentrate on them because of the role they have played in the literature on state politics and policy formation. We do not maintain that they are the only sources of cues or the dominant ones, but we do believe that they should demonstrate some patterned relationships to legislators' views on how legislative decisions should be made. Often we hear statements that the American parties are too weak (or, in some states and cities, too strong). Do members who believe in stronger party systems tend to seek out cues from party-related sources? We also hear that the power of governors far outweighs that of legislatures, as argued above. Do members who favor a more independent role for the legislature tend to look to their colleagues in the legislative branch for cues more than to those outside? And where do members with such orientations believe the centers of power actually are? We shall also examine at least briefly alternative sources of cues in the state legislative arenas, and, where possible, compare our results to the studies of Congress by Kingdon and Matthews and Stimson.

We are interested in the party system for several reasons: because support for a strong party system is associated with a view of democratic government that has been advocated by many reformers in twentieth-century America; because political parties are a major factor in recruiting candidates for office and—except for Nebraska—provide the electoral mechanism for the attainment of such office; and because in many state legislatures, the political party not only organizes the chambers but also controls committee assignments and whatever perquisites of office the member can obtain (see Jewell 1969; ch. 3). Even in states with weak legislative parties, we might expect party leaders to play a major role in cue giving simply by the nature of their official position. And, because state legislative turnover is so high—by any standards and particularly in comparison to the Congress (Rosenthal 1974a; 1974b), the need for reliable sources of information is critical. Turnover only increases the general level of uncertainty in the chamber. Familiar faces, the friends who gave you cues in the last session, are no longer in the state capital. It is as likely as not that the standing committee chairmen have changed since the previous session. In some states (such as Florida) there is an almost guaranteed discontinuity of leadership at all levels by informal provisions against any leaders seeking reelection to their posts. In such situations, the formal position of party leadership (as distinct from the occupants of the offices) appears to have the most salience for state legislators. Regardless of what else changes in the legislature—including but not limited to a revamping of the entire committee system—the party leadership posts continue from one session to the next.

The normative aspect of partisan cue giving, cue taking, and decision making in state legislatures stems from a broader concern in democratic theory. Reformers have argued that American politics is not marked by the clear-cut ideological divisions in the party system found in many other democracies (notably Western Europe). Furthermore, this lack of distinctiveness between the parties is not conducive either to policy innovation or electoral accountability. As a special Committee on Political Parties of the American Political Science Association stated:

> When there are two parties identifiable by the kinds of action they propose, the voters have an actual choice. On the other hand, the sort of opposition presented by a coalition that cuts across party lines, as a regular thing, tends to deprive the public of a meaningful alternative. When such coalitions are formed after the elections are over, the public usually finds it difficult to understand the new situation and to reconcile it to the purpose of the ballot. Moreover, on that basis it is next to impossible to hold either party responsible for its political record. (1950, p. 19)

The Committee took a strong stand in favor of the "doctrine of responsible party government." This doctrine maintains that: (1) political parties should be programmatic, that is, their chief function should be to develop policies to be implemented if elected (rather than to adopt any policies likely to lead to electoral success); (2) parties should be ideologically distinct from other parties in the system; and (3) parties should be internally cohesive in the legislature (see Ranney 1962). If these three conditions are not met, it is difficult for the voter to hold a particular party responsible for the actions of the government. To the extent that a legislator believes in such a strong legislative party system, we would expect him to seek out partisan cues more than alternative sources of information.

Jack Dennis, however, has argued that overall support for the American party system (which he calls "diffuse support") and adherence to the doctrine of responsible party government are quite distinct phenomena. In two studies (1966; 1975) he has found generally high levels of diffuse support for the American party system among the mass public (although these levels are declining), but considerably less enthusiasm for the idea of a more responsible party system. We believe that in the legislative arena, there are also various distinct indicators of support for the party system among elite groups and we sought to determine what these were. We followed the lead of Dennis in posing a set of questions to our respondents and employing factor analysis to determine the dimensions of support for the party system.

VARIABLE MEASUREMENT AND HYPOTHESES

Measurement of Dependent Variables

Two types of dependent variables are employed in this chapter and the following two. The first measures the use of information resources by our respondents and involves various operationalizations of cue seeking. The second measures the perceptions of the legislators as to which decision arena is the locus of power in the state legislative process.

Legislator responses to the following question were employed to construct the cue-seeking dependent variables for this book: "We are trying to get an idea of how a legislator goes about making up his mind when he is uncertain about whether he will support or oppose a bill. Who do you usually consult when making such a decision? Please rank the top five sources of information you consult with in deciding how to vote. Write '1' beside the source you consult most often, '2' beside the source next most important, '3' beside the source next most important, '4' beside the source next most important, and '5' beside the source least important."

The legislators were then presented with a list of 13 different possible sources of cues to use in making their rankings. The list of possible cue givers was as follows:

Committee chairman
Governor
Ranking minority member of committee
Party leaders in the legislature
Interest-group representatives
Personal friends in legislature
State party chairman
Precinct committeemen in my district
Legislators of my party from my district or adjacent districts
Administrator-specialist in policy
Legislators of both parties from my district or adjacent districts
County chairman in my district.

We also included an "other" category in our survey. Many of our respondents included constituents as a source of cues. Thus, the expanded list of 14 potential cue givers and the rankings yield the raw data we use to construct our dependent variables dealing with cues.

Our list of cue givers differs from that of Matthews and Stimson in several respects. Most importantly, they only consider information sources in the legislative and executive branches, while our question includes referents outside (such as state or local party leaders, interest groups, and administrator-specialists). Secondly, their list included informal groups in the Congress such as the Democratic Study Group, the Wednesday Group (liberal Republicans in the House), and the Conservative Coalition, while our study relied upon friendship networks in the legislature as the major informal groupings. In other respects, the cue givers are quite similar—although the difference in focus (state legislatures versus Congress) naturally dictated some differences in our lists. Kingdon's study, while not as similar to ours as that of Matthews and Stimson, did specifically include interest groups and constituents as sources of decision making by members of Congress.

Our other main dependent variable in this and the following two chapters, the major decision locus in the legislative process, was determined by responses to the following question: "In your legislature, where would you say the most significant decisions are made?" We asked our respondents to indicate only one answer to this question from the following decisional loci:

> Party caucus
> Regular committee meetings
> Prelegislative session
> On the floor
> In the governor's office
> In policy committee

In the case of both the cues received and the perceived decisional loci, we eliminate the responses that were noncodable (that is, did not fit any of our categories under the "other" option or elicited no response to the question). The decision locus question is identical to that posed by Francis in Legislative Issues in the Fifty States (1967; p. 73) and our criteria for coding followed his.

We employ five dependent variables in this chapter, four of which are alternative measures of the cues legislators take from party-related sources and the final one being a simple dichotomy between party-related and non-party-related decisional loci. Our first four dependent variables are, as stated, operationalizations of the cues legislators seek, and, in particular, the ways in which legislators rely upon partisan sources of information when making decisions on bills. Of the fourteen possible sources of cues, five refer to potential partisan cues. They are: party leaders in the legislature; state party chairman; precinct committeemen in my district; legislators of my party from my district or adjacent districts; and county chairman in my district.

The first party cue index we use grouped into one category all legislators who ranked first any one of the five party cue givers and into a second category all legislators who failed to rank first any of the party cue givers. Thus, the variable has legislators whose most important cue giver was a party source of information categorized against those whose most important cue giver was a nonparty source of information. The second party cue index is a variant of the first one. Here we array those legislators who ranked first as a cue giver the category party leaders in the legislator against those who rank first all other cue givers.

The third party cue index expands upon the second index by incorporating into its construction information on second, third, fourth, and fifth rankings on the party leaders in the legislature source of cues. For this index we created a six-category variable by simply placing every legislator who ranked party leaders in the legislature first into a first category, those who ranked party leaders in the legislature second into a second category, those who ranked this source third into a third category, those who ranked it fourth into a fourth category, those who ranked it fifth into a fifth category, and those who failed to rank it at all into a sixth category. This sixth-category index measures the degree to which the legislators see party leaders in the legislature as an important cue giver. The fourth party cue index is created by summing the number of different party cues each legislator mentioned in responding to the question. This index ranges from zero (those who name no party cue givers) to three (those who name three or more party cue givers).

Of the six distinct decisional-loci choices offered our respondents, we considered party caucuses and policy committees to represent partisan decisional loci. Policy committees were included in our categorization because they are generally (although not always) organized by the leadership of the majority party in state legislatures; moreover, in contrast to caucuses as well as congressional groups such as the Democratic Steering and Policy committee in the House of Representatives, they often involve gubernatorial participation and bridge the gap between members of bicameral legislatures by including members of both chambers. The other four decisional loci were considered not to be party-related. This measure is our fifth dependent variable.

Measurement of Independent Variables

In this chapter we use two scales discussed in Chapter 1 as our measures of legislator orientations toward political parties. The first scale, the GPO scale, measures the extent to which the respondent thinks that a legislator should vote with his party even if he disagrees with the party's position or if the vote will cost him support in his district. The second scale, the LPO scale, measures a legislator's feeling that he should look to the party's leadership in the legislature.

We hypothesize that legislators with high scores on both scales, but particularly on the LPO scale, will be more likely to seek partisan cues than other information; and be more likely to see the central decisional locus in the legislature in the party. In particular, we expect that members' subjective orientations toward the party system will affect both their behavior and their perceptions of power. With respect to behavior, members who are more positively disposed toward the party system should be more likely to seek out cues from party-related information sources, particularly party leaders in the legislature. To the extent that members do have such a positive evaluation of the party system, we would expect them to select as their sources of information their most-valued aspect of the legislative environment. This is consistent with our general argument that patterns of behavior are affected by members' subjective attitudes toward the institutions that are the source of that behavior.

We further expect that members' perceptions of power in the legislature, where the major decision loci are preceived to be, should vary directly with these subjective orientations. The rationale for this hypothesis is less direct, since it is plausible to maintain that members who oppose, for example, party-dominated leadership would nevertheless perceive power to reside in the party caucus. However, we maintain that even with respect to attributions of power, there is likely to be selective perception toward attributing more power to institutions that members believe ought to have the dominant role in decision making. The more party-oriented members thus are expected to perceive stronger party roles in the legislature on this account. To the extent that this is in fact the case, then our assumption is that subjective orientations toward the various institutions are major (if not the central) factors in legislative decision making. Furthermore, to the extent that our party orientation scales do measure attitudes about party government, this linkage would be expected empirically and would be a requirement for any system of responsible party government.

Such hypotheses are in need of qualification, however. Legislators in marginal electoral situations simply may not have the freedom to support party leaders at the expense of following the views of

their constituents (see Gilbert 1973; Mayhew 1974; pp. 30–31). We
do not posit a direct linkage between district competitiveness and patterns of cue seeking or perceptions of decision loci. Rather, we maintain that the basic relationship is between behavior (or perceptions of
power) and subjective orientations, which may be reinforced or de-
emphasized in alternative contexts. Thus, in competitive districts
we would expect a less pronounced relationship between party orientations and patterns of partisan cue seeking. In safe districts, on the
other hand, we would expect that there would be a stronger relationship between these variables than we would observe either for the entire sample or for the more competitive districts in particular. In
these safe districts, members are less cross-pressured between party and constituency factors, thus serving to enhance the effects of any
proparty orientations a member might have on cue-seeking behavior
(and the perception of power).

An even stronger control variable, which we shall also employ,
is not simply the extent of competition in a district, but competition
relative to the party representation the constituency has chosen at
the most recent election. This we call district "typicality." The most
typical district would find a Democratic legislator representing a
"safe" Democratic district (or a GOP legislator from a safe Republican seat); the least typical district would find a Democrat (Republican)
from a safe Republican (Democratic) seat. The more typical a district's representation, the stronger the relationship between party
orientations and cue-seeking behavior (or perceptions of decision loci) should be. A legislator from such a typical district has less need
to worry about the views of his constituents, on the one hand, and is
more likely than the marginal member (regardless of party affiliation)
to be vying for positions of influence within the legislature—particularly within the legislative party. This will be even more pronounced if
the members' sights are set on higher office. The control variables
we shall employ thus deal with competitiveness and typicality. The
two are certainly similar concepts, although the first has dominated
the literature. We believe that the second is a more useful analytic
concept of the relationship that district competition has on our other
hypothesized relationships, and, as we shall see below, is generally
a better predictor as well. The controls, while related, are analytically distinct. The first is nothing more than a measure of electoral
competition, as perceived by our respondents. The second, on the
other hand, is an interactive measure of perceived competition and
the party of the respondent. Particularly when measuring the impact
of subjective orientations on perceived influence or power, this seems
to be a more direct way of assessing the constraints of the electoral
system on attitudes and behavior.

The perceived competitiveness index is based upon responses
to the question: "How would you classify your legislative district—safe
Democrat, mostly Democrat, competitive, mostly Republican, or
safe Republican?" A three-category variable was constructed from
the responses. The first category (one-party district) includes those
legislators who perceived that their districts were either safe Democratic or safe Republican. The second category (mostly-one-party
district) includes the responses "mostly Democratic" or "mostly Republican." The third category (competitive district) encompasses the
"competitive" response.

The typicality of the legislator from the district index was created by combining information from the perceived competitiveness
question and on the party affiliation of the legislator. This index has
five categories running from the least typical to the most typical legislator. If the legislator is a Democrat and perceives that his district is safe Republican or if the legislator is a Republican and perceives that his district is safe Democratic, the legislator is placed
in the least typical category of the index. A legislator is classified
into the second least typical category if he is a Democrat representing a mostly Republican district or a Republican representing a mostly Democratic district. Any legislator perceiving that his district is
competitive falls into the middle category on this typicality index.
The fourth category is composed of Democrats coming from mostly
Democratic districts and Republicans coming from mostly Republican
districts. The fifth and most typical category contains Democrats
representing safe Democratic districts and Republicans from safe
Republican districts. Thus, a low value on this independent variable
indicates a low degree of typicality and a high value indicates a high
degree of typicality.

Hypotheses

The hypotheses we proposed to examine in this chapter are as
follows:

1. The higher the level of general support for the party system,
the more likely the legislator will be to seek partisan cues.
2. The higher the level of support for the legislative party system, the more likely the legislator will be to seek partisan cues. Furthermore, high support on the LPO scale is expected to be more systematically related to partisan cue taking than is general party support.
3. The higher the level of general support for the party system,
the more likely the legislator will be to perceive partisan arenas as
the major decision locus.

   4. The higher the level of support for the legislative party system, the more likely the legislator will be to perceive partisan arenas
as the major decision locus. Furthermore, high support on the LPO
scale is expected to be more systematically related to perceiving
partisan decision locus than is general party support.

   5. The effect of either party orientation scale on partisan cue
seeking will be moderated by the perceived level of competition in the
legislator's district. That is, the more competitive the district, the
less likely the member is to seek out partisan cues.

   6. The effect of either party orientation scale on perceived partisan
decision loci will be moderated by the perceived level of competition
in the legislator's district. That is, the more competitive the district,
the less likely the member is to perceive partisan arenas as the major
decision locus.

   7. The effect of either party orientation scale on partisan cue
seeking will be reinforced by the typicality of the member's district.
That is, the more typical a member's district is, the more likely he
will be (relative to the party orientation scales) to seek out partisan
cues.

   8. The effect of either party orientation scale on perceptions of
partisan decision loci will be reinforced by the typicality of the member's district. That is, the more typical a member's district is, the
more likely he will be (relative to the party orientation scales) to believe that the major decision locus is party-related.

And, finally, we propose another hypothesis, not explicitly commented
upon above but implied in our discussions:

   9. The more likely a legislator is to take partisan cues, the
more likely he will also perceive the major decision locus to be party-
related.

   We turn next to an examination of our findings. The first portion of the findings section will be descriptive, presenting the distribution of alternative cue givers and decision loci. An additional hypothesis will be suggested by these findings which we shall also examine in this chapter. Then we shall test each of these hypotheses
in this chapter.

                    THE SOURCES OF LEGISLATORS' CUES

   The primary sources of cues attributed by our 1,256 state legislators are presented in Table 2.1. The legislators were asked to
rank in order their five most important sources of information from
a total of 13 possible responses (chairman of committee and ranking
minority member have been combined, as have three sets of party
leaders outside the legislature). The cue givers are listed in the table

TABLE 2.1

Sources of Cues Attributed by State Legislators
(frequency of responses in percent)

Cue Givers	First Choice	Second Choice	Third Choice	Fourth Choice	Fifth Choice	Total Mentions	Weighted Total
Personal friends in legislature	17.4	14.4	10.6	7.7	6.0	56.1	39.6
Legislative specialist	14.3	10.8	7.8	7.3	5.5	45.7	35.7
Interest groups	8.4	9.8	11.4	11.9	9.6	51.1	29.7
Committee chairman/ranking minority member	11.9	8.2	8.2	10.1	9.4	47.8	29.3
Legislators of same party from same or adjacent district	8.6	9.2	11.1	8.4	4.5	41.8	28.3
Legislative party leaders	9.3	9.5	9.1	6.9	6.5	41.3	26.4
Administrator-specialists in policy area	4.9	10.8	8.2	8.1	6.5	38.5	23.0
Legislators of both parties from same or adjacent district	4.0	5.3	9.2	6.7	5.1	30.3	17.4
Party leaders outside legislature	2.0	2.7	2.3	4.7	10.1	21.8	9.5
Governor	1.4	2.7	4.0	4.2	5.8	18.1	8.8
Constituents	3.6	0.3	0.3	0.1	0.4	4.7	4.1
Others/no answer	14.1	16.1	17.8	23.8	30.7	NA	NA

in the order of their weighted totals (first mentions were weighted
by a factor of five, second mentions by a factor of four, and so on).
Perhaps the most surprising findings in this table are the relatively
low weighted totals for the legislative party leaders (ranking sixth
out of eleven cue givers) and state governors (tenth out of eleven) in
the analysis.

State legislators seem to rely most heavily upon personal friends
in the legislature. This set of cue givers ranks highest in terms of
first mentions, second mentions, third mentions, total mentions, and
the weighted total. With the exception of interest groups, it appears
that the dominant cue givers in state legislatures are to be found within the chambers themselves. Over half of the members cite personal
friends and committee leaders as important sources of information
in helping them decide on whether to support or oppose a bill. Over
40 percent of the respondents cited legislative specialists in the particular policy area under consideration, legislators of the same party
from the same or adjacent districts, and legislative party leaders as
important cue givers. The only nonlegislative cue giver mentioned
by more than 40 percent of the respondents is the interest group.
Specialists in policy areas working in the bureaucracy are another
significant source of cues, while members often consult legislators
from both parties with similar constituencies. On the other hand,
neither the governor nor party leaders outside the legislature (state
party chairman, precinct committeemen in the legislator's district,
and county party chairman) seem to be relied upon for information on
voting decisions.

While the role of party leaders—and indeed the legislative party
itself—may appear somewhat muted, it does not follow that such partisan ties are not important in state legislatures. In a study of socio-
metric relationships in the Wisconsin lower house, Samuel C. Patterson (1959) found that friendship cliques tended to be both party-oriented and leader-oriented (that is, members chose fellow party members, and particular party leaders, as their closest associates in the
legislature). Indeed, a comparison of Kingdon's findings on the importance of selected cue givers in the Congress with our data set indicates that legislative party leadership, though not the dominant
source of cues or even as important as we had hypothesized, is nevertheless considerably stronger among state legislators than among
members of Congress.

Table 2.2 presents the comparisons we have made between our
data and Kingdon's. We have weighted his data similarly to our coding scheme to allow for comparisons, although we do note that our
questions were somewhat differently phrased so that the inferences
we make are only approximate. Nevertheless, it does appear that
the importance of fellow legislators (as measured in our case by per-

TABLE 2.2

Comparison of State Legislator Responses on Cue Taking
with Kingdon's Sample of Congressmen
(weighted percentages)

Cue Givers	State Legislators	Congressmen
Fellow legislators	39.6	42.3
Party leadership	26.4	14.0
Interest groups	29.7	31.0
Governor/president	8.8	20.3
Constituents	4.1	22.2

sonal friends) and interest groups does not vary much from the Congress to the state legislatures. On the other hand, legislative party leadership receives almost twice as great a weighted score in the states as it does in the Congress. And, returning to Table 2.1, we note that only personal friends in the legislature has a much greater weighted total number of responses than does legislative party leadership. Indeed, over 9 percent of our respondents stated that the party leadership was their most important source of information, whereas none of Kingdon's congressional sample called this leadership group "determinative" and only 5 percent said it was of "major importance." Because of differences in the questions posed, it seems that we have underemphasized the extent to which legislative party leaders are important sources of information in the states in comparison to the Congress.*

In contrast, however, the executive does not appear to be a major source of cues for legislators in our sample. This is a somewhat surprising finding, since the literature on state policy formation has stressed the importance of the role of the governor in the decision-making process to an even greater extent than that of the president in Congress (Sharkansky 1968a; McCally 1966). Bureaucratic experts are considerably more important sources of information than are gov-

---

*Since we only asked our respondents to name those information sources consulted, we weighted each response by some positive integer (from one to five). We weighted Kingdon's responses of "not important" as a zero, "minor importance" as one, "major importance" as two, and "determinative" as three. We divided our total scores by five and our weighted version of Kingdon's scores by three to allow for comparability.

ernors—who rank next to last of our 14 cue givers (actually, last if
we remember that constituents as cue givers was not a category in
our original question).

To the extent that one views the bureaucracy as an arm of the
governor's office, the power of the executive branch of government
does seem stronger in the states. The weighted percentages of mentions for the executive branch using this broader concept of the administration (which seems to correspond to Kingdon's conceptualization) 31. 8 for the states and 20. 3 for the Congress respectively. Nevertheless, the relative weakness of the governor appears surprising.
Only 1. 4 percent of our respondents looked to the chief executive as
a primary cue giver, with an additional 4. 9 percent relying most
heavily upon administrator-specialists in particular policy areas.
The total of 6. 3 percent does not seem markedly different from the
4 percent of Kingdon's congressional respondents who stated that administration cues were "determinative."

Why the executive branch of state government does not dominate
the sources of cues is a fascinating question. In part, our results
will differ both from Kingdon's and from our own expectations about
the role of the governor because of differences in questions posed.
The governor's position on a bill may not be considered so crucial if
the legislators believe that the executive branch dominates the legislative process and is "determinative" in Kingdon's sense. This is in
fact not the case when we consider the arenas legislators in our survey considered to be the major source of decision making in the state
legislature. What we do find fascinating, however, is the rather close
correspondence between our measures of the importance of other legislators and interest groups between our study and Kingdon's despite
the different questions posed and the different legislative arenas studied. We were bound to underestimate the importance of constituents
as cue givers by not including this category in our original list of cue
givers, but even if we had, we would not have expected it to be as major a factor in state legislatures where members are even less likely
to be recognized by their constituents and where the business of the
chambers is even more remote from the average citizen's concerns
than that of the Congress.

Comparisons with the Matthews-Stimson study are somewhat
more complex. There are several reasons for this set of problems.
First, Matthews and Stimson employed both interviews and a simulation routine to assess the importance of alternative cue givers. Second, many of their findings are expressed as percentages of all responses, while we have not presented the data this way in Table 2. 1.
A third source of confusion is that Matthews and Stimson distinguish
between "initial" cue givers and "intermediaries," while we do not
do so. This distinction involves whether members responded affirma-

tively to the initial Matthews-Stimson question for a particular reference group, on the one hand, and whether they indicated that there were other sources of cues beyond the three they were allowed to rank order in the initial question. Finally, they draw a distinction between individual cue givers and collective groups (such as state party delegations, House majorities, and so on), which we do not.

The Matthews-Stimson interviews indicate that the individual cue givers who are the most important in the views of their colleagues are committee members, chairmen/ranking minority members, and party leaders respectively. Eighty-six percent of their respondents cited committee members, compared to 45.7 percent of ours who mentioned "legislative specialist in the policy area" as a reasonable surrogate measure. The very fact that 86 percent of the Matthews-Stimson sample of House members cited committee members in comparison to our figure of 45.7 percent indicates the greater importance of such bodies in the Congress than in the states. This is not surprising in itself, although the degree of concentration of cue givers in Congress compared to the state legislatures is more striking than we had anticipated. The reason for this finding, we suggest, lies in the relative degrees of institutionalization of the various legislative chambers (see Polsby 1968). In Congress, we find a highly structured pattern of decision making, reinforced by strong committees, strict adherence (at least until recent years) to the seniority norm, and the related phenomena of low rates of turnover and high rates of reelection. State legislatures, as we have suggested above, are lacking in many of these characteristics.

The second most important individual cue giver is the committee chairman, mentioned by 45 percent of the Matthews-Stimson (1975; p. 91) sample, and, together with the ranking minority member, accounting for over 38 percent of all sources of cues. Our findings for the combined category of chairman-ranking minority member indicate that almost 48 percent of the members seek cues from them, or 6 percent of all cues mentioned. Thus, we find that there is a slight tendency for state legislators to depend upon committee leaders more than upon legislative specialists—the opposite of what Matthews and Stimson found. Note, however, that in each study the differences are small and suggest relative equality of committee members and leaders rather than any pattern of dominance when one moves from the state legislature to the House of Representatives.

Party leaders appear less important than other members in leadership positions in the Matthews-Stimson study (1975; pp. 92-93). They account for 16 percent of all cue givers, as compared to 5.2 percent in our study. But, these overall figures may be misleading in making comparisons, for Matthews and Stimson report (1975; p. 102) that 46 percent of their respondents wanted to know the position of party leaders if they knew nothing else about a bill. This is a higher figure than the total percentage of state legislators who mentioned legislative party leaders at all. Given the differences in questions, we can reach no firm conclusions about the overall impact of party leaders as cue givers. It is rare indeed, either in Congress or state legislatures, that members are in such a state of ignorance that they know nothing whatsoever about a piece of legislation.

The most frequently mentioned cue giver in the Matthews-Stimson survey was the state party delegation (treated as an intermediary cue giver) (1975; p. 98). In state legislatures, the concept of a state delegation is obviously meaningless. We did, however, inquire about legislators from the same or adjacent districts. When we combine the percentage of mentions of members from both the member's party and the opposition party, we find that geography is also an important criterion in seeking out information. Over 80 percent of our respondents chose cue givers from the same or adjacent districts. When we restrict our attention to legislators from the same party (our closest approximation to a "state party delegation"), we find that only 41.8 percent mention this source of information, ranking fifth both in total mentions and in weighted totals in Table 2.1 above.

Personal friends in the legislature, cited by only 31 percent of the Matthews-Stimson sample (1975; p. 84), are considerably more important in state legislative decision making. They are mentioned by 56.7 percent of our respondents, are the most important group in terms of weighted totals, and clearly prevail over all other cue givers as both first and second choices. We expect that many of the respondents who rely upon personal friends also depend most heavily upon members from the same or adjacent districts, since most friendship patterns are likely to be based upon partisan and geographic considerations. We therefore hypothesize:

10. The greater the level of either general support for the party system or support for the legislative party system, the more likely a member will be to seek out cues from members of his own party from the same or adjacent districts.

11. The lower the level of support either for the party system overall or for the legislative party system, the more likely a member will be to seek out cues from legislators of either party from the same or adjacent districts, or personal friends in the legislature.

12. The lower the level of support either for the party system overall or for the legislative party system, the more likely a member will be to seek out cues from personal friends in the legislature.

The final two hypotheses are consistent with the argument of James Sterling Young (1966), who viewed friendship groups (members of early Congresses residing in the same boardinghouses) as alternative sources of influence to party leaders.

Consistent with our finding that the governor is not an important source of cues, Matthews and Stimson report that the president "was not voluntarily mentioned as a source of cues" except when members were given only a single potential source of information. Then, the president became the second most popular initial cue giver, with 40 percent of the respondents wanting to know his position if they could obtain no other information. The president still ranks below party leaders, however. The significance of these findings is that the executive's "position on legislative proposals helps define the nature of the issue more than it serves as an authoritative evaluation for them" (Matthews and Stimson 1975; p. 104). On the other hand, the position may indeed be determinative in Kingdon's sense without being considered a major source of information.

Finally, the Matthews-Stimson simulation results which can be directly compared to our findings indicate that there is a greater difference between Congress and state legislatures than our comparisons with Kingdon's study suggested. The cue givers in their simulation which are comparable to our survey results include regional party delegations (state versus district); legislative party leaders; committee chairmen and ranking minority members, and chief executives (the president versus the governor). The rank order of these cue givers in the congressional study is the same as the order in which they were listed. Our rankings, using either total mentions or weighted totals, are as follows: committee chairmen and ranking minority members; regional party delegations; legislative party leaders, and the executive. The relative ranking of regional delegations and party leaders in our study should be examined with caution, since both totals (weighted and nonweighted) are so close that differences may be due to sampling error.

What is striking about the comparisons, however, is the importance of committee chairmen in the states in contrast to the Matthews-Stimson data in the Congress. We have argued above that the role of committee leaders as sources of information is greater in Congress than in the states—indeed, by comparisons with the interviews conducted by Matthews and Stimson. How, then, do we reconcile these diverse findings? The answer lies, we believe, in the comments of a member of the House to Stimson:

> . . . I'd have to say the ranking minority member of the reporting committee would give me a lot of information. You don't necessarily follow—you like to at least think you are making up your own mind, even though that is influenced by the type of people you ask. (p. 429)

Cues can serve as negative references as well as positive, as the fa-
mous story about a member of Congress indicates: The member so
disliked a colleague that (according to a third source) if the colleague
would vote "present," the member would vote "absent."

Yet, differences between the Congress and state legislatures
cannot simply be explained away by the potential for negative cues.
Rather, we believe (along with Matthews and Stimson) that the survey
results are the more interesting ones to compare, since they tell us
how a member goes about making up his mind on a voting decision.
The simulation studies, on the other hand, only reflect the results of
the decision. And the comparative analyses for the Congress and the
states have suggested so far that we find stronger party leaders in the
states than in Congress. The relative strength of committee chairmen and regional delegations appears weaker in the states, as does
that of executives. Interest groups and fellow legislators appear to
be of relatively equal strength in the two arenas (comparing our data
with those of Kingdon). We shall return to our consideration of cues,
particularly partisan cues, shortly. We now turn to an equally if not
more important factor in the study of legislative decision making—
where legislators believe the major decisions in the legislature are
made.

ARENAS OF POWER IN STATE LEGISLATURES

Our analysis of sources of cues attributed by state legislators
indicated that the predominant information resources were personal
friends in the legislature and various committee-related positions
(including legislator-specialists). Party leaders in the legislature
ranked somewhat lower, and, surprisingly, the governor was the
least important cue giver of the 13 original choices given our respondents. The chief executive's position improves somewhat when we include the spontaneous mentions of constituents as sources of cues by
the legislators. Yet overall the executive branch did not serve as a
major cue giver in the responses we received and reported in Table
2.1. We hypothesized above that this may be because legislators may
feel that they do not "have to" look to the governor's office. That office may be viewed as so powerful that it controls much of state decision making in the final analysis and there may simply be no need
for legislators to seek out information on the governor's position.

To examine this question further, we shall analyze the responses
to our query, "In your legislature, where would you say the most significant decisions are made?" Here each respondent could name only
one primary decision locus. In addition to the governor's office, the
possible responses included: (1) party caucus; (2) regular committee

TABLE 2.3

Decision Loci Attributed by State Legislators

Decision Locus	Percent[a]	Adjusted Percent[b]
Regular committee meetings	35.7	38.5
Party caucus	24.7	26.6
Governor's office	11.4	12.3
On the floor	8.6	9.3
Policy committee	4.7	5.1
Prelegislative session	1.7	1.8
Other	5.9	6.4
No Answer	7.2	—
Partisan decision loci[c]	29.4	31.7
Executive decision loci[d]	16.1	17.4

[a]Column totals do not add to 100.0 because of rounding error.
[b]"No answer" responses excluded.
[c]Party caucus and policy committee.
[d]Governor's office and policy committee.

meetings; (3) prelegislative sessions; (4) on the floor; (5) in policy committee; and (6) other. Table 2.3 presents the responses to this question, both in terms of total figures and adjusted percentages excluding those members who did not answer the question.

It is clear from that table that our expectation about the limited role of seeking gubernatorial cues is not borne out by the data; only 11.4 percent of all respondents (12.3 percent when those who gave no answer are eliminated) believe that the governor's office is the major source of decision making in the legislature. Again, we should be cautious in interpreting this finding, since the question asked where the most important decisions are made in the legislature. It is very possible that we still face the problem of members believing that the chambers are not the site of most critical state decisions. However, given the pattern of responses we have observed so far, it appears that this is not the case. Members of state legislatures, both in terms of the cues they seek and the arenas of power they mention, tend to stress committees and party-related bodies (respectively) to a much greater extent than they do the role of the executive branch. Indeed, the governor's office does not appear to be that much more powerful (from the figures in Table 2.3) than does action on the floor of the legislature. We suspect that state legislators may actually see the legislative chambers as the major source of policy formation in the states. This may (or may not) be a naive view, but it does appear to represent the perspective of the decision makers we are studying.

Regular committee meetings seem to be the major decision locus in the states, not a surprising finding when one considers the importance of such bodies in Congress. Yet committees have not been investigated in great detail at the state level and theory development in this area is noticeably lacking. Tables 2.1 and 2.3 suggest, however, that we need to pay considerably more attention to committee behavior in the states. In comparison to the Congress (see Table 2.2 above), we find that the role of parties as the major decision locus is much stronger in the states. This is not unexpected, since party leaders often exercise more control over procedure and committee appointments in the states—some states (for example, Florida) give the party leadership the power to appoint not only committee chairmen but all committee members—than in Congress. What is intriguing is that the adjusted percentage of our sample who cite the party caucus as the major decision locus (26.6 percent) is virtually identical to the weighted percentage of mentions of the legislative party leaders as cue givers (26.4 percent). Since the questions are conceptually distinct, on the one hand, and the relative ranking of the party caucus is much higher on the decision-locus list than on that of cue givers, one should be cautious in making comparisons. This is particularly the case because only 9.3 percent of our respondents cited legislative party leaders as their first-choice cue givers, in comparison to 24.7 percent who believed that the major center of power in the state legislature was the party caucus.

How do we reconcile the differences that emerge, aside from citing dissimilarities in the questions posed? The most immediate answer seems to be that legislative party leaders do not in general (that is, across the 50 states) constitute a monolithic bloc dominating partisan activity in the chambers. The party caucus is composed of all party members and it appears that nonleaders have important roles in many state caucuses. The importance of the party caucus as a collective decision-making group, corresponding to the norms of the doctrine of responsible party government, should not be overlooked. Reformers who want to make the national party system more issue-oriented thus might want to look to at least some of the states for suggestions on implementing their goals.

The two major categories of committees and party caucuses appear to dominate the legislators' perceptions of the central arenas of power in state legislatures. The raw percentage totals indicate that these categories together account for over 60 percent of all decision loci. The adjusted totals for the two are more than 65 percent. Finally, if we exclude the "other" category, committees and party caucuses account for virtually 70 percent of all major decision loci.

The office of the governor and decision making on the floor appear to be of moderate importance as decision loci, comprising 12.3 and 9.3 percent of the adjusted percentages respectively. The policy committees are of lesser importance, while prelegislative sessions (which are not held in every state) account for less than 2 percent of the total. The partisan decision loci (caucus and policy committee) outrank the executive loci (governor's office and policy committee), but even the former combined total does not outrank the role of committees in the state legislative process.

Our next question is: what is the extent of overlap between seeking partisan cues and seeing partisan arenas as the major source of state decisions in the legislature? To assess the extent of overlap, we present in Table 2.4 the results of an analysis relating cue taking from legislative party leaders to perceptions of the party caucus as the major decision locus. We limit partisan cues to those from party leaders here (see, on the following pages, Tables 2.7 through 2.20) because our more general concept of partisan cues includes sources outside the legislative chamber. We restrict our concern for the partisan decision locus to the caucus because we believe that it is the most clearly party-related arena of power. By so doing, we are maximizing the possible correlation between sources of information and arenas of power. By deriving what we consider to be the strongest available relationship within our data set, we get the clearest idea of the correspondence between our two questions.

In the data reported in Table 2.4, we treat the decision locus as the "dependent" variable and the source of cues as the "independent" variable, although we are making no assumptions about the direction of causality. The measures of association we are employing are symmetric and the classification decision of dependent and inde-

TABLE 2.4

Decision Locus by Cues from Legislative Party Leaders

Decision Locus	Cues from Party Leaders in Legislature	Other Cues	N
Party caucus	44.2	25.5	286
Other	55.8	74.5	761
N	104	943	1,047

Note: phi = .126; Q = .397.

pendent variables is thus arbitrary. There does seem to be a slight
tendency for members who take cues primarily from party leaders
to see the party caucus as the major decision locus in the legislature,
but note that over half of our respondents who relied most heavily on
such cues saw other arenas as the places where the most important
decisions in the legislature are made. The two variables obviously
are measuring different phenomena. There is no evidence of a linear
relationship. The phi coefficient is only .126, accounting for less
than 2 percent of the total variance. Yule's Q is .397. Given the sample size and the values of gamma reported in the analyses of our hypotheses, this may not seem like a very small relationship. However,
we would have expected even higher values for the curvilinear coefficient if partisan cue seeking and the attribution of a partisan decision
locus were to measure a unidimensional party related pattern of decision making in state legislatures. The most that we can conclude,
then, is that the arenas are not entirely independent. However, they
hardly measure the same phenomenon.

Since these concepts are statistically as well as analytically
distinct, the question becomes: Which concept (since the source of
cues has several different operationalizations), if either, displays
the predicted pattern of covariation suggested earlier to a greater
extent? Does a legislator's orientation toward the party system (either in general or toward the legislative party in particular) have a
greater effect upon the member's behavior (the cues he seeks to help
him make up his mind in reaching a decision) or on his view of "real-
ity" (power relationships in the legislature)? We pose similar questions when these relationships are controlled by the degree of competition the member perceives in his district and the typicality of a
member's seat. These are questions that can be posed, of course,
about cue-seeking behavior and perceptions of decision loci which
are not necessarily partisan.

Earlier in this chapter, we presented nine hypotheses in relatively broad terms. The predictions were listed in the order we had
discussed the underlying logic behind each. The testing of the hypotheses, as well as others suggested in our discussion of cues, will not
follow the same order as the listing. Instead, we shall concentrate
first on the simple bivariate hypotheses related to cue taking and our
party orientation scales. Then we shall consider the relationship between cues and subjective feelings toward the party system, controlling for the competition and the typicality of a member's district.
Third, we shall consider the predictions about cue taking relating to
legislators from the same or adjacent districts and personal friends
in the legislature. After examining these hypotheses, we turn to an
examination of the posited relationships between party orientations
and perceptions of the most important decision locus in the legislature.

As we shall do with the cue variables, we shall first consider the bivariate relationships and then control for the typicality of the district and the perceived level of competition. Note that we have already tested hypothesis 9 above (see Table 2.4). With any semblance of order in our hypotheses, our luck should improve. We turn now to an examination of the hypotheses stated several pages ago.

SOURCES OF VARIATION IN PARTISAN CUES

We hypothesized in the Introduction that legislators who have a strong affective orientation toward the party system in general and the legislative party system in particular would be more likely to seek out partisan cues than would those who did not feel strongly about the party system. Tables 2.5 through 2.8 examine this hypothesis. We first consider all primary cue givers who are specifically related to partisan orientations: (1) legislative party leaders; (2) members of the legislature from the same party who are also from the same or adjacent districts; and (3) party leaders outside the legislature. In the analyses to follow, the sample size is reduced from the total of 1,256 owing to missing values on the dependent and independent variables. Each table will report both row and column marginals, the total sample sizes, the percentages down the columns, and values of tau-c and gamma.

TABLE 2.5

Source of Cues by GPO Scale, Party Cue Givers
Compared with Others
(in percent)

Source	High	Medium	Low	N
All party cue givers	30.3	21.2	19.5	244
Others	69.7	78.7	80.5	810
N	259	628	167	1,054

Note: For this and all succeeding tables, cases with missing values (no responses) have been excluded. Cases with missing values on the dependent variable have also been excluded.
    tau-c = .076; gamma = .187.

TABLE 2.6

Source of Cues by LPO Scale, Party Cue Givers
Compared with Others
(in percent)

Source	High	Medium	Low	N
All party cue givers	37.8	25.7	11.1	236
Others	62.2	74.3	88.9	799
N	136	582	317	1,035

Note: tau-c = .179; gamma = .437.

In comparing all party cue givers to all other cue givers in the remaining groups in Table 2.5 we find little relationship between partisan cues and the GPO scale discussed above. Neither tau-c nor gamma is impressive in Table 2.5, even given the large number of cases. On the other hand, the more specific LPO Scale presented in Table 2.6 does appear to be a reasonably good predictor of the taking of partisan cues, although the relationship appears to be more curvilinear than strictly linear. Partisan cue taking in general thus appears to be more a function of specific attitudes toward the legislative party system (gamma = .437) than toward political parties in more general terms (gamma = .187). Indeed, this is partly a function of the distribution of supporters of the two party systems: there is considerably more support among our respondents for the party system in general terms than for the legislative party per se.

These results become even more pronounced when we consider only party leaders in the legislature as cue givers compared to all other cue givers available to the members. These results are presented in Tables 2.7 and 2.8 and are considerably better than those for all party cue givers. Again, the relationships appear to be nonlinear. But the GPO scale predicts the choice of party leaders as the main source of information reasonably well (gamma = .420), even better than the LPO scale predicted the reliance upon all party cue givers.

However, the strongest relationship is between the choice of party leaders as information sources and the specific LPO scale, where gamma = .610. Overall, party leaders in the legislature are not the major source of cues, as the marginals in the tables demon-

TABLE 2.7

Source of Cues by GPO Scale, Party Leaders
Compared with Others
(in percent)

Source	High	Medium	Low	N
Party leaders in legislature	19.4	8.6	5.5	114
Others	80.6	91.4	94.5	940
N	259	628	167	1,054

Note: tau-c = .096; gamma = .420.

strate, but there is a much stronger tendency for those who pay hom-
age to the belief in a strong legislative party system to rely upon this
leadership group than there is among other members in the legislature. Indeed, only 2 percent of those with low affectation toward the
legislative party took their first cues from party leaders.

Having examined primary cues, we turn now to a more detailed
examination of the information-seeking process in the American state
legislatures. Our survey asked each respondent to name up to five
major sources of information regularly employed in the legislature.
Tables 2.9 and 2.10 examine the frequency with which partisan cues
were cited (as opposed to all others) and orientations toward the par-

TABLE 2.8

Source of Cues by LPO Scale, Party Leaders
Compared with Others
(in percent)

Source	High	Medium	Low	N
Party leaders in legislature	22.6	12.8	2.0	112
Others	77.4	87.2	98.0	924
N	136	582	317	1,036

Note: tau-c = .137; gamma = .610.

TABLE 2.9

Number of Party Cues Taken by GPO Scale
(in percent)

Number	High	Medium	Low	N
None	22.3	30.9	37.3	347
One	39.2	40.0	35.8	457
Two	31.2	23.0	22.6	292
Three or more	7.3	6.0	4.3	71
N	293	700	174	1,167

Note: tau-c = -.094; gamma = -.167.

ties. Our findings reinforce those of the previous tables: general party orientation (Table 2.5) does not have a measurable impact upon the frequency of party cues seeking, but there does appear to be a systematic, albeit not overwhelming, relation between the importance of partisan cues and a specific orientation toward the legislative party. This relation is once again nonlinear (tau-c = -.189, gamma = -.314).

We do find stronger linkages between support for the general party system and partisan cues when we consider another dimension of information gathering in the states: the frequency and rank order in which party leaders in the legislature are named as sources of cues. Tables 2.11 and 2.12 break down the extent to which party leaders are selected first, second, third, fourth, fifth, or not at all as important sources of information in the legislature. We hypothe-

TABLE 2.10

Number of Party Cues Taken by LPO Scale
(in percent)

Number	High	Medium	Low	N
None	21.8	25.8	43.8	352
One	33.8	39.0	40.7	449
Two	36.3	27.1	15.6	285
Three or more	8.1	8.1	1.7	70
N	150	640	366	1,156

Note: tau-c = -.189; gamma = -.314.

size that the stronger the affective orientation toward the party system, the higher the frequency of early mentions—and, of course, the lower the frequency of the party leader's not being cited at all.

Tables 2.11 and 2.12 provide support for this contention. For both general orientation toward the party system and specific orientation toward the legislative party system, we have moderate measures of association. There does appear to be some evidence of curvilinearity in the relationship (gamma = .337 and .441 respectively), but the tau-c coefficients are higher than we have found elsewhere (.193 and .257 respectively) and may even be considered respectable, given the tendency of this coefficient to be depressed and the large sample size. It is not surprising to find that the LPO scale is once again a stronger predictor of partisan cue seeking than the general orientation scale. Yet the respectable coefficient for the latter scale in this analysis provides even further support for the contention that this general partisan orientation is not a good predictor of the extent to which legislators rely upon party-related cue givers, except for party leaders in the legislature. The general support measure does not lead members to seek information from either legislators from the same or adjacent districts of the same party or from party leaders outside the legislative system. On the other hand, support for a more restricted party system (the party in the legislature) appears to be a good predictor for all types of partisan cues, and is particularly useful when related back to party cues from within the legislature. Before examining the relation between our party orientation scales and the decision loci in the legislature, we shall first examine the extent

TABLE 2.11

Rank Order of Cue Taking from Party Leaders in
Legislature by GPO Scale
(in percent)

Ranking of Party Leaders	High	Medium	Low	N
First	19.4	8.6	5.5	114
Second	16.2	9.6	5.3	111
Third	12.9	11.0	2.9	108
Fourth	7.4	8.7	6.3	84
Fifth	6.7	6.5	11.0	76
Not at all	37.3	55.7	68.9	562
N	260	629	167	1,056

Note: tau-c = .193; gamma = .337.

TABLE 2. 12

Rank Order of Cue Taking from Party Leaders in
Legislature by LPO Scale
(in percent)

Ranking of Party Leaders	High	Medium	Low	N
First	22. 4	12. 8	2. 0	112
Second	12. 6	13. 4	3. 7	107
Third	12. 6	12. 2	6. 5	109
Fourth	10. 1	9. 0	5. 3	83
Fifth	6. 8	6. 7	8. 5	75
Not at all	35. 5	45. 8	74. 0	551
N	137	583	317	1, 037

Note: tau–c = . 257; gamma = . 441.

to which each of our four indices of partisan cues covaries with our
party orientation scales, controlling for the legislators' perceived
level of competition within his district and the typicality of the district.

PARTISAN CUES, PARTY SUPPORT,
AND THE DISTRICT

We hypothesized that the member's perceived level of party
competition should have a dampening effect on partisan cue taking (to
the extent that the member perceives his district to be competitive).
On the other hand, districts that are most typical of a party's legislative contingent (a Democratic member elected from a safe Democratic district or a Republican member elected from a safe Republican district) should be more likely to seek partisan cues than a legislator from an atypical district (a Republican from a safe Democratic
district). We examine each of the hypotheses from the previous section once again here, controlling for the perceived competitiveness
and the typicality of the district. We have divided the competition variable into a trichotomy: safe districts, mostly one-party districts,
and competitive ones. The more competitive the district, the less reliance we expect on party cues. Thus, unless otherwise noted, we
posit that negative relationships should obtain between the most competitive districts and the extent of partisan cue taking. The typicality
of a district is, as stated above, a five-category variable. The most

typical district would be one represented by a Democrat (Republican) who perceived his district as being safely Democratic (Republican). The least typical district would be represented by a Democrat (Republican) who perceived his district as being safely Republican (Democratic). There are very few cases in the latter category; depending upon the number of missing values on the dependent and independent variables, the number of cases ranges from 17 to 19, clearly too few for analysis.

It is not difficult to see why the number of cases in this category of our typicality variable should be so small. In the first place, we would not expect, for example, very many Democrats to be elected from safe Republican districts. Second, and even more critically, those members of the minority party who did achieve electoral success would hardly be likely to perceive their districts as safe for the opposition party. If the district were actually safe, the member might legitimately ask himself, how did he get elected at all? Now, it is not at all uncommon for members who might represent what might even be generously called "marginal" districts to agree that their district is generally supportive of the opposition party's candidates, but not safe for that party. Indeed, we find (partially, as one might expect from the facts of political life, particularly at the low-salience level of the state legislature) a distribution skewed toward more typicality. This is not unexpected given Kingdon's "congratulation-rationalization" effect in political campaigning. This effect posits that the victorious candidate believes that his victory reflects support for himself (or possibly his party) and that defeated candidates tend to blame their losses on the inability of the electorate to comprehend the most fundamental issues in the campaign. The distribution is less skewed in the extreme category of greatest typicality, perhaps a reflection of the fact that most legislators see some threat to their reelection prospects.

TABLE 2.13

All Party Cue Givers as Source of Cues by GPO Scale,
Controlling for District Competitiveness

	Safe	Mostly One-Party	Competitive
Tau-c	.129	.024	.088
Gamma	.262	.065	.241
N	294	466	291

TABLE 2.14

All Party Cue Givers as Source of Cues by LPO Scale,
Controlling for District Competitiveness

	Safe	Mostly One-Party	Competitive
Tau-c	.260	.171	.103
Gamma	.545	.424	.293
N	285	459	289

We choose not to collapse the two least typical districts into a
single category, however, because to do so would destroy the sym-
metry in the categorization of the typicality variable; and more importantly, the tau-c and gamma coefficients for the second least typical districts were virtually unaffected by collapsing these categories.
In the tables below, we report the tau-c and gamma coefficients for
each control category corresponding to the analyses of the previous
section. In the case of the atypical districts with too few cases to
make analysis meaningful, our comparisons will be made over the
four categories of typicality that have sufficient cases. This method
of presentation is, we believe, the most parsimonious. It spares the
reader the bother of attempting to make comparisons across rows
and down columns for each subgroup we are analyzing. It also provides more information than a simple partial coefficient would in each
case, since it allows us to make more detailed comparisons across
subgroups than partial coefficients would. In particular, we can examine the extent to which our hypotheses might be supported in the
more extreme categories, even though the relationship we posited
might not be strictly monotonic across all categories. In several
cases, this will turn out to be the case. The drawback of this approach
is that we can compare our measures of association only within tables. Such measures for subgroups are not directly comparable with
the overall coefficients in the previous section in terms of the impact
of our control variables. To measure the extent of impact, we need
measures such as regression coefficients instead of the correlation-
type measures we are employing. The capacity to make comparisons
across subgroups is, however, sufficiently worthwhile from our perspective to proceed in the way we have outlined.
     We first turn to a reexamination of the data in Tables 2.5 and
2.6 applying our controls. The results of these analyses are reported
in Tables 2.13 through 2.16 respectively. Tables 2.13 and 2.14 cor-

respond to tables 2.5 and 2.6 (relating, first, cue taking from all partisan sources by the GPO scale and, secondly, by the LPO scale), controlling for the perceived level of party competition in the member's district. Tables 2.15 and 2.16 similarly correspond to Tables 2.5 and 2.6, but the control variable here is the typicality of the district. The other tables employing controls will be grouped similarly.

TABLE 2.15

All Party Cue Givers as Source of Cues by GPO Scale,
Controlling for District Typicality

	Least Typical				Most Typical
Tau-c	.238*	.001	.087	.025	.118
Gamma	.543*	.005	.239	.062	.239
N	18*	.08	286	353	276

*In this and succeeding tables asterisk indicates there were too few cases for analysis.

In Tables 2.5 and 2.6, we found that there was at best a very weak relationship between the GPO scale and the taking of cues from all party cue givers, but a considerably stronger correlation between this pattern of cue taking and the LPO scale. Controlling for perceived party competition, we find that there is no overall pattern for the general party scale (see Table 2.13). Both tau-c and gamma are higher for safe and competitive seats than either coefficient is for mostly one-party districts. Furthermore, the magnitudes of the coefficients for safe seats and competitive ones are not large.

On the other hand, Table 2.14 indicates that party competition does affect the relationship between all party cue givers and the LPO scale. There is a monotonically decreasing relationship between the all party cue givers variable and the legislative party scale as we move from the least competitive to the most competitive districts. We find strong relationships for safe seats, moderate ones for mostly one-party districts, and lower coefficients for the competitive seats. Thus, as hypothesized, members from safe seats who have high scores on the LPO scale are more likely to take any type of partisan cues than are legislators from the more competitive seats. We had hypothesized that this would be the case because members from the less competitive districts would have greater freedom to look to party leaders for cues rather than focusing their attention on their constituents. This pattern holds only for the LPO scale—not for the GPO scale.

We observe a similar set of findings for the typicality of districts. There is no overall pattern for the typicality control. Indeed, the measures of association increase from the second category to the third, drop from the third to the fourth, and increase again for the most typical districts. (Recall that we shall not consider the first category because there are too few cases to make the analysis meaningful; the relatively high values of tau-c and gamma in the first column of Table 2.15 are artifacts of the small sample size.) Table 2.15 does report a value of gamma of .239 for the most typical districts in comparison to that of .005 for the second least typical ones; but the value of the curvilinear measure for the middle districts is identical to that for the most typical ones!

In contrast, Table 2.16 shows that there is a monotonic increase in the relationship between partisan cue seeking and support for the legislative party system as a member's district becomes more typical.

TABLE 2.16

All Party Cue Givers as Source of Cues by LPO Scale,
Controlling for District Typicality

	Least Typical	- - - - - - - - - - - - - -→			Most Typical
Tau-c	-.003*	.013	.103	.216	.279
Gamma	-.009*	.043	.291	.495	.576
N	17*	108	285	347	268

Members from the second least typical district are no more likely to take partisan cues than would be expected by chance, according to their scores on the LPO scale (tau-c = .013); this relation is considerably strengthened for the most typical districts. It also appears that the overall relationship is curvilinear since the values of gamma, beginning with the middle category, are considerably higher than those of tau-c. Yet even the values of the latter coefficient are respectable for the two most typical district types. It thus appears that the overall tendency for members who have high scores on the LPO scale to seek out all types of available partisan cues is accentuated when we control for the perceived competitiveness of the district and also the district's typicality.

The strongest relationships we have found so far involve those between the two party orientation scales and the searching for cues from legislative party leaders (see Tables 2. 7 and 2. 8 above). These findings are reinforced in Tables 2. 17 through 2. 20, in which the same data are analyzed with controls for competition and typicality.

TABLE 2. 17

Party Leaders in Legislature as Source of Cues by GPO Scale, Controlling for District Competitiveness

	Safe	Mostly One-Party	Competitive
Tau-c	.172	.048	.074
Gamma	.554	.254	.390
N	294	466	291

As we go from the safe to the competitive districts and from the least typical to the most typical ones (Tables 2. 17 and 2. 19), we do not find a monotonic pattern of increases or decreases in either measure of association for the GPO scale. Yet it is hard to escape the conclusion that the safe seats and the most typical ones display much stronger patterns of covariation between cue sources and diffuse support toward the party system than do other types of districts. Competitive districts, then, have stronger patterns of interrelationships than do mostly one-party ones and districts in the middle of the typicality scale display similar patterns in comparison to those which are not very typical and quite typical (the second and fourth categories, respectively). Yet the coefficients for the safe and most typical districts are so much larger than any in the other categories that the most appropriate conclusion is that our hypothesis holds at least for the extreme cases.

For the LPO scale (Tables 2. 18 and 2. 20), we do find overall support for our hypotheses that seeking partisan cues within the legislature will covary systematically with support for the legislative system, and that this relationship will be strongest in districts that are safe and most typical of the party's basis of support. Again, the relationships are not always monotonic, but they are relatively easy to distinguish. There does seem to be a monotonic decline in the measures of association when we control by competition. However, the overall relationship seems curvilinear (as it did in the analysis of the entire sample). The slight difference in the values of gamma from the safe to the mostly one-party districts, in comparison to the decline when one moves to the competitive districts, suggests that there is a competitive-noncompetitive distinction on the relation between our dependent and independent variables. For all types of districts, there does appear to be a patterned relationship between cue seeking among legislative party leaders and support for the party system in the chamber. It is found to be greatest, however, in the noncompetitive seats.

There is a similar phenomenon at work when we control for typicality. The most typical districts actually have a value of gamma which is less than that for the very typical ones (.701 compared to .724). If we accept the general premise that the underlying relationship is curvilinear, then the distinction we make is between typical and atypical districts. The somewhat typical (that is, median category) districts have much smaller coefficients than the typical ones; the atypical districts almost wipe out any relationship between the LPO scale and the seeking of information from legislative party leaders.

TABLE 2.18

Party Leaders in Legislature as Source of Cues by LPO
Scale, Controlling for District Competitiveness

	Safe	Mostly One-Party	Competitive
Tau-c	.200	.122	.091
Gamma	.672	.622	.479
N	285	459	289

The above findings represent the strongest relationships we have reported between any of our measures of information seeking and the subjective orientations of members toward their party. The tables that follow are, like Tables 2.9 through 2.12, not as striking in terms of the magnitudes of the coefficients. However, the patterns of relationships are quite interesting; we shall turn to an examination of them now.

TABLE 2.19

Party Leaders in Legislature as Source of Cues by GPO
Scale, Controlling for District Typicality

	Least Typical				Most Typical
Tau-c	.106*	.043	.075	.054	.176
Gamma	.515*	.268	.389	.273	.557
N	18*	108	286	353	276

Tables 2.21 to 2.24 show the relationships, when controlled, between the number of party cues a member mentioned and his scores on the two party orientation scales. Table 2.9 above indicated that there was not a systematic correlation between the number of party cues and the general party scale, while Table 2.10 indicated a moderate relationship with the legislative party scale. For these tables, we expect negative measures of association since the number of cues variable ranges from zero to three (or more).

Table 2.21 indicates that the control for the perceived level of party competition is not very useful if we consider competition to be a strictly increasing phenomenon. The relationship between the number of cues sought and the general party orientation is highest in the safe and the competitive districts and lowest in the mostly one-party areas. We have no ready explanation for this set of findings. Perhaps it simply reflects the lack of overall relationship between the two variables. This interpretation is given further support by examining Table 2.23, in which the typicality of the district is the control variable. The not very typical districts display positive coefficients (tau-c = .094, while gamma = .193); the most typical districts, on the other hand, have negative values (tau-c = -.166, gamma = -.265). But so do the median districts, and the values of the measures of association for these districts are not so different from those of the most typical districts that no firm conclusions can be drawn. There is certainly no monotonic trend for either the linear or the curvilinear measure of association. What we have here is chaos, and the appropriate conclusion is that our controls do not tell us more than the original analysis did.

We found moderate relationships between the number of party cues and the LPO scale above (tau-c = -.189 and gamma = -.314). The patterns of covariation when controls for competition and typical-

ity are employed are consistent with our hypotheses, if not dramatic.
For example, the control for competition (Table 2. 22) reveals a small
but steady decline in the strength of the relationships for both tau-c
and gamma as we move from the safe to the competitive districts.
Members from safe districts who have high (low) scores on the LPO
scale are more likely to seek multiple party cues than colleagues
with similar scores from more competitive districts.

TABLE 2. 20

Party Leaders in Legislature as Source of Cues by LPO
Scale, Controlling for District Typicality

	Least Typical				Most Typical
Tau-c	-.003*	.035	.091	.148	.215
Gamma	-.009*	.206	.478	.724	.701
N	17*	108	285	347	268

The control for typicality also suggests that members who represent districts most typical of their party's voting behavior (at least
as perceived by the legislators) are also more likely to seek multiple
cues from partisan sources in the legislature in comparison to other
members with the same level of support for the legislative party. The
pattern of coefficients is once more monotonic and the cut-off point
seems to be at the median level of typicality. Members from atypical
districts are considerably less likely to seek out many sources of
party cues (relative to their orientation toward the legislative party)
than do members from the median district and the more typical ones.
This tendency is not overwhelming. For the most typical districts,
tau-c = -. 274 (a very respectable figure for that coefficient) and gamma = -. 422. The number of cues from party leaders does not seem
to be predicted as well as the simple question of whether primary cue
givers are related to the legislative party—although any such comparisons should be taken with caution. Yet we have found a systematic
pattern of covariation underlying the more general relationships discussed above.

The rank ordering of cue taking from legislative party leaders
was found to be moderately related to the GPO scale and somewhat
more strongly correlated with the LPO scale (gamma = . 337 and . 441

TABLE 2.21

Number of Party Cues Taken by GPO Scale,
Controlling for District Competitiveness

	Safe	Mostly One-Party	Competitive
Tau-c	-.160	-.039	-.109
Gamma	-.252	-.073	-.188
N	332	520	311

respectively; tau-c = .193 and .257 respectively), as Tables 2.11
and 2.12 indicate. When we control for the perceived level of competition in a member's district, we find that the values of both tau-c
and gamma are considerably higher for the safe districts than they
are for the more competitive seats for both party orientation scales.
However, note that the GPO scale does not display a monotonic pattern of declining measures of association as we move from the least
competitive seats to the most competitive ones (see Table 2.25). The
relationship suggests that the pattern of covariation between support
for the general party system and the ranking of cues from legislative
party leaders is (relatively) high, low, moderate. Yet the magnitude
of the coefficients for the safe seats is quite high even in comparison
to those for the competitive ones, suggesting once again that the distinction which is most appropriate is safe seats/competitive districts
(including mostly one-party ones).

TABLE 2.22

Number of Party Cues Taken by LPO Scale,
Controlling for District Competitiveness

	Safe	Mostly One-Party	Competitive
Tau-c	-.246	-.178	-.139
Gamma	-.379	-.304	-.237
N	325	516	311

On the other hand, the coefficients for the LPO (see Table 2.26) scale do decrease monotonically, as predicted, although the magnitude of the differences from one category to the next are not as great as we have found elsewhere. Overall, it appears that both scales, and the controls, have moderate-to-high relationships with the ranking of cues from legislative party leaders.

The control for the typicality of the legislator's district displays very similar patterns to that for competition. Table 2.27 indicates modest values for both tau-c and gamma for the not very typical and median districts, reduced relationships for the quite typical ones, and much stronger values for the most typical seats on the GPO scale. Members from districts most typical of their parties, then, tend to rank cues from party leaders in the legislature as important if they have positive orientations toward the party system in general.

TABLE 2.23

Number of Party Cues Taken by GPO Scale,
Controlling for District Typicality

	Least Typical	– – – – – – – – – – – – – – – →			Most Typical
Tau-c	-.060*	.094	-.110	-.067	-.166
Gamma	-.094*	.193	-.192	-.122	-.265
N	19*	119	305	395	313

Furthermore, this relationship is considerably weaker for members from districts that are not safe for party members. On the other hand, support for the legislative party does display the expected relation with the ranking of cues from legislative party leaders, and the relationship is accentuated when the control for typicality is added. There is a monotonic increase in the pattern of coefficients and the sharpest increase in the relations displayed in Table 2.28 (for both tau-c and gamma) occur in the two most typical district types.

We have thus seen that there is an identifiable pattern of relationships between support for both the general party system and the legislative party system. The relationships, not surprisingly, are stronger for the LPO scale. We expected these results because the latter scale is particularly concerned with member's orientations toward party leaders in the legislature. Furthermore, we have found

TABLE 2.24

Number of Party Cues Taken by LPO Scale,
Controlling for District Typicality

	Least Typical	- - - - - - - - - - - - - - - →			Most Typical
Tau-c	.204*	-.049	-.142	-.212	-.274
Gamma	.300*	-.088	-.243	-.358	-.422
N	18*	121	306	391	305

support for most of our predictions regarding the impact of our control variables, the perceived level of competition and the typicality of the district, as intervening factors in the linkage between partisan cue taking and support for the party system. Most notable has been the effect of the most consistent control (typicality) for the best predictor (LPO scale) on the most clear-cut measure of partisan cue seeking (whether a member employs cues from legislative party leaders).

TABLE 2.25

Rank Order of Cue Taking from Party Leaders in
Legislature by GPO Scale, Controlling for
District Competitiveness

	Safe	Mostly One-Party	Competitive
Tau-c	.284	.134	.185
Gamma	.437	.254	.335
N	294	467	291

When there has been a failure of our predictor variable to display a relationship with our operationalization of cue taking (such as the general party orientation versus all party cue givers or versus the simple number of party cues taken), the control variables do not appear to be of much help in resolving the disorder. For the inter-

TABLE 2.26

Rank Order of Cue Taking from Party Leaders in
Legislature by LPO Scale, Controlling for
District Competitiveness

	Safe	Mostly One-Party	Competitive
Tau-c	.310	.257	.203
Gamma	.492	.451	.358
N	285	460	290

mediate situations, we find that the controls for competition and typicality generally do sharpen our ability to predict the pattern of co-variation between information seeking and support for the party system, although the relations are not always monotonic (as hypothesized). Simply stated, legislators' orientations toward political parties, and toward the legislative parties in particular, are systematically related toward the taking of cues from party-related sources (party leaders in particular); and the rank order of importance of cues from

TABLE 2.27

Rank Order of Cue Taking from Party Leaders in
Legislature by GPO Scale, Controlling for
District Typicality

	Least Typical				Most Typical
Tau-c	.235*	.150	.185	.130	.290
Gamma	.356*	.331	.335	.236	.457
N	18*	108	286	354	276

TABLE 2.28

Rank Order of Cue Taking from Party Leaders in
Legislature by LPO Scale, Controlling for
District Typicality

	Least Typical				Most Typical
Tau-c	.133*	.162	.213	.283	.322
Gamma	.186*	.322	.357	.479	.514
N	17*	108	287	348	268

legislative party leaders also varies with the legislator's support for
the party system. Finally, the electoral situation of the member
(most critically, the typicality of the district) has an important intervening effect on the relation between partisan cue taking and support
for the party system.

Every operationalization of our cues variable has indicated that
at least moderate relationships hold for one (sometimes both) of our
party orientation scales. Do these patterns continue to hold for perceptions of the most important decision locus in the legislature? We
shall answer this question after considering the other hypotheses on
information seeking in the legislature suggested above. It is to these
latter hypotheses, dealing with colleagues from the same or adjacent
districts and with personal friends in the legislature, that we now
turn.

FRIENDS AND NEIGHBORS IN THE LEGISLATURE

Since personal friends are the primary cue givers and legislators from the same or adjacent districts also constitute a sizable proportion of the cues sought by members, we hypothesized that there
should be a relation between use of these information sources and orientations toward the party system. With respect to legislators from
the same or adjacent districts of the same party as the respondent,
we expected that this type of cue would be the closest thing in a state
legislature to a "state party delegation," one of the most critical information resources in the Congress. Thus, we hypothesized a positive relationship with the two party orientations and the seeking of
cues from legislators of the same party who are "neighbors."

On the other hand, we consider the general reliance upon friends and neighbors to be indicative of dependence on non-party-related information resources, that is, to reflect an independence based upon peer groups in the legislature (friends) or upon constituency-oriented connections (neighbors). Thus, we expect negative relationships between each of our party orientation scales and the seeking of cues from: (1) all "friends and neighbors" (friends and legislators of either party from the same or adjacent district) cues; and (2) those that rely exclusively upon personal friends in the legislature. We expect that this latter category, if it does measure reliance upon information specifically removed from formal leadership positions (such as parties in particular), will display the strongest of the entire friends and neighbors relationships.

The results for the hypothesis tests are presented in Tables 2.29 through 2.34 below. Each pair of tables, respectively, reports

TABLE 2.29

Cue Sources from Legislators of Own Party from Same
or Adjacent District by GPO Scale
(in percent)

Source	High	Medium	Low	N
Legislators of own party from same or adjacent district	9.4	10.2	10.7	106
Others	90.6	89.8	89.3	948
N	259	628	167	1,054

Note: tau-c = -.009; gamma = -.042.

the results of our analysis by cue giver for the both party-orientation scales. For the GPO scale, Table 2.29 indicates a pair of slightly negative correlations with cues from party sources from the same or adjacent districts, contrary to our expectation. The correlations are miniscule, however, and are reversed for the LPO scale, where we obtain a tau-c of .030 and a gamma of .146. While these coefficients are in the predicted direction, they are also very small. Either regional delegations do not mean the same thing (in comparison to the total party delegations) in the states as they do in the Congress or our hypothesis is not adequately tapping the regional cleavage. We believe that there is a degree of each explanation in the low relationships we observe. On the one hand, regional groupings in the states are not as

TABLE 2.30

Cue Sources from Legislators of Own Party from Same
or Adjacent District by LPO Scale
(in percent)

Source	High	Medium	Low	N
Legislators of own party from same or adjacent district	12.3	10.4	7.9	102
Others	87.7	89.6	92.1	934
N	136	582	317	1,036

Note: tau-c = .030; gamma = .146.

likely to be as cohesive as they are in Congress because sessions are generally shorter as is tenure in office—both factors reducing the amount of patterned interaction among fellow legislators from the same areas. On the other hand, regional conflict may not be revealed

TABLE 2.31

Cue Sources from Personal Friends and Legislators
from Same or Neighboring Districts by GPO Scale
(in percent)

Source	High	Medium	Low	N
Friends and neighbors	27.8	35.8	37.7	360
Others	72.2	64.2	62.3	694
N	259	628	167	1,054

Note: tau-c = -.070; gamma = -.140.

by this analysis because the most appropriate affective response on the part of the individual legislator may be to the regional delegation rather than to the general or the legislative party system. The independent variables here may not be measuring the specific commitment to a subset of the member's party. The situation is further compounded by the fact that regional conflicts may be strong in some states but not in others.

We do find the expected negative relationships with both party orientation scales for our composite friends and neighbors variable, but again the magnitude of the coefficients for both scales is not large. For the GPO scale, tau-c = -.070 and gamma = -.140, while we find very similar values (-.084 and -.164 respectively) for the LPO scales in Tables 2.31 and 2.32. Thus, it does not appear that orientations

TABLE 2.32

Cue Sources from Personal Friends and Legislators
from Same or Neighboring Districts by LPO Scale
(in percent)

Source	High	Medium	Low	N
Friends and neighbors	22.9	34.1	37.9	350
Others	77.1	65.9	62.1	685
N	136	582	317	1,036

Note: tau-c = -.084; gamma = -.164.

toward the party system have a systematic impact on the general seeking of cues from personal friends and legislators from the same or adjacent districts in the state legislatures. The lack of a relationship is probably due to the different orientation which would be expected to affect this type of cue seeking. Hence, we can reject the hypothesis that low support for the party system will lead members to "substitute" personal friends and neighboring colleagues rather than other groups or individuals as their primary information source.

Finally, when we consider only personal friends in the legislature (Tables 2.33 and 2.34), we find at best a modest relationship in the posited direction between taking cues from such colleagues and orientations toward the party system. "Diffuse" support for the party system does not seem to be related to cue taking from friends at all;

TABLE 2.33

Cues from Personal Friends by GPO Scale
(in percent)

Source	High	Medium	Low	N
Personal friends	15.5	20.6	21.4	205
Others	84.5	79.4	78.6	849
N	259	628	167	1,054

Note: tau-c = -.042; gamma = -.120.

tau-c = -.042 and gamma = -.120. On the other hand, there is some tendency for members who rely primarily upon personal friends in the legislature to have negative orientations toward the legislative party system. We caution that this is not a strong relationship; tau-c = -.106 and gamma = -.297. Yet only for personal friends is there any pattern of covariation with party orientation, and, here, the relationship is restricted to orientations toward the legislative party system. This is not surprising. Diffuse support for the parties is less likely to have an impact on cue taking because both concepts—diffuse support and the American party system—contain elements of ambiguity.

On the other hand, support for the legislative party system implies a stronger commitment to the role of the party in the legislature as a source of information which the member relies upon—and actively pursues. While a member's personal friends in the legislature may be—indeed, are likely to be—members of his own political party, it is not necessarily the case that this friendship group will include the party leaders. Thus, the LPO scale is a more clear-cut measure of subjective attitudes toward this critical information source. And the modest negative correlation with the latter scale indicates that at least for a member's personal friends in the legislature, there is some conflict between party-related sources of information and ones that are clearly more individualistic (that is, salient to each member in a different way).

The findings for this source of information, compared to our earlier discussion of partisan cues, provide a generally consistent conclusion that members who have strong feelings in favor of the party system are more likely to look to party-related cue givers (particularly if they are from typical and/or safe districts) and legislators who are less committed to the parties will tend to seek out other cues, among them personal friends in the legislature. We turn now to an examination of alternative decision loci in the legislature.

TABLE 2.34

Cues from Personal Friends by LPO Scale
(in percent)

Source of Cues	High	Medium	Low	N
Personal friends	9.5	18.0	25.9	200
Others	90.5	82.0	74.1	836
N	136	582	317	1,036

Note: tau-c = -.106; gamma = -.297.

DECISION LOCI AND ORIENTATIONS
TOWARD THE PARTIES

We have found low-to-moderate relationships between the taking of cues from all party cue givers and members' orientations toward the general party system and the legislative party system. The correlations were considerably stronger when we considered only legislative party leaders as sources of information. We had hypothesized that members' perceptions of where the most important decisions are made in the legislature should also vary systematically with their evaluations of the parties. Our expectations are somewhat tempered by the only moderate relationship between seeking cues from party leaders and the propensity to see party-related decision loci (party caucuses and policy committees) as the major arenas of power in the legislature. We turn now to an examination of the hypotheses on perceptions of decision loci.

Table 2.35 indicates a weak relationship between diffuse support for the parties and the propensity to perceive the caucus or the policy committee as the major decision locus (tau-c = .140, gamma = .282). There are moderate relationships between perceptions of partisan decision loci and support for the legislative party system (tau-c = .182, gamma = .351). These figures are not appreciably affected if we consider only the party caucus as the source of partisan decision

making in the legislature (figures not presented here). Thus, our
findings on orientations toward the party system and perceptions of
decision loci seem much closer to those of all party cue givers than
to those of legislative party leaders as the major information sources.
The arenas of power in the state legislatures are thus different aspects of decision making in the states and the sources of cues members seek.

TABLE 2.35

Source of Decision Locus by GPO Scale
(in percent)

Source of Decision Locus	High	Medium	Low	N
Party caucus or policy committee	44.3	29.8	23.5	358
Others	55.7	70.2	76.5	747
N	272	667	166	1,105

Note: tau-c = .140; gamma = .282.

It is not surprising that there are at least moderate relationships between party orientations and our decision-locus variable.
However, the decision-locus variable appears to measure what legislators see as the way the chambers work rather than how they might
work if cue taking were the dominant factor in decision making. Now
we know of no student of cue giving and taking who maintains that the
exchange of information can serve as a unidimensional explanation
for the decision-making process in any legislative body. However,
for the states, at least in comparison to the findings for Congress,
it appears that cue taking constitutes only a small portion of decision
making. Perhaps because state legislative positions are not full-time
positions in many states, turnover is much higher, and the decision-
making structure may be less open to the influence of the individual
member (as opposed to the leader of the party, the committee, or the
state—the governor), the role of information in the states may not be
as critical as in Congress. We can only speculate on this, but it does
seem that decision making in state legislatures would be more decentralized (and like that of Congress) if members could make such a
choice.

Tables 2.37 to 2.40 demonstrate the relationships between perceived decision loci and the party-orientation scales, controlling for the perceived level of district competition and the typicality of the

TABLE 2.36

Source of Decision Locus by LPO Scale
(in percent)

Source	High	Medium	Low	N
Party caucus or policy committee	47.1	36.2	21.1	357
Others	52.9	63.8	78.9	732
N	142	597	350	1,089

Note: tau-c = .182; gamma = .351.

TABLE 2.37

Source of Decision Locus by GPO Scale, Controlling
for District Competitiveness

	Safe	Mostly One-Party	Competitive
Tau-c	.190	.081	.176
Gamma	.353	.183	.338
N	316	492	296

member's district. Each table reveals a curvilinear relationship, with the mostly one-party districts displaying the lowest correlations with both the GPO scale (tau-c = .081, gamma = .183) and the LPO scale (tau-c = .136, gamma = .282). For the former scale, the relationship with partisan decision loci is strongest in the safe seats. The LPO scale, on the other hand, is most strongly related to perceptions of decision loci in the competitive districts, contrary to our hypothesis.

For neither scale is the pattern clear enough to warrant any conclusions that the controls are adding to our knowledge about the perceptions of state legislators.

Similarly, the relationships between both scales and decision loci, controlling for typicality, do not clarify the relationships very much. We can state that the second least typical districts (the least typical ones have too few cases for analysis) do appear to display lower correlations than do any of the other types of districts. This is not terribly informative and we would have to maintain that there is no support for our hypothesis regarding the typicality control.

TABLE 2.38

Source of Decision Locus by LPO Scale, Controlling
for District Competitiveness

	Safe	Mostly One-Party	Competitive
Tau-c	.202	.136	.236
Gamma	.365	.282	.439
N	308	486	294

Our conclusion, then, is that the sources of information members seek are, at least from the partisan perspective, more predictable than the sources of power in the legislature from the orientations

TABLE 2.39

Source of Decision Locus by GPO Scale, Controlling
for District Typicality

	Least Typical				Most Typical
Tau-c	.148*	-.065	.176	.139	.205
Gamma	.235*	-.139	.338	.325	.392
N	18*	114	291	372	298

TABLE 2.40

Source of Decision Locus by LPO Scale, Controlling
for District Typicality

	Least Typical				Most Typical
Tau–c	.149*	.121	.235	.138	.202
Gamma	.232*	.244	.437	.301	.370
N	17*	116	290	366	290

of the legislators toward the party system, either in general or with
respect to legislative party leaders in particular. This pattern is not
surprising, since both the cue-seeking variable and the two party-
orientation scales requested subjective evaluations from our respondents. The party-orientation questions specifically asked for value
judgments; the sources of information implicitly raised evaluative
questions, since each member could choose any information giver he
felt most reliable or closest to. The question on decision locus is,
of course, subject to some coloration by one's perspective. Yet, it
is a much more objective instrument than any of the other questions
we have employed. It did not ask the member to state where he believed decisions should be made, but rather where he thought they
are made. The correspondence between members' goals and the decisional structure of a legislative body may be one of the most critical questions in the study of such institutions. Yet this has not generally been the focus of reformers who propose to redesign legislative systems.

3

DECISION-MAKING SOURCES WITHIN STATE LEGISLATURES: THE COMMITTEE PERSPECTIVE

INTRODUCTION

In the previous chapter, we found moderate-to-strong relationships between orientations toward the party system and the seeking of legislative cues and somewhat lower correlations between party as the major decision locus in the legislature and our party orientation scales. Yet political parties are not the most salient sources of information for our respondents, nor is the political-party caucus the dominant locus of decision making in the states. For our cue-seeking question, 47.8 percent of our respondents mentioned (among their top five information sources) committee leaders, compared to 41.3 who cited legislative party leaders. The weighted totals were 29.3 and 26.4 percent respectively (see Table 2.1 above). Even more revealing is the pattern of responses to our question on the major decision locus in the legislature. For party caucuses, we obtained a weighted percentage of 26.6; for committees, 38.5. Committees were by far the dominant decision loci within state legislatures (see Table 2.3 above). We are thus led to the immediate question: what are the patterns of variation in committee-leader cue seeking or perceptions of committees as the major source of power in the legislature?

We are struck once again by the relative standing of committee chairmen and ranking minority members when we compare our cue-seeking results to those of Matthews and Stimson (1975). Recall that the relative standing of committee leaders was considerably higher in our ranking than it was in theirs. And these findings certainly do not run contrary to the report of the Committee on American Legislatures of the American Political Science Association over two decades ago, which maintained that "the most important work of the

state legislatures, like that of Congress, is conducted by standing
and special committees" (Zeller 1954; p. 95). The power of committees in Congress, particularly in relation to the political parties, was
the dominant theme of Woodrow Wilson's Congressional Government,
originally published in 1885 but still considered one of the major
works on Congress and perhaps the entire legislative process. It was
Wilson who first referred to the committees as "little legislatures"
which serve to decentralize the legislative system and thus to prevent
overall policy coordination in that branch of government (1885; p. 113).
Viewed from the perspective of the doctrine of responsible party government, this is clearly an undesirable state of affairs. Even without
the normative perspective of the doctrine of responsible party government, the emphasis on committee decision making rather than party
decision making has clear implications for policy formation in the
chamber. Members will not base their decision-making strategies on
what they believe will constitute "good public policy," so much as on
what sorts of action will win favor with their legislative colleagues
and perhaps their constituents as well (see Fenno 1973; ch. 1 for a
discussion of these alternative member goals).

Wilson argued in particular:

> Power [in Congress] is nowhere concentrated; it is rather
> deliberately and of set policy scattered amongst many
> small chiefs. It is divided up, as it were, into forty-seven
> seigniories, in each of which a Standing Committee is the
> court-baron and its chairman lord-proprietor. These petty
> barons, some of them not a little powerful, but none of
> them within reach of the full powers of rule, may at will
> exercise an almost despotic sway within their own shires,
> and may sometimes threaten to compulse even the realm
> itself; but both their mutual jealousies and their brief and
> restricted opportunities forbid their combining, and each
> is very far from the office of common leader. (1885, p.
> 92)

In the same work he stated:

> The leaders of the House are the chairmen of the prin-
> cipal Standing Committees. Indeed, to be exactly ac-
> curate, the House has as many leaders as there are
> subjects of legislation for there are as many Standing
> Committees as there are leading classes of legislation.
> . . . It is this multiplicity of leaders, this many-headed
> leadership, which makes the organization of the House

too complex to afford uninformed people and unskilled
observers any easy clues to its method of rule. (pp. 60-
61)

Wilson not only deplored the decentralization of power which
the committee system fostered and the accompanying lack of accountability for overall policy formation in a single set of leaders (Wilson
1885; pp. 92ff.), but he also saw the committee chairmen as a set of
oligarchs largely removed from any sanctions. He stated:

There are no screws of responsibility which [the people]
can turn upon the consciences or upon the official thumbs
of the congressional Committees principally concerned.
Congressional Committees are nothing to the nation; they
are only pieces of the interior mechanism of Congress.
To Congress they stand or fall. And, since Congress itself can scarcely be sure of having its own way with them,
the constituencies are manifestly unlikely to be able to
govern them. . . . Each branch of the government is fitted
out with a small section of responsibility, whose limited
opportunities afford to the conscience of each many easy
escapes. (p. 281)

Wilson was not alone in his condemnation of the policy autonomy
of the committee system in Congress. Eighty years later, V. O. Key,
Jr., stated: "A first essential in the execution of a program in the
general weal is the power to batter down the more outrageous demands
of narrow interests. The strategic advantages enjoyed by committee
chairmen handicaps efforts in that direction" (1964, p. 672). It was
not only among critics of the committee system that the conflict in
roles between such a system and more cohesive party system was
noted. Ralph K. Huitt, who was more inclined to extol the virtues of
a decentralized legislative arena, maintained that "the committee
chairmen, especially when they are clothed with the immunity of a
seniority rule, are chieftains to be bargained with, not lieutenants to
be commanded. A party leadership of formal power, as distinguishable from one of persuasion and accommodation, is incompatible with
specialized committees" (1961, p. 335, emphasis added). And a somewhat more dispassionate observer, Alan Rosenthal, noted that in the
50 states, a measure of the "performance" of committee systems was
negatively related to the strength of parties in the legislature. Rosenthal concluded: "Although weak parties or factions do not guarantee
better performance by committees, significant influence by parties
or factions almost precludes effective policy and program formulation
by standing committee systems" (1974a; p. 58).

It should be clear, then, that committees and cohesive parties are not generally compatible (see Uslaner 1974 for a more detailed discussion of this point). Indeed, there appears to be an inverse relationship between a member's party orientation and his committee orientation, given the above discussion. How accurate is this prediction? We shall examine it in this chapter after first considering the potential impact of orientations toward the committee system upon cue seeking and upon perceptions of committees as the major decision locus in state legislatures. Before directly proceeding to a discussion of our hypotheses and a description of our variables, we should first note some of the differences between contemporary work on the role of committees in Congress and earlier treatments; and variations in committee characteristics from the national to the state level. Both of these considerations will allow us to refine our hypotheses and to get a better perspective on how strong a set of relationships we should expect before even commencing our analysis.

VARIATIONS IN COMMITTEE SYSTEMS: COMPARISONS ACROSS TIME AND SPACE

Perhaps the major conclusion reached by Wilson that has gone unchallenged in studies of Congress is that strong committees produce weak parties (or vice versa). On a priori grounds, as we shall see below, there is less reason to expect this to be the case in the states—even given Rosenthal's findings with respect to committee performance. But we have little basis for deriving any firm hypotheses about committees in state legislatures at all—they simply have not been studied in any depth. As Rosenthal stated in a review of the literature on state legislatures:

> . . . there is as little developed knowledge on state legislative committees as there is on state legislative leadership. When it comes to committees, congressional research is far ahead. . . . The contemporary study of committees in Congress appears to have started with the examination of assignment criteria and processes. . . . The study of committees in state legislatures seems to be starting in about the same way. . . . Although there is available information on the number, the size, the assignment of members, and other variables such as these, there are no systematic analyses [of propositions dealing with such variables] and no studies of committee strength or weakness from state to state. (1973a, p. 67)

Rosenthal then cites Dye (1971) to reinforce the basic hypothesis that committees are weaker when parties are stronger. And Rosenthal's own subsequent work on state legislative committees (1973b; 1974a) has begun to examine the overall performance of committees in the state legislative process. Yet a selected bibliography on state government research from 1959 to 1972, compiled by the Council of State Governments (1972; p. 17), lists only six studies of committees—all of which deal with single states and only four of which examine the assignment process.

Obviously, we have much to learn about state legislative committees. What hypotheses have been formulated will thus be derived from the literature on congressional committees. This is not the most satisfactory way in which to proceed, but it does provide a method of escaping a theoretical vacuum. The obvious place to begin any examination of the committee systems in the Congress is the work of Wilson, but even here potential hypotheses are in need of qualification. As the work of Richard F. Fenno, Jr. (1966; 1973) and John F. Manley (1970) demonstrates, committee leaders are no longer the monolithic power brokers that Wilson depicted in the late nineteenth century. Indeed, Fenno's comparative study of House and Senate committees (1973) indicates that the currently prevalent style of leadership is based on fairness and equity rather than dominance by the chairman—a trend likely to be accentuated even more by recent reforms in the committee assignment process among Democrats (see Rieselbach 1977; ch. 3). As David Price (1972) has shown, some Senate committee chairmen simply do not even attempt to "lead" their committees. They either accept a role as one among equals or devote the greater share of their attention to their other assignments, particularly if a chairmanship on a more desirable committee will soon be within their grasp. The Wilsonian argument about dominant chairmen has not been totally shattered; rather, we are now forced by Fenno's analysis of six House committees and their Senate counterparts (1973) to recognize that different patterns of behavior mark different committees. Furthermore, different institutional arrangements between the House and the Senate are likely to lead to different styles of committee behavior—and therefore of committee leadership.

Fenno stresses three alternative goals, which all members share to some extent but which different members emphasize to different extents. These goals are reelection; the making of good public policy; and seeking institutional power within one's chamber (1973, ch. 1). In each case, the member is looking to a somewhat different constituency. Members seeking reelection as their primary goal, as Mayhew (1974) claims every member does, look to the voters of their district as their primary constituents. A legislator seeking to make good public policy will have as a primary reference group a much

broader and less geographically based constituency—the supporters
of the policy or policies emphasized by the member. Finally, the
representative seeking institutional power has as his primary constituency other members of the same legislative body. Clearly, each
of these ideal types will not behave in the same way as others. A
pork-barrel project will help a member seeking reelection, but it
will not benefit a member seeking institutional power (who might better profit by "awarding" the project, if possible, to another legislator whose continued support he needs). A member who wants to make
good public policy (however defined) will perhaps object to the pork-
barrel project on the grounds that it does not constitute part of his
desired agenda.

Because of the relatively low stature and salience of state legislatures (see our discussion in Chapter 5), we assume that the primary orientation of members toward their committee assignment is
related to their geographical constituency (the voters who elect the
legislators). We do not stress the reelection goal here because of the
high turnover, mostly voluntary, in state legislatures. But there is
even less evidence to suggest that the goals of making good public
policy or seeking institutional power are likely to be fostered by the
state committee system. Malcolm E. Jewell described the situation
aptly:

> In some states relatively few legislators serve for more
> then three terms. A study in 1950 showed that in eight
> states, less than one-fifth of the committee chairmen
> had served in the legislature more than three terms. A
> Missouri study showed that chairmen of important com-
> mittees were sometimes freshmen in the legislature and
> were often serving their first terms on the committee.
> It also showed that chairmen often shifted from one com-
> mittee to another . . . the seniority principle, though
> often observed in committee assignments, is not an iron-
> clad rule as in Congress. The dominant leaders on a
> committee may be removed in the next session if they
> act too independently. The committee, in short, is not
> a stable base on which legislators may build their power.
> (1969, p. 53)

Thus, our working assumption that the primary committee orientation is related to the legislator's geographical constituency is
given some credence by what we do know about state legislatures.
We need such an assumption, since the orientation scale to be employed in the analyses in this chapter, discussed in Chapter 1, emphasizes
such factors as the provision of money to set up district offices, staff

and office space for individual legislators (especially those who are not part of the formal leadership), and committee staffing. There is a distinct constituency orientation in this variable—even more so than a committee perspective.

Not only is there a constituency orientation; there is a reform perspective as well. Many of the services such as individual offices (both in the legislature and in the district) and staffs (both the individuals and committees) are lacking in state legislatures, particularly in comparison to the Congress. These are areas highlighted by the Citizens' Conference on State Legislatures (1971) as in great need of reform. Indeed, the development of this scale and an associated one occurred within the context of the analysis of "legislative professionalism" and legislative reform, our concern in Chapter 5. We did not ask our respondents specific questions about their attitudes toward the committee system. But, given the overlap between what students of professionalism consider desirable in the congressional arena, on the one hand, and in state legislatures, on the other, it does not seem unreasonable to consider a committee orientation to be basically a staff and services perspective.

The most professionalized legislature in the United States, of course, is the Congress—and Congress functions primarily through committees (as Wilson maintained), which in turn rely most heavily upon staff. The weaknesses of state legislatures are generally associated with poorly constructed committee systems, which often have too many committees, badly defined jurisdictions, little continuity of membership or leadership, and insufficient resources. In fact, Rosenthal has argued: "The existence of a larger number of committees appears to be a serious obstacle to performance. . . . With many committees there is a tendency for individual legislators to have too many assignments" (1974a; p. 46). A criticism often made of the U. S. Senate, in comparison with the House, in that Senators serve on so many committees and subcommittees that meetings of such bodies often are attended by only a handful of members.

Thus, we view committees as basically oriented toward a member's constituency rather than toward other goals. State legislators may not provide the type of "constituency service" (see Fiorina 1977) that members of Congress do, but the criteria for appointment to committees is largely based on constituency characteristics. Furthermore, should the members be interested in seeking higher office— such as a seat in the Congress—their assignments to congressional committees are at least in part determined by previous committee experience (Masters 1961). Yet, the state legislative committee structures are quite different even across the states. Some bodies may meet for only a few months a year, others may meet throughout most of the year. And the professionalism of the legislature is direct-

ly tied to the status of its committees. Legislatures in the more professionalized states of New York and California are likely to have
full-time staffs, adequate office space, a reasonable number of committees, and some continuity in committee service. On the other
hand, less well-supported legislatures may have committees with
very restricted powers; may delegate much of the actual decision
making to "special" or "select" committees rather than the standing
committees (as occurs in West Virginia); or may have committees
that are dominated by factions or parties. Jewell cites Florida, where
"an interlocking directorate of a dozen or more members in each
house held the most important legislative posts and served as chairmen or members of key committees" (1969; p. 55) before the legislature was reapportioned. Yet, even after reapportionment, the power to appoint committee members (and particularly chairmen) remained with the party leaders in each house. During the 1975 session,
for example, the senate majority leader was engaged in a bitter strug-
gle for control of the state Democratic party with the governor, and
he simply replaced chairmen who voted with the governor and against
his own positions with stalwarts who were more loyal.

One does not need to have an "underdeveloped" legislature to
have a strong role for parties in the committee system. States in
which there is a strong role for the parties will yield, as Rosenthal
and Dye have suggested, less-independent committee systems. But
this does not imply that such committees are in any way inferior to
those found in other states. Despite the lack of uniformity among
state committee systems, we still hypothesize that members who look
to the committee system will be less likely to have strong partisan
orientations. If a member favors strong partisan committees, then
we would expect that his first commitment should be toward the party
caucus and party system rather than the committee system. Particularly because our Committee Orientation (CO) scale is composed of
many constituency-related items and similarly because we maintained
in the previous chapter that party orientations indicate some independence from one's constituency, there should be a different pattern of
support for the committee system per se than for the party system.

It is this expected pattern of primary support for the party system or the committee system that to some extent permits us to dis-
count variations within the states in terms of the composition of committees and even the behavior of such bodies. We do not maintain that
such differences are not important, but rather that they should also
be reflected in the orientations that members have toward the institutions of the legislatures in which they serve. A state such as Wisconsin, in which party ties are quite strong, would be expected to
produce legislators who are more strongly oriented toward the parties than toward the committees. We shall thus posit a set of relation-

ships similar to those hypothesized for the party system in the previous chapter. Members with the strongest positive orientations toward the committee system should be most likely to perceive the committees as the major source of power in the state legislature. We shall also employ the same controls as in the previous chapter (the competitiveness and the typicality of a member's district) and shall consider the relationship between support for the committee system and the party system. This linkage will be the last we shall test, expecting to find negative relationships.

We do not believe, however, that the data analysis in this chapter provides as comprehensive a test of the hypotheses presented below as did that in the previous chapter because (1) interstate variations with respect to support for the party system are less likely to be based upon idiosyncratic factors such as support for the committee system; (2) our measure of committee support, based upon a series of questions primarily dealing with legislative professionalism (which nevertheless seem to have implications for the committee system as well) is not ideal; (3) the hypotheses on the committee system were drawn from literature on the Congress and we have no assurance that committee systems are similar enough to make comparisons meaningful. Yet, it is precisely for this final reason that the question becomes so interesting: how similar are the state legislatures to the Congress, based upon what we know about the latter institution? We turn now to a discussion of our hypotheses and variables before presenting the results of the analysis.

HYPOTHESES AND OPERATIONALIZATIONS

Our hypotheses are similar to those in the previous chapter, with a few interrelated additions. In particular, we hypothesize:

1. The more likely a legislator is to seek cues from committee leaders, the more likely he will be to perceive the committees as the major decision locus in the legislature.
2. The higher the level of support for the committee system, the more likely the legislator will be to seek cues from committee leaders.
3. The higher the level of support for the committee system, the more likely the legislator will be to perceive the committees as the major decision locus in the legislature.
4. The effect of the CO scale on committee cue seeking will be reinforced by the perceived level of competitiveness within the legislator's district.

5. The effect of the CO scale on the perceived committee-oriented decision locus will be reinforced by the level of competitiveness in the legislator's district.

6. The effect of the CO scale on committee cue seeking will be reinforced by the typicality of the member's district.

7. The effect of the CO scale on the perceived committee-oriented decision locus will be reinforced by the typicality of the legislator's district.

8. Members who have high scores on the CO scale will have low scores on both the GPO scale and the LPO scale.

9. Members who depend most heavily upon party-related leaders for cues will depend least heavily upon committee leaders for information.

The first two hypotheses are straightforward and do not require any elaboration. We expect that members from the more competitive districts who also have strong committee orientations will be the most likely to look to committee leaders for cues and also to perceive committee meetings as the major decision locus in the legislature. This expectation is based upon our assumption that for state legislators, at least to as great a degree as members of Congress, committees are constituency-related bodies. Thus, we expect the members who are in the more competitive districts, to the extent that they either intend to seek reelection or have a career in politics beyond the state legislature in mind, to be more committee-oriented than members from safe districts. The opposite prediction was made with respect to the party orientation scales and party cue seeking. And this is consistent with our earlier argument that the pull of partisan forces leads a member to be somewhat independent of his constituency, whereas committee ties reinforce constituency demands.

Our predictions for the typicality control are not as easily reconciled with those for the party orientation variables. In the respective cases of the parties and the committees, we expect that the level of cue seeking and also the extent of perception of the major decision locus with respect to committees to increase (relative to overall orientations toward the party and committee system) in the more typical districts. For the typicality control, we have a different concept than we did for the competitiveness variable. For the parties, we expect that members with strong partisan orientations from districts which are the most typical will have the greatest freedom to seek out partisan cues. Constituency voting patterns do not conflict with member orientations. In fact, there is a clear case of reinforcing orientations toward party-related cues. For the committees, on the other hand, members from the most typical districts will be most likely to be serving on committees which overlap with the member's personal interests (Jewell 1969; pp. 55-56) and therefore also with his constituency's interests. But we do not expect that members will reflect such latter interests in the broadest sense—that is, overall constituency opinion. Rather, it is more likely that the committees a member chooses (to the extent that there is the opportunity for choice) will reflect the concerns of an "active constituency," that is, of the groups most directly responsible for the member's winning electoral coalition (Markus 1974). Thus, typicality in the context of committee orientations tends to reinforce a member's constituency orientation, perhaps to a greater degree than does the perceived level of competition. For this reason, while our predictions on the effects of the typicality control are the same for party and committee orientations, the analytical difference in the concept of typicality differs from one arena to the other. Hence, our arguments are consistent with those that we have made above and in the previous chapter.

Our last two hypotheses relate to the hypothesized inconsistency between strong partisan orientations and strong committee perspectives. Both subjective orientations toward each system and the pattern of cue seeking should display negative correlations with the other, if the arguments of Wilson and virtually every observer who has followed him at both the congressional and state levels are correct. We did not present any hypotheses on party versus committee sources of decision making because our data simply do not permit such comparisons. Our questionnaire asked each respondent simply to state where he thought the major decisions were made in the state legislature, not to rank order power centers. Thus, there is no basis of comparison between the two loci. A member who said that the major decision locus was in committee meetings could not have also answered that the party caucus was the center of power in the legislature.

The dependent variables for the hypotheses presented above do not need much elaboration. We have discussed the construction of the decision-locus and cue-seeking variables in the previous chapter. We shall employ two further operationalizations of the cue-seeking variable here: committee leaders as primary cue givers; and the rank order of mentions of such leaders. The main independent variable, committee orientations, is the Legislator Staff Orientation (LSO) scale presented in Chapter 1. The controls, perceived competitiveness and district typicality, are the same ones that we employed in the previous chapter.

SOURCES OF CUES AND DECISIONS AND
COMMITTEE ORIENTATIONS

We found in the previous chapter that members' attitudes toward the party system, and the legislative party system in particular, did affect their propensity to seek cues from party leaders. The relationship between a member's perception of the primary decision locus in the legislature and party orientations is somewhat lower. What was initially most surprising was that members who relied upon legislative party leaders as their primary cue givers did not display a strong tendency to see the party caucus as the major decision locus in the legislature. We now turn to an examination of similar factors with respect to the committee system.

First, we consider the posited relationship between committee leaders as primary sources of cues and member's perceptions that the committees are the major decision loci in their chambers. After that preliminary question, we shall examine the relation between cue-seeking behavior for committees and orientations toward the committee system. We shall then consider the relation between these subjective orientations and the propensity of legislators to perceive committee meetings as the major focus of legislative activity. To the extent that our hypotheses about both the LSO scale and the various controls employed should be the same for cue-seeking behavior and perceptions of power in the legislature, we would expect that these latter

TABLE 3.1

Decision Locus by Cues from Committee Leaders
(in percent)

Decision Locus	Cues from Committee Leaders	Other Cues	N
Committees	43.5	38.1	406
Other	56.5	61.9	642
N	132	916	1,048

Note: phi = -.037; Q = .112.

variables are themselves strongly related. Furthermore, we have an a priori reason for expecting cue-seeking behavior and perceived decision locus to be related. If members perceive the sources of power in a legislature to be, for example, primarily committee-oriented, then we should expect that they would also rely upon the "most powerful" members for information. In the case of political parties, we found that there was only a moderate relationship for our measures of cue-seeking behavior and perceptions of the major decision locus.

In the previous chapter, we argued that members may look for cues to those members whom they believe should have the major share of power in the legislature rather than the arenas that they believe actually exercise this power. In this situation, there is likely to be some underlying dissatisfaction with the overall workings of the legislature. We have not been able to identify this directly, since we have no specific questions on the sources of members' evaluations of the legislative processes in their states.

As Table 3.1 indicates, however, there is even less of a patterned relationship between primary cue givers and perceptions of the main decision locus than we found for the party leaders in the previous chapter. While a larger percentage of those members who sought primary cues from committee leaders (43.5 percent) also saw committees as the major decision locus in the legislature compared to those who sought other primary sources of information (38.1 percent), these differences are not large. The nominal measures of association, phi and Yule's Q, are .037 and .112 respectively (see Table 3.1). These

TABLE 3.2

Source of Cues by LSO Scale
(in percent)

Source	High	Medium	Low	N
Committee leaders	15.5	9.3	15.3	129
Others	84.5	90.7	84.7	933
N	238	569	255	1,062

Note: tau-c = -.001; gamma = -.002.

values are lower than we reported in the previous chapter for party-related cues and ones we shall report in the next chapter for executive-related cues; in fact, not even the curvilinear measure, Q, is increased by the skewed row marginals, as we find for both party and executive information sources. We are led to the inevitable conclusion that perceptions of power are not at all linked to sources of information for state legislative committees, but we do not have an immediate answer as to why this is the case. We shall examine this question in greater depth after we investigate the predicted relationships for our other hypotheses.

We turn now to an examination of the relationship between the LSO scale and the cues sought by our legislative respondents. In Table 3.2, we present the results of our analysis of the effects of subjective orientations toward the committee system and the primary cue sources of the respondents. Contrary to our hypothesis, there is virtually no relationship between the orientations toward the committee system and primary cue givers (tau-c = -.001, gamma = -.002). In fact, almost as many of our respondents who fell into the lowest category of support for the committee system relied primarily upon committee leaders as did members who had high scores on the LSO scale. Are the relationships that we posited hidden by patterns of covariation which are revealed through our control variables?

TABLE 3.3

Rank Order of Cue Taking from Committee Leaders in
Legislature by LSO Scale
(in percent)

Ranking of Committee Leaders	High	Medium	Low	N
First	15.5	9.3	15.3	129
Second	8.0	9.1	8.6	93
Third	6.7	8.9	7.0	85
Fourth	10.0	10.0	10.2	107
Fifth	5.9	9.8	9.0	93
Not at all	53.8	53.0	50.0	557
N	238	570	256	1,064

Note: tau-c = -.017; gamma = -.027.

Before turning to this question, we shall first examine the relationship between subjective orientations toward the committee system and the rank order of mentions of committee leaders. Table 3.3 reports the results of this analysis, and they are no more encouraging than our previous table. The linear coefficient is a miniscule -.017 and gamma is not much higher (-.027). For both the primary cue givers and our rank ordering of mentions of committee leaders, we find virtually no relationship with the LSO scale. Indeed, the miniscule coefficients that we do find are in the wrong direction! We turn now to an examination of our control variables to see if the relationships can be clarified.

TABLE 3.4

Committee Primary Cue Givers by LSO Scale:
By Competitiveness of District

Measure of Association	Safe	Mostly One-Party	Competitive
Tau-c	.022	-.035	.032
Gamma	.069	-.143	.121
N	297	469	294

In Table 3.4, where we control for the perceived level of competitiveness in the members' districts for primary cue givers and the LSO scale, we note a nonmonotonic pattern. Members from safe and competitive districts tend to display the expected positive correlations, although they are quite modest. The members from mostly one-party districts account for most of the cases in the table—and their behavior is, albeit only slightly, contrary to the hypothesized direction. Overall, there is weak support for hypothesis 4, since the positive relation is strongest for the competitive districts. Yet we should not overemphasize the import of these findings, given the sizes of the measures of association.

There is more order to the pattern of covariation when we consider the control for perceived competitiveness for the rank order of committee leaders as sources of information in the legislature. We observe a monotonic increase from negative to positive relationships as we move from the safe seats to the competitive ones. But again we do not find very strong relationships, even though they are consistent with our expectations. Members from the more competitive districts display a very slight tendency to seek cues from committee leaders if they also have positive orientations toward the committee system. There is a similar slight tendency for members from safe districts to take cues from committee leaders when their LSO scale scores are low. In the middle category, however, no relationship exists between the two variables, as the overall findings in Table 3.3 indicated. The controlled results are reported in Table 3.5. If members of state leg-

TABLE 3.5

Rank Order of Committee Leader Cues by LSO Scale:
By Competitiveness of District

Measure of Association	Safe	Mostly One-Party	Competitive
Tau-c	-.074	-.008	.027
Gamma	-.116	-.014	.045
N	297	470	294

islatures do in fact perceive committee posts to be useful for fostering good constituency relationships, the perceived level of party competition by the respondents does not seem to discriminate well as a control variable between information sources and attitudes toward the committee system.

The typicality of a district was a more discriminating control with respect to information sources and orientations toward the party systems than simple competitiveness. Does it also prove to be a better control for the relationship, if any, between the LSO scale and committee leaders as a source of cues? We present the results of employing this control in Tables 3.6 and 3.7. The former table is based upon primary cue givers only, the latter on the rank order operationalization. For members from somewhat atypical districts (either a Democrat from a mostly one-party GOP district or a Republican from a generally Democratic seat), we do find a moderate negative relationship (gamma = -.247) for primary cue givers. This relation is clearly curvilinear. However, the other categories simply do not display any discernible pattern between the LSO scale and information seeking.

When we consider the control applied to the rank order of cues, every category of typicality except the middle one displays the slight negative relationship we found for the simple bivariate case. Indeed, the strongest set of coefficients we observed (tau-c = -.067, gamma = -.101) occurs in the most typical districts. This is again contrary

to our prediction that members from the more typical districts will
be more responsive to their voting constituency through the committee system—and, therefore, through the committee leadership. If any

TABLE 3.6

Committee Primary Cue Givers by LSO Scale:
By Typicality of District

Measure of Association	Least Typical				Most Typical
Tau-c	—†	-.058	.026	-.028	.026
Gamma	—†	-.247	.100	-.109	.078
N	18	108	288	356	279

†No measures of association could be computed since all cases
fell into a single cell.

TABLE 3.7

Rank Order of Committee Leader Cues by LSO Scale:
By Typicality of District

Measure of Association	Least Typical				Most Typical
Tau-c	-.136*	-.003	.028	-.007	-.067
Gamma	-1.000*	-.006	.046	-.012	-.101
N	18*	109	289	356	279

results emerge from this final column of Table 3.7, it is that members with the strongest electoral base are the most independent in
their choice of information sources. They do not, that is, look primarily to committee leaders even if they are supportive of the committee system.

How do we account for these findings? Our first inclination is
to reject the LSO scale as a valid measure of the subjective attitudes

of our respondents toward the committee system. We have noted above that the scale was not originally designed to measure attitudes toward committees and our speculation may provide the basis for explaining our poor results. Yet, we are reluctant to do so, not because we insist that the LSO scale is the most desirable measure of committee orientations, but rather because neither of our control variables displays much stronger relationships with the pattern of primary cue seeking. As Table 3.8 indicates, a slight positive relationship exists between competition and cue sources, while we observe only a small negative correlation between this cue variable and district typicality

TABLE 3.8

Source of Primary Cues by District Competitiveness
(in percent)

Source	Safe	Mostly One–Party	Competitive	N
Committee leaders	14.5	11.1	11.6	129
Others	85.5	88.9	88.4	930
N	296	469	294	1,059

Note: tau–c = .024; gamma = .086.

TABLE 3.9

Source of Primary Cues by District Typicality
(in percent)

Source	Least Typical	- - - - - - - - - - - →			Most Typical	N
Committee leaders	0.0*	11.2	11.1	11.5	18.1	127
Others	100.0*	88.8	88.9	88.5	81.9	922
N	18*	109	288	356	278	1,049

Note: tau–c = -.043; gamma = -.137.

in Table 3.9. Even if the LSO scale were an unreliable measure of members' attitudes toward the committee system, we would still expect some pattern of covariation between each of our control variables and our principal dependent variable. If this were not the case, then the logic behind our hypothesized relationships would have to be called into question as well as our use of the LSO scale. In fact, we shall reconsider our logic on the sources of cues later in this chapter. It is clear, however, that the relationships between our measures of information sources, committee orientations, and the competitiveness or typicality of a district are not in accord with our hypotheses.

DETERMINANTS OF COMMITTEE POWER

Before attempting alternative explanations of sources of cues within the legislature, however, we shall turn to an examination of the perceived decision loci. Do our predictions fare better for this variable, employing the same predictory and controls? We have no reason to expect similar patterns of covariation with our information-seeking measures because of the virtually nonexistent relationship between primary committee cue givers and perceptions of the major arenas of power in state legislatures. Thus, we begin our analysis with at least some hope of improvement in predictive potential.

TABLE 3.10

Source of Decision Locus by LSO Scale
(in percent)

Source	High	Medium	Low	N
Committees	31.4	37.8	45.2	425
Others	68.6	62.2	54.8	691
N	258	588	270	1,116

Note: tau-c = -.100; gamma = -.173.

Our predictions with respect to the perceived major decision locus in a state legislature are similar to those for our cue-seeking variable. Specifically, we expect that members who have high scores on the subjective committee-orientation measure will also be more likely to perceive committees as the major sources of power in the legislature. Furthermore, we expect that this relationship should be reinforced in both the more competitive districts and the more typical districts, as discussed earlier.

Table 3.10 indicates, however, that there is a weak relationship (which is basically linear) in the opposite direction. Members with low scores on the LSO scale compose a greater proportion of the respondents who believe that committee meetings are the major source of power in the chamber then members with high scores. These findings are not spurious in that they are not affected by the marginals for high and low scorers on the LSO scale, since Table 3.10 indicates that there is almost an identical number of respondents in each category. Overall, 31.4 percent of the members with high LSO scores perceived committee meetings as the major sources of power, in contrast to the 45.2 percent with low scores who had such perceptions. Our predictive success has improved somewhat, but not in the direction posited. We are once again tempted to dismiss these results as potentially spurious because the LSO scale was not initially designed as a measure of committee orientations. The components of the meas-

TABLE 3.11

Source of Decision Locus by LSO Scale,
Controlling for District Competitiveness

	Safe	Mostly One-Party	Competitive
Tau-c	-.149	-.076	-.080
Gamma	-.268	-.129	-.139
N	319	496	300

ure only roughly tap a subjective committee evaluation. Do we, then, reject these results? Again, before doing so, we should consider whether the controls employed better follow our predictions, or have any independent relationship with our decision-locus variable. Also, we shall investigate other potential predictors of the decision locus before making any judgments on the suitability of the LSO scale as a measure of committee orientations.

We examine the relationship between perceived decision locus and the LSO scale, controlling for perceived district competitiveness, in Table 3.11, while the control for district typicality is reported in Table 3.12. For perceived competitiveness, we find some support for our hypothesis. Legislators from competitive districts are less

TABLE 3.12

Source of Decision Locus by LSO Scale,
Controlling for District Typicality

	Least Typical	----------------→			Most Typical
Tau-c	.030*	-.030	-.091	-.089	-.163
Gamma	.062*	-.050	-.159	-.154	-.290
N	18	116	294	375	300

likely to have divergent relationships between their perception of the major arena of power in state legislatures and their evaluations of the committee system than members from safe districts. In particular, the dividing line appears to be between safe districts and all other districts, both for the linear measure of association and the curvilinear one. Yet, despite support for our hypothesized order of the relationships, note that every coefficient in Table 3.11 is nevertheless negative. We had hypothesized that the level of party competition in a district would reinforce a positive relationship between perceptions of power and subjective orientations of the committee system. However, we found no positive relationship to reinforce. Nor did any subsample in our analysis yield such a positive correlation. Thus, while there is some support for our hypothesis in Table 3.11, it is at best mildly reassuring.

The control for typicality, however, leads to even greater skepticism regarding our initial hypotheses and/or our measurement techniques. For the cue-seeking variables, we found that there was a slight tendency for the most typical districts to have the strongest negative relationships with our LSO scale. For the decision-locus variable, this order (see Table 3.12) is even more pronounced, with moderately negative relationships (tau-c = -.163, gamma = -.290) in the most typical districts. The only positive relations are found in the least typical districts, but here the number of cases (18) is too small for meaningful comparisons with other columns in the table. Thus, we are once again presented with negative relationships within each subgroup—and, in fact, considerably higher coefficients for the most typical districts than for others. Unlike the information-seeking variables, we cannot explain away a set of null findings by another set of null findings—that is, the relationships between perceived decision loci and competition and typicality respectively. While, there is virtually no relationship between these controls and our dependent variable (see Tables 3. 13 and 3. 14), we still have to account for a more structured set of findings, as reported in Table 3. 11 and particularly in Table 3. 12.

TABLE 3. 13

Source of Decision Locus by District Competitiveness
(in percent)

Source	Safe	Mostly One-Party	Competitive	N
Committees	34. 1	41. 9	37. 6	447
Other	65. 9	58. 1	62. 4	713
N	331	518	311	1, 160

Note: tau-c = -. 030; gamma = -. 049.

If we maintain that the LSO scale does indeed measure subjective orientations toward the committee system, then we must attempt to account for its lack of patterned relationships with information sources, the negative correlations found between it and decision loci, and the incorrect predictions made for the typicality control. We shall examine the first two questions in the context of the relationships among party orientations, committee cues, and committee decision loci below. The typicality control is somewhat easier to explain. Rather than representing a response to a member's group-related constituency (that is, his specific supporters within a district), the typicality variable may operate similarly to the competitiveness control, as it did for party-related cues and perceptions of arenas of power.

We found considerable support for the hypothesis that cue seeking from legislative party leaders according to their scores on the LPO scale would be reinforced by the safety of their districts and the typicality of such districts. These relations were maintained over a variety of alternative measures of cue-seeking behavior from partisan information sources. The controls were less helpful in determining the relationship between support for the legislative party system and perceptions of the party caucus as the major decision locus in the legislature. In each case, however, we maintained that members were responding to <u>overall</u> competitiveness of their districts. Members from the competitive seats were less likely to seek out partisan cues because there was posited to be a tension between loyalty to one's party and adherence to one's district. Similarly, the typicality control was also considered in the context of overall competitiveness. Members from the less typical districts would tend to seek out cues from nonparty sources, whereas those from the most typical districts would have their partisanship reinforced by the lack of electoral sanctions.

TABLE 3.14

Source of Decision Locus by District Typicality
(in percent)

Source	Least Typical	- - - - - - - - - - - - - →			Most Typical	N
Committees	22.2	35.0	36.8	43.8	34.9	439
Other	77.8	65.0	63.2	56.2	65.1	708
N	18	120	304	393	312	1,147

<u>Note</u>: tau-c = -.009; gamma = -.014.

Our data for committee orientations, cue seeking, and decision loci suggest that the competitiveness and typicality controls yield similar results and thus should be viewed as general measures of competition. Specifically, for the typicality control, we have found at least a slight tendency for members from the most typical districts to be less likely to seek cues <u>and</u> to perceive power in committee-oriented terms, given their scores on the LSO scale. These members, then, may feel more secure in their electoral status (should they choose to run for another term) and thus would be less subject to constituency constraints. The committees do not serve as a vehicle for constituency service for such members to the same degree that they do for members from less typical districts. While we have found negative relationships for <u>all</u> categories of typicality for our decision-locus

variable, this is not the case for our measures of cues. The rank
ordering of cues does display negative relationships for three of the
four comparable subgroups, but the largest values are found for the
most typical districts. Primary cues display such an erratic pattern
of subgroup correlations that we believe that further discussion is
simply unwarranted.

What we emphasize, then, is that the patterns that do emerge
are in fact consistent with the treatment of typicality as a general
measure of competition. State legislators may respond less to particular groups within constituencies because they have little opportunity (in comparison with members of Congress) to perceive demands
within their electorate. Nor is there any evidence that constituents
"target" state legislators for electoral defeat based upon their records
or constituency service. To the extent that there is any electoral connection between state legislators and their constituents, we would expect that partisan swings in the national vote or statewide trends, particularly at the gubernatorial level, are important. One only has to
note, for example, that the Iowa legislature in 1965 had a more than
two-thirds Democratic majority following the national Democratic
landslide in 1964. Two years later, a two-to-one GOP advantage was
restored in a more typical year for the Republicans in that state.
Similarly, the 1965 Democratic sweep of New Jersey gave the party
overwhelming control of the legislature, only for the more normal
1967 off-year state legislative elections to restore the GOP to dominance there. The Democrats did not take control of either house in
New Jersey until the 1973 landslide, which outdid the two previous
record-setting elections (1965 for the Democrats and 1969 for the Republicans), so that the party was able to maintain a reduced majority
in the 1975 legislative elections.

There is simply little evidence of strong electoral sanctions for
state legislators based upon constituency-oriented behavior in the
chamber. Thus, members with the greatest electoral security tend
to look to party leaders for cues, even though they may not perceive
the party as the major source of power in the legislature. These members appear less likely to look to committee leaders for cues or to
perceive committee meetings as the major source of power in the
chamber. They are more independent than members who have similar scores on the LSO scale. While they may be more supportive of
a strong committee system, they do not appear to believe that committees are or should be the major sources of power and/or information. Other members may not be as dependent upon the legislative
committees, for we do not observe as strong negative relationships
for them.

Even if we can make sense out of the controlled relationship,
we still have to account for the absence of any relationship between

the LSO scale and cue sources, and the weak negative relationship
between the LSO scale and members' perceptions that committees
are the major decision loci in the legislature. We propose to examine next the relationships among party and committee orientations,
sources of cues, and decision arenas to see if there are more systematic patterns of covariation for our information sources and power arenas.

PARTIES AND COMMITTEES IN
STATE LEGISLATURES

First, we shall examine the interrelationship of support for the
party system and our measures of support for the committee system.
We then move to a set of propositions not included in our initial list
of predictions: do members' cue sources for committees vary inverse-
ly, as we would expect, with their support for the party system? If
parties and committees are more than different sources of power, we
would expect members who strongly support the party system to look
for cues from almost any other source of information than committee
leaders. We know that such members do in fact tend to seek out partisan cues to a greater extent than other members. Thus, if any pattern of covariation is predictable, it should be found through either a
committee measure or a party measure. Since we have more established validity for our party orientation scales, we believe that such
a test is appropriate. Finally, we shall examine the extent to which
members who rely upon party cues also depend most heavily upon

TABLE 3.15

Legislator's Position on the LSO Scale by the GPO Scale
(in percent)

Position on LSO	High	Medium	Low	N
High	24.3	20.8	26.0	261
Medium	52.4	54.9	46.1	616
Low	23.3	24.3	27.9	286
N	294	699	172	1,163

Note: tau-c = .015; gamma = .030.

committee-oriented information sources. Again, we expect a negative
relationship between our two rank orders. We cannot test directly for
the overlap, if any, with perceptions of where the major decisions are
made in the legislature because this question involves a simple dichotomy and therefore comparisons would not be meaningful.

We begin by analyzing the relationships between the LSO scale
and our two party orientation scales—the GPO scale, measuring diffuse support for the party system, and the LPO scale, tapping our respondents' belief that the role of the parties in the legislature should
be strengthened and that members should be subject to greater pressure to conform to positions taken by the party leadership. We expect
a negative relationship between the LSO scale and each party scale,
with the LPO scale displaying a stronger correlation than the GPO
scale. Tables 3.15 and 3.16 present the results of these analyses,
and they are not heartening. The GPO scale is almost completely unrelated to the LSO scale, even by the generous gamma measure (.030).

TABLE 3.16

Legislator's Position on the LSO Scale by the LPO Scale
(in percent)

Position on LSO	High	Medium	Low	N
High	34.6	20.4	21.5	261
Medium	46.5	55.5	51.4	611
Low	18.9	24.1	27.1	281
N	150	640	363	1,153

Note: tau-c = .060; gamma = .113.

There is a stronger relationship for the LPO scale (tau-c = .060;
gamma = .113), although the curvilinear measure might be inflated
because of greater skewness of the marginals. Yet, note that both
party scales are positively correlated with LSO, not negatively as
hypothesized. The coefficients are, however, so low that we should
regard them as basically nil. While this test does not provide any
evidence for the validity of the LSO scale, it does indicate that the
hypothesized relationship between support for the party system and
support for LSO items must be rejected. We have thus rejected the

first seven of our eight hypotheses. Perhaps we have to turn to other variables to seek determinants of cue seeking and perceptions of decision loci.

In Tables 3.17 and 3.18, we examine the relationship between our two party orientation scales and the primary cue givers' variables dichotomized according to whether the cue givers are committee leaders or others. (We do not report on committee leader rank-order cue sources, since the findings are quite close to those for the primary cues.) Here, we find positive relationships between the GPO scale and committee-oriented cues. And we also find positive coefficients, though reduced in magnitude, for the LPO scale. A possible explanation for these findings involves rejection of the claim that a strong committee system is incompatible with a strong party system in the

TABLE 3.17

Source of Cues by GPO Scale
(in percent)

Source	High	Medium	Low	N
Committee Leaders	16.2	11.9	6.6	128
Others	83.8	88.1	93.4	926
N	259	628	168	1,054

Note: tau-c = .062; gamma = .259.

TABLE 3.18

Source of Cues by LPO Scale
(in percent)

Source	High	Medium	Low	N
Committee Leaders	16.2	11.8	11.0	126
Others	83.8	88.2	89.0	910
N	136	583	317	1,036

Note: tau-c = .028; gamma = .110.

states. We might posit that committees in state legislatures are quite different from those at the national level, so that the arguments of Wilson and Huitt simply do not apply to state politics. However, such

TABLE 3.19

Source of Decision Locus by GPO Scale
(in percent)

Source	High	Medium	Low	N
Committees	27.6	40.9	44.6	422
Others	72.4	59.1	55.4	683
N	272	667	166	1,105

Note: tau-c = -.119; gamma = -.229.

an argument would also refute the suggestions of Dye (1971) and Rosenthal (1974a) that committee systems do appear to be incompatible with strong party systems in state legislatures.

We do not accept this argument because we find moderate relationships between perceptions of the major decision locus in the legislature and first, the GPO scale (tau-c = -.119, gamma = -.229) and second, the LPO scale (tau-c = -.163, gamma = -.295) in Tables 3.19 and 3.20. These relationships are in fact in the predicted direction. For the LPO scale, we find a stronger pattern of covariation with perceptions of the major source of decision making in the legislature than the GPO scale, also as expected. Indeed, 23.9 percent of members with high scores on the former scale perceive committee meetings as the major source of power in the state legislature, compared to 35.2 percent with medium scores, and 48.0 percent with low scores. These figures, perhaps to an even greater degree than the measures of association, clearly indicate that support for the party system does lead members to attribute less power to the committees. We have already noted in the previous chapter that there is at least as strong a tendency for high scores on the LPO scale to be associated with perception of the party caucus as the major arena of power in state politics. For the decision-locus variable, then, we have found support for the proposition that a strong party system is incompatible with a strong committee system.

What do these tables tell us about patterns of cue taking with respect to committee leaders and the validity of the LSO scale among our legislative respondents? The answer is quite simply not very much. While the decision-locus variable casts some suspicion on the validity of the LSO scale as a committee-orientation measure, none of our results in the search for determinants of committee-oriented cues has led very far. In particular, the lack of any systematic pattern of covariation between the perceived decision locus and the sources of cues suggests that the validity of the LSO scale cannot be

TABLE 3.20

Source of Decision Locus by LPO Scale
(in percent)

Source	High	Medium	Low	N
Committees	23.9	35.2	48.0	412
Others	76.1	64.8	52.0	677
N	142	597	350	1,089

Note: tau-c = -.163; gamma = -.295.

determined by a direct comparison with findings for the committee decision-locus variable. We do not reject the LSO scale as a measure of subjective member orientations toward the committee system because we have not found any alternative determinant of cue seeking that is more successful in predictive power. Our control variables do not have any direct correlation with sources of cues. Thus, the most plausible explanation for our poor findings is that the committee systems of the legislatures of the 50 states vary not only from state to state, but perhaps also from committee to committee within the states. This is essentially the same conclusion reached by Fenno (1973) in his analysis of congressional committees. Members may in fact perceive the committee system to be more or less powerful than the party system, particularly when a few prominent leaders dominate the decision-making process both for parties and committees. On the other hand, members may seek cues from whichever committee leaders they serve with or whichever handle legislation of importance to the individual legislators. The strength of committees within state legislatures is even more difficult to discern than that of political parties; but it does appear that committee power does vary over a much greater range than does party power. Furthermore, as we have maintained, even within a chamber with generally powerful committees, there will be some bodies with great advantages over others.

CONCLUSION

In the previous chapter, we maintained that perceived decision locus is a measure of how members perceive power to be distributed, whereas the cue variable is an indicator of how power ought to be distributed. Given the rather well-defined orientations toward the party system among our respondents, we were better able to predict cue-seeking behavior than perceptions of power for party leaders. For committee leaders, on the other hand, our strongest predictive success came in the area of the perceived decision-locus variable rather than on any of our measures of cue seeking. We attribute this result to the fact that members do not have well-developed conceptions of how the committee system ought to operate. Reinforcing this is the fact that committee experience as found in the legislature is not paralleled by any aspect of a member's life before entrance into the legislature, particularly compared to one's prior knowledge of the party system. While committee leaders were among the more frequently mentioned sources of information, there simply did not appear to be any pattern among members with respect to the LSO, the GPO, or the LPO scales. We do not believe that the distribution of cue-seeking behavior is random, but rather that it probably varies according to the structure of the committees within and across states rather than according to any subjective orientations toward the entire committee system. Members thus will seek out cues from committee leaders who have access to important information, and this access will depend upon the structure of the committee system in the state. Cue seeking among our legislative respondents also undoubtedly varies according to the personal relationships of the members to the chairmen and ranking minority members. If the subjective orientations of members were of major importance in determining cue-seeking behavior, then we would have expected that the party scales would provide an indication that this was the case. Yet they did not. Thus, we maintain that the relationship between subjective orientations and cue seeking is not obscured by whatever deficiencies the LSO scale might have as an indicator of committee support. In fact, the relationships uncovered by our control variables for the LSO scale with our cue measures are stronger than the simple ones for committee orientations with perceived competitiveness and typicality.

It thus does not appear that we could better predict the information-seeking behavior of our respondents with a more refined committee orientation scale. Thus, we have no overall conclusive evaluation of the LSO scale as such a scale—except to note that it is all too simple to dismiss it as inappropriate because it does not predict committee cue seeking or perceptions of decision loci very well.

We stressed in the previous chapter our predictive success with respect to cues from legislative party leaders. If similar factors were to have the opposite relationships with committee-leader cues, then there should be, as hypothesized, a negative relationship between the rank order for each set of cues. Table 3.21 indicates that there is no such relationship: tau-c = .053 and gamma = .096, both slightly positive, but neither is strong enough to warrant any conclusion but one of nonassociation between these alternative cue sources.

TABLE 3.21

Rank Order of Cue Taking from Committee Leaders in
Legislature by Rank Order of Cue Taking from
Party Leaders in Legislature
(in percent)

Ranking of Committee Leaders	First	Second	Third	Fourth	Fifth	Not at All	N
First	0.0	24.8	12.7	10.7	14.1	13.9	148
Second	16.9	0.0	11.2	8.4	7.4	8.0	94
Third	13.0	13.3	0.0	19.5	6.9	5.4	86
Fourth	18.8	12.2	12.3	0.0	12.0	8.2	110
Fifth	11.6	8.6	10.1	14.9	0.0	8.3	98
Not at all	39.7	41.1	53.8	46.5	59.6	56.1	582
N	117	116	114	86	81	603	1,117

Note: tau-c = .053; gamma = .096.

For the decision-locus variable, however, we did find some support for the proposition that a strong party system is incompatible with a strong committee system. Party orientations appear to predict perceptions of committee decision loci better than our LSO scale, even though we did not find much interrelationship between either party measure and the LSO scale. What this chapter has shown is that the committee systems in the states are important sources of cues and particularly critical arenas of power. Yet, the diversity of these bodies within and across states suggests that we are more likely to account for variations in perceptions of committee influence (cues) and power (decision loci) by examining types of committees, as Fenno (1973) does for the Congress, than all such bodies as responses to subjective stimuli. This will require an intensive microlevel analysis of state legislative systems to examine patterns of similarity within states of committee structures and jurisdictions. This is a task beyond the scope of this study, but it seems necessary if we are to arrive at a more comprehensive understanding of these important chambers in the states.

4

PATTERNS OF GUBERNATORIAL POWER AND INFLUENCE IN THE STATES

INTRODUCTION

If one had to select a single dominant theme characterizing the literature on legislative-executive relations in the United States in recent years, it would be executive dominance of the legislative branch. At the national level (discussing the role of Congress relative to that of the president), we speak of the "imperial presidency" (Schlesinger 1973), the "arrogance of [presidential] power" (Fulbright 1966), "[t]he loss of congressional control over the substance of policy" (Huntington 1973)—underscoring decline of legislative power at the expense of the executive. The state of the balance of power at the national level has been documented at length elsewhere; here we are concerned with the situation in the states. As Malcolm E. Jewell and Samuel C. Patterson note: "Programs to reorganize the state administrative structure and the development of the executive budget system, paralleling trends at the national level, strengthened not only the governor's administrative control but also his ability to influence legislative development" (1972, p. 301).

When one considers the resources at the governor's disposal, particularly in terms of formal powers, this pattern of executive dominance becomes readily understandable. Jewell notes that in most states the governor has complete control of the budget submitted to the legislature. Furthermore, he adds:

> While the governor's positive influence over legislation is considerable, his negative authority is massive. In every state except North Carolina, the governor has the veto power, and in most states a vote of more than a ma-

106

> jority of the legislature is required to override the veto.
> A study published in 1950 showed that slightly more than
> 5 percent of bills passed by state legislatures were ve-
> toed and only 1 or 2 percent of the vetoes were overridden.
> . . . There are several reasons why the governor in most
> states can nearly always make his veto stick. His politi-
> cal power is usually great enough so that he can maintain
> the support of the one-third or two-fifths majority to up-
> hold a veto. Moreover, a large proportion of bills are
> passed in the closing days of a session, and on these the
> governor can exercise his veto after the legislature has
> adjourned. (1969, pp. 65-67)

The part-time legislature, which we shall discuss in greater detail
in the next chapter, is another indicator of the relative weakness of
the state chambers in comparison to the Congress, relative to the
executive branch. Furthermore, four states (Alabama, New Jersey,
Massachusetts, and Virginia) grant the governor the power of executive amendment; and 41 states give the chief executive an item veto
over appropriations measures. The president has neither of these
powers.

Given this enormous potential power base, we were somewhat
surprised by our findings, as discussed in Chapter 2, and those of
others as well, that the governor does not appear to be an extremely
important factor in legislative decision making (at least from the perspective of other decision makers in the states). We are reminded
that even in the case of the federal government, presidential power
is the power to persuade (Neustadt 1964) rather than to dictate. And,
of course, the governor does not have control over foreign-policy decision making, which tends to widen the power gap between the president and Congress, and accentuate the former's control of public
opinion.

Yet, the absence of gubernatorial authority over such an issue
area would not necessarily detract from the overall power of a governor. One only has to realize that the issues raised at the national
and state level are often quite different and that the level of public
concern will vary with the salience of these issues. As V. O. Key,
Jr. stated, "The American people are not boiling with concern about
the workings of their state government" (1956, p. 3). A decade later
(still more than ten years ago), there was no appreciable shift in the
public's pattern of concern (Jennings and Ziegler 1970), with a slight
decrease occurring a few years later (Beyle and Williams 1972). Yet,
the overall level of knowledge among the mass public and the pattern
of positive and negative attitudes toward national and subnational institutions indicate that the governor fares reasonably well in compar-

ison with other institutions on both questions (Lehnen 1972). There is no comparable data on state legislators (or state legislatures as institutions).

The ability of governors to play a major (if not _the_ major) role in state decision making depends upon the way in which the individual occupying the office perceives his role and deals with members of the legislature and other decision-making bodies in the state. An index of the governor's formal powers in the states, including indicators of budget, appointive, and veto powers as well as tenure potential, has been developed by Joseph A. Schlesinger (1965; pp. 217-32). Brian R. Fry and Richard F. Winters (1970) found virtually no relation between the Schlesinger index and a composite measure of "redistribution" from the more advantaged to the less advantaged groups in the states. Thomas R. Dye (1969) found some moderate relationships between Schlesinger's index and various measures of education, health and welfare, taxation, and highway policy, but concluded that these correlations were spurious, owing to the intervening effects of economic development.

Somewhat greater support for the idea that the formal powers of office have a significant impact on policy formation was found in a study by Ira Sharkansky (1968a). Examining the relationships between the budget requests of 592 agencies in 19 states, the response of the governor to agency requests, and the appropriations decisions of the legislature, Sharkansky did find that the veto and tenure powers of the governor are systematically related to gubernatorial success in the appropriations process. However, a study by Deil S. Wright (1967), in which 933 state executives in the 50 states were interviewed, indicated that more bureaucrats believed that the legislature "exercises greater control over your agency's affairs" than the governor; the figures were 44 percent for the legislature and 32 percent for the governor, with 22 percent believing that the relative power balance was equal (2 percent did not respond to these categories).

The question, "How powerful is the governor?" thus does not admit of a simple answer. Just as the power of the president is the power to persuade, so is that of the governor and here we find variations from state to state, as Coleman B. Ransone, Jr., noted over two decades ago (1956). Similarly, Sarah McCally Morehouse (1966; 1973) has argued that the support received by a governor, particularly among Democrats, from his legislative party varies with the strength of the gubernatorial candidate's electoral strength in a member's district in primaries held _after_ legislative sessions. On the other hand, her study indicated that for northern legislatures (in the 1946-60 period) there was little relation between the legislator's district primary or general election competition and his support for the governor's requests (1973, p. 71).

The power base of the governor, to a greater degree than that of the president, appears to depend upon the chief executive's role as a party leader. Jewell (1969, pp. 77-80) notes that two of the most potent weapons a governor has at his disposal (in terms of influencing members of the legislature) are patronage and control over local legislation affecting a member's district. Both are clearly partisan tools and Jewell's discussion makes it clear that they are generally used in that manner. That is, a Democratic governor is simply not likely to have much influence over a Republican legislator (and vice versa). It is therefore little wonder that Key considered the degree of centralization of the party system the most critical element affecting the strength of state government—particularly when the same party maintained control of the legislative and executive branches (1956, ch. 3).

The governor does have a reservoir of good will, at least among state bureaucrats. Even though there was an imbalance of power relationships in favor of the legislature in Wright's study (1967), and particularly when the question involved reduction-of-budget requests, there was a substantial basis of support for the governor—particularly when compared exclusively with the legislature—among executives when they were asked which institution (person) was more sympathetic to the goals of the agency and which type of control they preferred.

In Chapter 2 above, we found that state legislators were least likely to mention the governor of the 13 possible choices we gave them. Indeed, only the constituency response, which was spontaneously mentioned (as part of our "other" category) by a total of 4.7 percent of our respondents falls below the total of 18.1 percent of the legislators who cited the governor as a desired source of information. When we simply look at first-place mentions, the governor falls to fourteenth place, again behind party leaders outside the legislature (2.0 percent) and now behind constituents (3.6 percent), with only 1.4 percent of our legislative respondents selecting the chief executive.

If we broaden our concept of the executive branch to include administrator-specialists in a policy area, we find considerably more support for the executive branch within the legislature as a source of information: a total of 38.5 percent of our respondents cited such specialists. These two sources of executive cues total 56.7 percent of all respondents—a figure identical to that of our principal source of cues, personal friends in the legislature. Even so, we did not find much evidence for an hypothesized strong relationship on executive domination of the legislature, at least as perceived by our respondents.

When asked where they believed the most important decision locus in the legislature was, only 11.4 percent mentioned the governor's office. If we delete the respondents who did not answer the question, the weighted percentage is 12.3 percent of our state legislator sample who saw executive influence to be the dominant one in state legislative decision making.

Because of the wording of each question, however, we have probably underemphasized the importance of the executive branch in the state policy-making process. A legislator may not look to the governor for information on a given piece of information because the chief executive may simply be more difficult to reach than the chief cue giver, personal friends in the legislature, or even administrator-specialists in a policy area (who may testify before committees of the legislature or interact with members in other ways). Similarly our question on the major decision locus specifically asked members to cite the major source of power within the legislature. We thus may have failed to pick up indicators of the governor's influence in policy formation outside the chamber.

We thus argue that two factors in particular should affect the status of the governor and other members of the executive branch from the perspective of state legislators: (1) members' orientations toward the legislative-executive competition for power; and (2) the political party of the members. With respect to the seeking of cues and the perception of the major source of decision making in the legislature being executive-oriented, we hypothesize:

1. The greater the support for a strong role for the governor in the policy-making process, the more likely a member will be to seek cues from the executive branch.

2. The greater the support for a strong role for the governor in the policy-making process, the more likely a member will be to see the major decision locus as executive-oriented.

3. Legislators from the same party as the governor will be more likely to seek cues from the executive branch than will members from the opposition party.

4. Legislators from the same party as the governor will be more likely to see the major decision locus as executive-oriented.

5. The greater the support for a strong role for the governor in the policy-making process, the more likely a member will be to seek cues from the executive branch if he is a member of the governor's party. That is, the pattern of cue seeking from the executive branch is posited to be greater among members of the governor's party than among all members and particularly among members of the opposition.

6. The greater the support for a strong role for the governor in the policy-making process, the more likely a member will be to see the major decision locus as executive-oriented if he is a member of the governor's party.

7. The more likely a member is to seek cues from the executive branch, the more likely he will be to see the major decision locus as executive-oriented, and this relationship will be accentuated for members from the same party as the governor.

Thus, our major control variable is the party of the legislator compared to that of the governor. Unlike the previous chapter and the next one, we do not control for the level of competition in a district or its typicality because Morehouse's findings (1973) on competition suggest that at least the former control is not supported in her study; and our control for the party-match of the legislator and his governor, particularly given the multiple indicators of the cue-giving variable (to be discussed below), would simply make such controls unmanageable in this chapter. We do not argue that the controls are irrelevant; quite the contrary. Rather, we limit our analysis in order not to overwhelm the reader with table upon table.

We also want to look at another—and from our perspective—more interesting question in this chapter which would preclude further hypothesis testing. This question, identical to that used by Wayne Francis (1967) in his national sample of state legislators over a decade ago, asks each respondent to select the most important policies to come before recent sessions of the legislature (we asked our respondents to name up to four such areas), and, taking one policy area at a time, to check (when the respondent believed appropriate) whether "the Governor was pressing hard for legislation in this area." Which areas do our respondents believe are of greatest concern to their respective governors? Are there some areas of concern that we find throughout our sample, or is the power and influence of the governor's office so varied that we do not obtain a single response? We offer no specific hypotheses on this question, but believe that it will be instructive to examine the results.

After a section in which we describe the construction of our variables, we shall proceed as follows in the analysis: first, we shall test the relationship between the seeking of executive cues and the perception that members who are most likely to seek such information will also perceive the major decision locus to be executive-oriented. Second, we shall examine the posited relationship between executive cue seeking (through our series of multiple indicators) and the orientations of members toward the legislative-executive balance of power. Third, we shall consider the direct relationship between cue seeking and the legislator-governor party linkage. Fourth, we shall reconsider the relationship between information seeking and members' orientations toward the balance of legislative-executive power, controlling for whether the member is from the same party as the governor. Fifth, we shall examine the sources of major decision loci as perceived by the members according to legislators' orientations toward the balance of power, the party-match with the governor, and orientations controlling for the party-match variable, as we have proposed for the cue variable. Finally, we shall seek to determine whether there is a coherent pattern of responses to gubernatorial action on matters of policy believed to be the most important by members of the legislature. We turn now to a discussion of our operationalizations of the variables in the analysis.

OPERATIONALIZATION OF THE VARIABLES

Our first dependent variables measure in a number of ways the manner in which legislators rely upon executive-branch cues when making decisions on bills. In the list of thirteen possible sources of cues, two refer to potential sources of executive-branch cues. They are the governor and administrator-specialist in policy. The first executive-branch cue index we use grouped into one category all legislators who ranked first any one of the two executive-branch cue givers and into a second category all legislators who failed to rank first any of the executive-branch cue givers. Thus, the variable has legislators whose most important cue giver was an executive source of information categorized against those whose most important cue giver was a nonexecutive source of information. The second executive-branch cue index expands upon the first by incorporating into its construction information on a second, third, fourth, and fifth rankings on the executive-branch source of cues. For this index we created a six-category variable by simply placing every legislator who ranked executive-branch cue givers first into a first category, those who ranked executive-branch cue givers second into a second category, and so on, with those who failed to rank them at all constituting the sixth category. This six-category index measures the degree to which the legislators see the executive branch as an important cue giver. The decision-locus variable is measured employing responses to our query, "In your legislature, where would you say the most significant decisions are made?" We shall consider the governor and the policy committee to be the executive sources of decision loci in the legislature. Thus, this dependent variable is a dichotomy: either the member perceived the major decision locus to be executive-oriented or he did not.

Our first independent variable is the member's orientation toward the balance of power between the legislative and executive, the Gubernatorial Orientation (GO) scale discussed in Chapter 1. The higher the score on this scale, the more supportive a member is of a strong gubernatorial role (and a weaker legislative one). Thus, we expect positive relationships between this scale and our cue-taking and decision-locus variables. The party-match variable categorizes into one group all of the respondents who are of the same party as the governor and into another group all those who are of a different party from the governor. Finally, we have already discussed the last "variable" to be analyzed—the responses to our question on the most important problems facing a state.

LEGISLATIVE CUE SEEKING, PERCEPTION OF DECISION LOCI, AND ORIENTATIONS TOWARD THE EXECUTIVE

We begin by examining the relationship between the propensity of a legislator to take cues from the governor or from an administrative specialist in a policy area and those who believe that the major decision locus in the legislature is gubernatorial power. We have noted that members who perceive the major decision locus as the governor's office constitute a small percentage of our total sample (only 12.3 of those who responded to this question), while there was a similarly small figure for members who relied primarily (that is, as their first choice) on executive cues—only 6.3 percent. While these figures are quite small, we do seek to determine whether there is a substantial overlap in the two groups: those who actively seek out information from the executive and those who believe that the power of this branch of state government is a fact of life in legislative politics.

Our results, presented in Table 4.1, are somewhat difficult to interpret, given the skewed marginals for both the row and column variables. We observe a very low value of phi, the linear measure of association, indicating a virtually random pattern of covariation within the table. The curvilinear measure, Yule's Q (the equivalent of gamma for a two-by-two table), is a respectable .347. But this measure is sensitive to skewed marginals and can be easily inflated under such circumstances. The appropriate course here is to examine both coefficients, with particular emphasis on phi, which is less subject to inflation because of unequal marginals. We thus conclude that there is very little relationship between cue taking from the executive branch and perception of the governor's office as the major decision locus in the legislature.

Yet an examination of the first row of Table 4.1 indicates that there is some pattern of relationship between the two groups. The percentage of members who see the governor as the major decision locus in the legislature is twice as great as that for members who perceive other loci as the major centers of power in the legislature. Similarly (although the data are not presented in the table), almost twice as large a percentage of members who rely most heavily upon executive-oriented cues see the governor as the major source of power in the legislature, compared to those who depend primarily upon other sources of information. (The respective percentages are 21.3 and 11.6.)

The raw figures are of course not nearly as impressive. But there does appear to be some overlap in the two groups which is ob-

TABLE 4.1

Source of Cues by Perception of Decision Locus
(in percent)

Source	Executive-Oriented Decision Locus	Other Decision Locus	N
Executive-oriented	12.3	6.4	74
Other	87.7	93.6	974
N	129	919	1,048

Note: phi = .076; Q = .347.

scured by the linear measure of association because of the skewness in both variables. Table 4.1, then, shows that there is some pattern of covariation between the two groups, but also that this pattern is obscured by the propensity of our respondents to perceive power in the legislature as insulated from the executive branch and for cue-taking behavior to be similarly perceived. Indeed, only 16 of the 1,048 respondents in Table 4.1 were "executive-oriented" on both questions. This low set of relationships suggests that perception of decision locus and the primary cue source are distinguishable constructs. Despite some of our earlier hesitation, it seems that the decision-locus question may reflect perceptions of gubernatorial power. If this were not the case, then we would expect stronger patterns of covariation with the cue-seeking variable.

Concentrating on cues, we now examine the relationship between executive cue seeking and support for a strong role for the governor among our legislative respondents. We first consider only those re-

spondents who cited executive-oriented cues as their primary source
of information. This operationalization of the hypothesis is examined
in Table 4.2. Here, we again find a very weak linear relationship between our cue variable and our predictor, the GO scale, with tau-c =
.043. We cannot attribute this result to skewed distributions on both
variables, since there is considerable variation in support for a strong
role for the governor. Even the curvilinear measure, gamma, is not

TABLE 4.2

Source of Cues by GO Scale
(in percent)

Source	High	Medium	Low	N
Executive-oriented	11.5	4.8	8.9	76
Other	88.5	95.2	91.1	991
N	314	660	93	1,067

Note: tau-c = .043; gamma = .269.

very strong, despite the tendency of this coefficient to be inflated with
a marginal distribution such as we have for the cue variable. Examining the percentages in Table 4.2, we find that there is simply little
variation in the extent of executive-oriented cue-seeking behavior, a
finding consistent with an earlier analysis we conducted which demonstrated virtually uniform patterns of information gathering within the
legislature (as opposed to outside sources, such as our executive cue
givers) regardless of the subjective orientations of the members
(Uslaner and Weber 1975b).

The marginals are not as skewed for our cue-taking variable
when we operationalize it in terms of the rank order of mentions of
executive cues, as the data in Table 4.3 demonstrate. While executive sources are not often cited as primary cue givers, they are relied upon for information as second, third, fourth, or fifth choices
to a much greater extent. This is particularly the case for administrator-specialists in a policy area—in contrast to the governor himself—who were tied for second place with legislative specialists (but
behind personal friends in the legislature)—as the second choice of
our respondents for information when a member goes about making
up his mind.

TABLE 4.3

Rank Order of Cue Taking from Executive Branch
by GO Scale
(in percent)

Ranking of Party Leaders in Legislature Cue Taking	High	Medium	Low	N
First	5.7	4.3	6.4	52
Second	15.3	11.3	10.0	132
Third	9.9	11.1	10.6	114
Fourth	17.8	11.0	8.9	137
Fifth	13.0	15.6	6.6	150
Not at all	38.4	46.6	57.5	482
N	314	660	93	1,067

Note: tau-c = .080; gamma = .138.

Executive-oriented cues, when rank ordered, then, are even more a function of the informational role of the bureaucracy than are the primary cues. The governor was mentioned by more than 5 percent of our respondents only as a fifth choice. This greater reflection of the role of administrator-specialists may account for the lower value of the curvilinear measure of association (gamma = .138), even though the marginals are not as unevenly distributed as we found in Table 4.2. The linear measure is, however, slightly higher at tau-c = .080. Nevertheless, this alternative conceptualization of the extent of executive cue seeking is not strongly associated with the GO scale. Even the less skewed distribution in Table 4.3, compared to Table 4.2, cannot hide the basic pattern of cue-seeking behavior within the confines of the legislatures of our respondents.

We turn now to an examination of the impact of legislators' subjective orientations toward gubernatorial power and their perception of the major decision locus in the legislature. In Table 4.4, we find only a weak linear relationship (tau-c = .095), but a much stronger curvilinear one (gamma = .396) between our decision-locus variable and the GO scale. While the value of gamma might be inflated because of the marginals for the decision-locus variable, an examination of the percentages in Table 4.4 indicates that there is indeed a systematic pattern of perceptions in our data. The percentage of members who perceive the decision locus to be executive-oriented and who rank high on the GO Scale—that is, who believe that the major role in the state policy-making process should be played by the governor rather than the legislature—is more than twice as great as that for those with "medium" scores. This is the sharpest division we observe in Table 4.4 and it indicates that members' subjective orientations toward gubernatorial power do seem to have at least a moderate impact on the more objective measure of where power in the legislature is believed to lie.

TABLE 4.4

Perception of Decision Locus by GO Scale
(in percent)

Decision Locus	High	Medium	Low	N
Executive-oriented	19.5	9.7	5.5	137
Other	80.5	90.3	94.5	983
N	332	691	97	1,120

Note: tau-c = .095; gamma = .396.

For two reasons, we interpret these results somewhat differently from those of the second chapter, in which similar values of gamma and even higher tau-c coefficients were said to represent less clearcut linkage patterns. First, the executive-oriented perceptions of decision loci are less prevalent (and, hence, the data in the tables are more skewed) than were partisan attributions of the major source of decision making in state legislatures. Second, the two party orientation scales had reasonably strong predictive success with respect to the cue-taking variables, which was not the case for the GO scale. Thus, we see perceptions of gubernatorial power, as reflected in our decision-locus variable, as more indicative of how members perceive the decision-making process than the partisan responses to the same question. The justification for this argument is that the office of the governor is a more readily identifiable source of power for legislators than is the party caucus or the policy committee. This is particularly the case since executive decisions are extralegislative, at least in origin. The party caucus and the policy committee are part of the legislative process, and, as such, may involve the members attributing power to themselves.

The thrust of our argument is that there is a more clear-cut conceptual distinction between executive cues and executive decision loci, on the one hand, and similar partisan variables, on the other. Parties, even "party leaders in the legislature," are amorphous in comparison to the office of the governor—just as committees and party organizations in the Congress each represent multiple information sources, whereas the office of the president seems to speak with one voice to a much greater extent. Thus, executive power may be more clearly isolated by the members than party-related power. On the other hand, attitudes toward the parties are more likely to shape the cue-seeking behavior than are gubernatorial orientations, since the latter may not reflect the relative closeness of the member to cues from the executive branch.

CUES, DECISION LOCI, AND THE LEGISLATOR-GOVERNOR PARTY-MATCH

Our first two hypotheses have received, at best, only moderate support from the analysis reported so far. There does not seem to be a systematic relationship between cue taking from the executive and subjective support for a strong decision-making role for the governor. There is some evidence, however, that members who perceive the major decision locus in the legislature to be the office of the governor are also those most likely to support a strong role for the chief executive in the policy-making process. We hypothesized, however, that these relationships should be strengthened when we control for the party of the governor and of our legislative respondent.

TABLE 4.5

Source of Cues by Governor-Legislator Party-Match
(in percent)

Source	Governor/Legislator of Same Party	Governor/Legislator of Opposition Party	N
Executive-oriented	7.3	6.9	80
Other	92.7	93.1	1,037
N	640	477	1,117

Note: phi = .008; Q = .033.

Specifically, we expect there to be stronger patterns of covariation when the governor and the legislator are of the same party than when they are not. The third and fourth hypotheses presented above simply employ the party-match variable as a determinant of cue-seeking behavior and of the attribution of gubernatorial power by our respondents. The fifth, sixth, and seventh hypotheses employ the party-match as a control variable, with the GO scale still serving as our major predictor.

Table 4.5 indicates that the party-match variable has virtually no impact on cue-seeking behavior. The linear coefficient phi indicates a virtually random pattern of cue-seeking behavior relative to the party-match predictor (phi = .008), while the curvilinear measure Yule's Q does not appear to do much better. Examining the percentages of those who seek cues primarily from the executive branch, we find that 7.3 percent of the respondents from the same party as the governor depend most heavily upon such information, compared to 6.9 percent from opposition parties. Contrary to our hypothesis, then we find no relationship whatsoever between the seeking of executive-oriented cues and the party-match variable.

TABLE 4.6

Perception of Decision Locus by Governor-Legislator
Party-Match
(in percent)

Decision Locus	Governor/Legislator of Same Party	Governor/Legislator of Opposition Party	N
Executive-oriented	14.2	9.9	143
Other	85.8	90.1	1,018
N	652	505	1,161

Note: phi = .065; Q = .202.

There is some evidence of a stronger relationship for the perception of the major decision locus in the legislature and the party-match predictor (phi = .065, Q = .202) in Table 4.6. But, even here, the effect of the legislator-governor party-match is relatively small. Only 14.2 percent of our matched respondents depended primarily upon executive cues, not dramatically higher than the almost 10 percent of legislators from parties different from those of the governor. Tentatively, we thus argue that members who look to the executive branch for information or who perceive the governor's office as the major source of power in the legislature are not affected by partisan factors.

Members, for example, who want to know what the position of the governor is on a piece of legislation may either use that information as a negative cue or as reflecting the judgment of a staff much larger than that of their own or their party's, if they are of the opposition party. Similarly, members who perceive the governor's office as the major source of power in the legislature may simply be expressing the view that the executive dominates the legislative branch and this situation would not change if party control of either branch were to be altered. These are of course speculations, but they do seem to correspond to the claims of those who proclaim the weakness of our legislative institutions, and particularly they seem to reflect the attitudes of the dispirited Republican minority in the United States Congress (Jones 1970).

TABLE 4.7

Sources of Cues by GO Scale:
Members of Governor's Party
(in percent)

Source	High	Medium	Low	N
Executive-oriented	12.4	4.0	9.9	43
Other	87.6	96.0	90.1	560
N	202	357	44	603

Note: tau-c = .058; gamma = .359.

When we examine the sources of cues and their relationship to support for a strong role in the state policy-making process by the governor, controlling for the party of the member (Tables 4.7 and 4.8), we find only slight differences in cue-taking behavior. The relationship between executive cue taking and the GO scale appears somewhat stronger for members of the governor's party than for opposition members, particularly when we concentrate on the curvilinear measure (gamma = .359 and .149, respectively) rather than the linear one (tau-c = .058 and .021, respectively).

Yet, an examination of the percentages in Tables 4. 7 and 4. 8 for executive-oriented cues does not reveal a strong pattern of covariation at all. For members who rank high on the GO scale, 12. 4 percent of the party-match legislators rely primarily upon executive cues,

TABLE 4. 8

Sources of Cues by GO Scale:
Members of Opposition Party
(in percent)

Source	High	Medium	Low	N
Executive-oriented	9. 9	5. 8	8. 1	33
Other	90. 1	94. 2	91. 9	431
N	112	303	49	464

Note: tau-c = . 021; gamma = . 149.

compared to almost 10 percent of the members from opposition parties. This is the largest percentage gap in the two tables. Indeed, a slightly higher (5. 8) percentage of opposition members with medium scores from opposition parties seek out information from the executive branch than do their party-match colleagues with similar scores (4 percent). The differences in the gamma coefficients for these tables can thus be attributed to the skewed marginals for the dependent variable.

What we do find interesting, and not entirely unexpected, is that a larger percentage of our respondents from the same party as the governor scored high on the GO scale than did opposition-party legislators: the respective figures are approximately one-third compared to one-quarter. Thus, our expectation about the general nature of the party-match effect on some aspect of gubernatorial support has been borne out, although our specific predictions have not fared as well.

The answer to this dilemma is not complex. Simple party identification may well predict one's attitude toward executive power. During the period of our survey (1973-74), a preponderance of both state houses and legislatures were controlled by the Democrats, the party that has been most supportive of a strong executive at the national level since World War II. This undoubtedly had some effect on the strength of the relationship between the party-match variable and high scores on the GO scale. However, such support for the concept of a strong governor does not imply that members will seek out information from the executive branch, as we have seen. It is thus not surprising that the control for party-match would not contribute much to our understanding of the factors that induce members to seek executive cues. Before concluding our examination of the effect of party-match on cue behavior, we turn now to a reexamination of the effects of this control on the rank ordering of executive cues.

The rank ordering of executive cues displayed a somewhat lower linear relationship with the GO scale, but a higher curvilinear one without the party-match control. When we divide our sample into those respondents of the same party as the governor and those from opposition parties, the pattern of relationships is not as clear-cut from the perspective of comparing the linear-curvilinear hypotheses across the sets. What we do find, however, is at least a modicum of support for our hypothesis that the party-match control affects the overall relationships. For the members of the same party as the governor, both tau-c and gamma are higher than we observed for the uncontrolled rankings in Table 4.3. Table 4.9 presents these results: tau-c = .115 and gamma = .184 for the party-match respondents. In

TABLE 4.9

Rank Order of Cue Taking from Executive Branch by
GO Scale: Members of Governor's Party
(in percent)

Ranking of Party Leaders in Legislature Cue-Taking Mention	High	Medium	Low	N
First	4.1	3.0	6.3	22
Second	18.5	10.6	9.4	80
Third	12.6	13.9	17.8	83
Fourth	22.5	12.8	10.5	96
Fifth	13.3	17.7	8.7	94
Not at all	28.9	42.0	47.3	229
N	202	357	44	603

Note: tau-c = .115; gamma = .184.

contrast, both the linear and curvilinear coefficients are greatly reduced (.018 and .037, respectively) for the members from opposition parties, as Table 4.10 indicates.

We thus have some partial confirmation of our hypothesis on the effect of the party-match variable, whether we operationalize cue-seeking behavior exclusively in terms of primary information sources or by the rank orders of our respondents. In each case, the linear and curvilinear coefficients are highest for the party-match control, somewhat reduced for the entire data set, and lowest for the members

TABLE 4. 10

Rank Order of Cue Taking from Executive Branch by
GO Scale: Members of Opposition Party
(in percent)

Ranking of Party Leaders in Legislature Cue-Taking Mention	High	Medium	Low	N
First	8. 5	5. 8	6. 5	30
Second	9. 3	12. 2	10. 6	52
Third	5. 1	7. 8	4. 1	31
Fourth	9. 1	8. 9	7. 4	41
Fifth	12. 5	13. 2	4. 6	56
Not at all	55. 4	52. 1	66. 9	252
N	112	303	49	463

Note: tau-c = . 018; gamma = . 037.

of opposition parties. These comparisons, as noted above, ignore the relative values of tau-c and gamma within each operationalization, which are not needed to provide confirmation for our hypothesis. But the confirmation must be interpreted cautiously because of the over-all low correlations between our cue variables (however measured) and support for a strong governor.

We return to our consideration of the decision-locus variable. Although the direct relationship between executive-oriented perceptions of the major source of power in the legislature and the party-match variable was not strong, we did observe at least a moderate relationship with the GO scale. In Tables 4. 11 and 4. 12, we reconsider the relationship between the perceived decision locus and the member's subjective orientation toward gubernatorial power. In the former table, we consider the relationship for legislators of the same party as the governor. The latter table displays the same results for members of different parties. In both, we note that the observed patterns in Table 4. 4 above continue to hold. For our overall sample of

legislators, tau-c = .095 and gamma = .396. For party-match legislators, tau-c = .100 and gamma = .367. The relationships for members of different parties from that of the governor are .081 and .416

TABLE 4.11

Perceptions of Decision Locus by GO Scale:
Members of Governor's Party
(in percent)

Decision Locus	High	Medium	Low	N
Executive-oriented	21.1	10.9	7.6	88
Other	78.9	89.1	92.4	536
N	210	368	47	624

Note: tau-c = .100; gamma = .367.

respectively. The higher value of gamma for the nonmatched members is somewhat surprising and seems to run contrary to our sixth
hypothesis. Note, however, that this result is a statistical artifact
of the very small number of cases for both subsets of our sample who
perceive the governor to be the major factor in legislative decision
making but who have low scores on the GO scale (eight in the matched
subset and only two in the nonmatched group).

There is a slight tendency for members of the same party as
the governor who score high on the subjective gubernatorial scale to
see the major decision locus as the governor's office more than do
those members who are of a different party, but even here the differences are not large. The tau-c values for the two groups do not de-
viate much from the overall value reported in Table 4.4. Members'
perceptions of the relative degrees of power of the governor in legislative politics are moderately affected by their scores on the GO scale,
but they are not differentiated (either directly or when controlling) by
the party-match variable. Legislators who perceive power to be main-
ly gubernatorial, even within the context of the legislature itself, also
do not seem to be differentiated by party. This confirms our earlier
findings that simple party identification is too broad a concept to be
of much utility in determining members' perceptions of the workings
of the legislative system—particularly in comparison to the subjective
orientations of the members about how the legislature ought to be

structured. These subjective perceptions color a member's view of the "objective" situation better than the more "objective" measures we have examined.

TABLE 4. 12

Perceptions of Decision Locus by GO Scale:
Members of Opposition Party
(in percent)

Decision Locus	High	Medium	Low	N
Executive-oriented	16. 9	8. 4	3. 6	50
Other	83. 1	91. 6	96. 4	446
N	123	323	50	496

Note: tau-c = . 081; gamma = . 416.

Finally, we turn to our seventh hypothesis, in which we posited that there should be a systematic pattern of covariation between the sources of information a member seeks and his propensity to attribute power to those sources in the legislative arena. The uncontrolled version of this hypothesis was the first one examined in this chapter. We found only slight support for this hypothesis when examining the percentage distributions in Table 4. 1. Tables 4. 13 and 4. 14, which replicate Table 4. 1 for the party-matched and nonmatched members respectively, indicate that once again, there is not a linear relationship between cue sources and decision loci for either subset (phi = . 108 and . 028, respectively). The percentages for each table, together with the very different values of Yule's Q (. 434 for the party-match group, . 161 for the other group) indicate that there is at least some pattern of interrelationship of cues and decision loci for members of the same party as the governor. Even with the skewed marginals on both variables (and particularly on the decision locus one), we find that the party-match control does discriminate among members who rely primarily upon executive-oriented cues and those who perceive that the major source of power in the legislature does not come from the governor's office.

The same pattern of relationships holds if we operationalize executive cue-seeking behavior in terms of rank orders rather than reliance on primary cue givers. We do not report the data in tabular form, as we did for the rank orders reported earlier (see Tables 4. 3, 4. 9, and 4. 10 above), but we do present the values of tau-c and gamma for the entire sample, the party-match subgroup, and the opposi-

TABLE 4. 13

Source of Cues by Perception of Decision Locus:
Members of Governor's Party
(in percent)

Source	Executive-Oriented Decision Locus	Other Decision Locus	N
Executive-oriented	14. 1	6. 1	43
Other	85. 9	93. 9	546
N	83	506	589

Note: phi = . 108; Q = . 434.

tion party members in Table 4. 15. The linear measures are somewhat stronger for the full sample and the party-match group (but quite lower for the nonmatched members), while the curvilinear measures are not as dramatically different since the marginals are not as skewed. It is clear, however, that regardless of how we measure cue taking, the relationship with perceived decision locus is moderate, with the highest values observed for the party-match subsample.

While this relationship is not overwhelming, we are left with, in the language of The King and I, a "puzzlement." The party-match control did not seem particularly useful in examining either executive-oriented cues as the primary source of members' information or legislators' perceptions of where the major power source in the legislature is. Yet it does appear to have at least some nontrivial relationship to the relationship between cue seeking and perceptions of gubernatorial power among legislators.

These findings can be reconciled; they are not as anomalous as they may first appear to be. The low correlations between the party-match dichotomy, on the one hand, and patterns of cue seeking and perceptions of decision loci, on the other, did not consider the conjoint effects of the latter variables. Recall, furthermore, that we did observe a rather modest (particularly given the skewed marginals) curvilinear relationship between party-match and decision locus, particularly when compared to sources of cues (Q = .202 and .033, respectively). Thus, for members of our legislative sample affiliated with the same party as the governor of their state, there is a greater overlap between the perception of decision locus and cue-seeking behavior. For these members, then, there is greater "constraint" in their concept of legislative-executive relations (on "constraints" in "belief systems," see Converse 1964; Nie with Andersen 1974; Achen 1975), as we had hypothesized.

TABLE 4.14

Source of Cues by Perception of Decision Locus:
Members of Opposition Party
(in percent)

Source	Executive-Oriented Decision Locus	Other Decision Locus	N
Executive-oriented	9.1	6.7	32
Other	90.9	93.3	428
N	46	414	460

Note: phi = .028; Q = .161.

This raises the further question of why the party-match controls were ineffective for both the information-seeking variable and the one dealing with centers of power. The answer seems to lie in the skewed distributions in the direction of nonexecutive responses to both questions. Our legislative respondents simply did not seek out cues from the executive branch or believe that the governor's office was the primary decision locus in the state legislature. Indeed, there was not much variation in the pattern of responses we obtained, particularly in the case of the primary information source. What small variations we have observed are somewhat related to orientations toward gubernatorial versus legislative power.

Thus, the overall conclusion regarding our hypotheses is that attitudes toward the executive branch are not only more uniform but also less variable (that is, subject to predictability across subgroups in our analysis) than are orientations toward the party system. We also realize that we are underestimating the role of the governor as a formal leader and a party leader in our analysis. Since we did not ask our respondents about their orientations toward the chief executive of their state in particular, we cannot evaluate the very reasonable argument of Ransone (1956) that gubernatorial success varies with the

TABLE 4.15

Source of Rank-Ordered Cues by Perception of Decision
Locus: Summary Measures for Full Sample
and Subgroups

	Tau-c	Gamma
Entire sample	.072	.220
Party-match members	.121	.310
Members of opposition parties	.004	.017

personality of the executive officer. To compensate, in at least some small part, for this, we now move to a consideration of the issues that our legislative respondents believed to be important and the extent to which the governors in the 50 states were actively attempting to influence such legislation.

GUBERNATORIAL ACTIVITY ON POLICY AREAS
IN THE STATES

While our questions may not have indicated the extent to which the governor actually plays a major role in the state policy-making process, we do have a way of assessing the extent to which members saw the governor as active in particular policy areas: whether or not he was actually influential when the members made their own decisions on these policy areas. Following the design of the original Francis study (see Francis 1967; pp. 8ff., 110-11), we asked each respondent, "What would you estimate to be the most important matters of policy to come before the most recent regular session of your legislature?" and requested that each member list four such issues, not necessarily ranked in order. Then, taking each issue separately, the respondent could either answer affirmatively or not at all to the statement, "The governor was pressing hard for legislation in this area."

Francis measured the salience of each of the 20 issues he analyzed through a construct called the "index response value," a summary measure he found useful in making comparisons across differently worded questions (Francis 1967; pp. 16-18). In the present context, the index response value reduces to the simple proportion of times respondents indicated strong gubernatorial action on the issues. The mean across the 20 issues Francis studied was .45 (Francis 1967; p. 15) for gubernatorial action. We have added 2 categories to his initial set of 20—energy and environment. Nevertheless, the mean value has fallen to .40, ten years after the Francis survey was conducted.

Either figure is impressive, however, in contrast to the much smaller proportions of cues or perceptions of gubernatorial power within the legislature we have noted. The governor may be working quite hard to get a bill enacted. If this is the case, cues from the executive branch may be superfluous. They might not provide enough detailed information to be of use to the legislator. The member might find it more profitable to turn to a surrogate for the governor who is managing the legislation in the chamber—either a party or a committee leader, in particular. Similarly, members may acknowledge that the governor was attempting to use his influence on members quite frequently, but they may make the same distinction that academics have stressed: influence and power (which implies some element of coercion) are quite different things. If these speculations are correct, then studies that have attributed so much power to the governor at the expense of the legislature may have overstated the case.

Before attempting to examine the areas in which the chief executives attempted to exercise influence on legislators, we should first consider the relative salience of the 22 issues we are considering, both in 1963 (when the Francis study was done) and in 1973-74, the years of our study. The issue categorizations were, with two exceptions, identical to those of the Francis study. First, we wanted comparability with the only other such study (and the one upon which this one is in part based). Second, we believe that in general the Francis categories tapped the major dimensions of policy formation in the states. The categories are as follows: taxation; apportionment; education; finance; labor; health; business; civil rights; highways-transportation; administration (including questions of reorganization of state government); local government; social welfare; courts-penal-crime; liquor; gambling; land use; elections-primaries-conventions; constitutional revision; water resources; and agriculture. To these issue areas, we added energy and environment, two policy areas that

did not have the salience in the early 1960s that they did in the 1970s
(see Jones 1974). In considering the overall salience of these issues
(based upon the frequency of mentions by our respondents), we would
hypothesize:

8. The more salient an issue is, the greater influence the governor would be expected to attempt to exercise on that policy area.

We turn now to an examination of the importance attached to each issue area by our respondents and to their perceptions of gubernatorial
activity on these policies.

Table 4.16 presents the distributions of mentions by policy area
for the original Francis survey and for this study. The figures were
obtained from a paper by Weber and Francis (1975), employing the
original 1963 survey by Francis and the data base we are employing
here. Table 4.17 presents the distributions of attributions of gubernatorial activity on the policy areas from the two studies; figures from
the Francis study were either taken directly from his book (Francis
1967; pp. 76-78) or were computed from the data set he gathered. To
test hypothesis 8 we employ Spearman's rank-order correlation coefficient. We do not use the more familiar Pearson product-moment
correlation, even though the data are expressed as proportions, because comparisons of such coefficients across variables with different
numbers of cases and different variances are risky at best (see Rao
and Miller 1971; p. 16). Furthermore, if the data are to be construed
as meeting the assumptions of interval-ratio scales, then the Spearman and Pearson coefficients are identical.

Examining the data in Table 4.16, we note that there is substantial continuity in issue salience from 1963 to 1973-74. Of course, there
is an increase in the salience of some issues—notably, education (stim-
ulated by the passage of the Elementary and Secondary Education Act
of 1965 by the 89th Congress, administration (as more and more governments became concerned with internal reorganization), courts-
penal-crime (as the question of "law and order" became increasingly
salient to the public), land use, and elections-primaries-conventions.
Issues such as gambling and liquor regulation became considerably
less important as the major moral issues involved were resolved
in earlier years, while social welfare programs may have lost some
of their earlier salience because of the greater federal role taken in
the years following the Francis survey. There was a sharp drop in
the number of references to apportionment as a major state issue, indicating that the issues raised by the Supreme Court decisions of the
early 1960s had largely been settled by the 1970s, during which time
the periodic and routine redrawing of district lines every ten years
has replaced the more frequent and hectic pace of earlier years. Fi-

nance, taxation, and education are among the most important issues
in both our study and that of Francis; while constitutional revision,
water resources, and agriculture were mentioned by 1 percent or less

TABLE 4.16

Distribution of Issue Mentions by Policy Area:
1963 and 1973-74

Policy Area	Francis Study	Current Study
Taxation	.192	.132
Apportionment	.137	.026
Education	.135	.104
Finance	.132	.162
Labor	.060	.055
Health	.046	.049
Business	.046	.075
Civil rights	.033	.021
Highways-transportation	.032	.024
Administration	.035	.091
Local government	.019	.011
Social welfare	.035	.020
Courts-penal-crime	.018	.049
Liquor	.015	.001
Gambling	.015	.007
Land use	.017	.059
Elections-primaries-conventions	.010	.060
Constitutional revision	.010	.006
Water resources	.008	.006
Agriculture	.006	.004
Energy	n.a.	.009
Environment	n.a.	.030

Note: n.a. indicates data is not available, area was not surveyed in the Francis study.

of the respondents in each study. The rank-order correlation, r_S,
between the two studies for the 20 policy areas common to both is an
impressive .672.

The issues on which gubernatorial activity was notable were
not, however, so constant over time. By 1973-74, land use had become the major issue on which governors attempted to exercise in-

fluence: 61. 7 percent of our respondents who mentioned this as an important question believed that there was strong gubernatorial pressure in this area. Administration issues, however, continued to rank second. But the major issue of the Francis study in terms of gubernatorial activity, highways-transportation, fell to fifth place in our survey, perhaps because most of the interstate highway system has been completed and fewer states are spending their increasingly tight

TABLE 4. 17

Distribution of Gubernatorial Activity by Policy Area:
1963 and 1973-74

Policy Area	Francis Study	Current Study
Highways-transportation	. 709	. 483
Administration	. 618	. 598
Civil rights	. 615	. 262
Finance	. 592	. 443
Social welfare	. 538	. 313
Water resources	. 522	. 421
Courts-penal-crime	. 510	. 314
Taxation	. 492	. 446
Health	. 490	. 249
Land use	. 474	. 617
Education	. 450	. 364
Constitutional revision	. 433	. 393
Local government	. 400	. 486
Gambling	. 367	. 138
Apportionment	. 326	. 238
Liquor	. 320	. 000
Labor	. 290	. 228
Business	. 282	. 363
Agriculture	. 222	. 333
Elections-primaries-conventions	. 091	. 379
Energy	n. a.	. 500
Environment	n. a.	. 328

Note: n. a. indicates data is not available, area was not surveyed in the Francis study.

resources on transportation. Liquor and gambling, two of the three issues mentioned as least frequently involving the governor in the

Francis study, again rank at the bottom of our list—but note the striking drop in the proportion of members who cite gubernatorial activity on such issues. The least important question as far as governors were concerned in the Francis study was elections-primaries-conventions. But in the intervening ten years, this issue area has moved into the top half of our rank ordering. Undoubtedly contributing to this change was the report of the McGovern-Fraser committee of the Democratic National Committee after the party's divisive 1968 convention. The report urged states to adopt more open systems of nominating candidates for the presidency and the number of state primaries almost doubled from 1968 to 1976. On the other hand, civil rights, third in Francis's list, fell to seventeenth on our list. Here the role of the states has largely been eclipsed by that of the federal government; the courts particularly have been more active than chief executives. Of issues on which the governors "pressed hard" the correlation of rank orders for the two data sets is .402.

It is thus not surprising that we do not find much support for the eighth hypothesis in either data set. The rank-order correlation for 1963 is .226, while that for 1973-74 is .222. While the signs are in the expected direction, the magnitude of the coefficients is small indeed. It is not the salience of issues to the members which appears to determine whether a governor takes an active or passive role. Furthermore, as Francis (1967; p. 76) noted, the formal powers of the governor across the states do not correlate strongly with an overall measure of gubernatorial activity aggregated to the state level. Outside the South, there was a moderately strong relationship with an overall measure of the centralization of decision making in the state, but as Francis noted when examining data for the South: "Centralized decision-making is likely to focus on the Governor, but not necessarily" (p. 76). As the states have become more homogeneous, we would expect that the relationship with centralization would become more uniform. We do not have a comparable measure of centralization for the later time period.

Those students of state politics who have concentrated their efforts on analyzing the role of the governor in the budgetary process (see Sharkansky 1968a) may have made too strong an inferential leap from the salience of a policy area such as taxation and finance to legislators (see Table 4.16) and bureaucrats (see Wright 1967) with the propensity of the governor to make an actual attempt to influence policy on such fiscal matters. We do not mean that the budget is not of great concern to the governor, as Table 4.17 clearly indicates (taxation and finance are the sixth and seventh most frequently mentioned policy areas, respectively).

Yet, the role of the governor goes considerably beyond that of the realm of fiscal affairs. Indeed, the chief executive is perceived as being most involved in matters that are of greatest concern to the state—that is, those that least involve other officials, either national or local. In particular, there is the policy area of land use, in which interstate planning has greatly increased over the last decade. The natural issue for gubernatorial attention is administration, that is, the running of the state government itself. The increased rank and percentage of governors becoming involved with elections, primaries, and conventions further highlights the role delegated to the states in determining the shape of their electoral mechanisms, the strong gubernatorial interest in questions of energy policy indicates the ways in which the chief executives have, of necessity, become involved in attempts to achieve greater parity among the states in a resource-scarce area. Gubernatorial activity is weakest in those issue areas with little conflict (liquor and gambling), primarily within the confines of the legislature (apportionment), and, most notably, those which have become the predominant domain of the federal government (labor, health, civil rights, social welfare).

Governors, then, are most active in the policy areas most demanding their attention—and also in the arenas with the least potential for negative reactions. Government administration is not a highly salient issue to most voters—unless a governor successfully brings off a major state reorganization, as did Governor Jimmy Carter of Georgia in the early 1970s. Land-use questions cannot be avoided by contemporary chief executives, but a resourceful leader can gain political advantage by directing planning efforts which are most favorable toward the more established residents of the state. Similarly, many governors gained popularity in the 1970s by their demands for either greater parity in energy resources (leaders from the Northeast and Midwest in particular) or by their defenses of the rights of their states to the energy resources that the federal government may have proposed to claim (the Gulf Coast and Pacific states).

Gubernatorial activity, as perceived by the legislators, is less tied to explicitly partisan considerations, to power relationships (in which a chief executive attempts to impose his will upon a pliant legislature), budgetary matters (which often raise questions the governor might just as well prefer avoiding), or even the willingness of members to support the concept of a strong legislative role for the executive leader—although we have found a modicum of support for the last thesis. The strongest statement about gubernatorial activity is that state executives take the lead on issues where leadership is the most likely to be productive, both in terms of policy success and future electoral results. Thus, Morehouse (1973) has suggested that governors (at least among Democrats) who have the best primary records are likely to achieve the most success with the legislature. We suspect that the phenomenon she observed may hold for just the opposite reasons: governors with the greatest policy success relative to their legislatures may (at least among their partisans) be the "best politicians," in every sense of that phrase.

5

LEGISLATIVE PROFESSIONALISM AND LEGISLATIVE REFORM: A RECONSIDERATION

INTRODUCTION

The collective judgment of many observers of the legislative process, both academics and political leaders, has virtually identified the state legislature as the Stepin Fetchit of decision arenas within the American federal system. Unlike the U. S. Congress, salaries are generally quite low, staff is almost nonexistent, research facilities are scarce, and the level of job satisfaction is often not very high. While local legislatures (city and county councils or boards of aldermen) face many of the same problems, these bodies do not require members to be away from home for considerable periods of time (sometimes two months, perhaps as many as eight to nine). Thus, it is not surprising that the rate of turnover in state legislatures is very high, particularly in comparison to the Congress (Rosenthal 1974a; pp. 180-84; Rosenthal 1974b).

Students of state legislatures have tended, like doctors, to not only diagnose the disease but also to prescribe the cure. Before discussing the many cures suggested, we wish to address ourselves to the nature of the problem as seen by several of these students. Consider, then, the following statement by the Citizens' Conference on State Legislatures in a book aptly titled The Sometime Governments:

> State legislatures would undoubtedly rank low on most
> Americans' lists of governmental institutions that make
> a difference in dealing with the issues and problems that
> bother us. The legislatures are the least visible of those
> institutions, commanding neither the national attention
> that the Congress does nor the local attention that the

city council or the board of supervisors gets. The legislatures meet infrequently—many of them for only a few
months every other year. And when they do meet, their
deliberations and decisions generally take place behind
a pall of public ignorance and indifference. (Bums 1971,
p. 2)

James David Barber has stated, "The scope, volume, and complexity
of legislation have increased tremendously in the last fifty years, but
the number of congressmen has remained about the same and the number of state legislators has actually decreased" (1965, p. 6). Indeed,
Alexander Heard commented, "State legislatures may be our most
extreme example of institutional lag. In their formal qualities they
are largely nineteenth century organizations and they must, or should
address themselves to twentieth century problems" (1966, p. 3); he
then posed the question of whether this is a possibility.
    We should not leave this cursory glance at the problems of state
legislatures without considering the comments of V. O. Key, Jr.,
the foremost student of American state politics:

Many factors have conspired to produce the low status
of the American state legislature. Yet, among these
factors, its unrepresentative character must be assigned
a high rank. A body that often acts reluctantly under executive pressure and whose chief purpose often seems
to be one only of negation cannot but in the long run lose
prestige. A body that is condemned by its constitution
to the defense of a partial interest in the state becomes,
if not a council of censore, something other than a representative body in the conventional sense. (1956, pp.
76-77)

The problem specifically discussed by Key is the "unrepresentative"
character of most state legislatures (at least before Baker v. Carr,
which mandated that both houses of a state legislature be apportioned
on the basis of population) in terms of biases toward one party or the
other in the apportionment schemes of the various states (some even
mandated by the respective constitutions). We shall not be concerned
with the unrepresentative character of state legislatures owing to malapportionment or gerrymandering here, but we believe that we cannot
discuss legislative reform without at least citing this critical problem.
    In summary, then, the literature on state legislatures does not
rate these bodies very highly in terms of what an ideal legislature
should be. But what is our ideal legislature? How could it be brought
into being? Finally, will the proposed reforms have an impact on the

policy-making process itself? This latter problem is itself too complex to admit of a simple answer, for it includes evaluations of the process of policy making (for example, strengthening the legislature in dealing with the executive branch) and with the substance of the decisions reached by the legislature (which in some way are expected to be more representative of a state's public opinion or addressed to some broader concept of the public interest).

Students of state legislatures have tended to be optimistic on the prospects for reform. The Citizens' Conference on State Legislatures, for example, has commented:

> During the last decade, the fog has begun to lift. State legislatures have begun to show new signs of life. Innovative policies and programs in such fields as education, air pollution, mental health, and transportation have begun to emerge. Legislatures have also begun to gear themselves up—to cast off crippling constitutional restrictions, to overhaul their structures and procedures, to hire more and better staff, to meet more often and to stay on the job longer, to pay their members better—so that they can, in fact, function as one of the most important institutions of government. (Bums 1971, p. 3)

In particular, the Citizens' Conference noted that between 1966 and 1970, the number of states meeting in annual session rose from 20 to 31 and average salaries for members jumped from slightly under $10,000 to over $13,000 (p. 7). The group, not content to let this increasing professionalization of state legislatures take its course, has made specific recommendations for each state (Burns 1971, pp. 151-336; Citizens' Conference on State Legislatures 1971, pp. 93-369), and, through the more popular-oriented Sometime Governments, has attempted to reach the mass public in much the same way as the Ralph Nader Congress Project (Green 1975) has done. The group also has published an evaluation of the determinants of its performance measures which has drawn directly on the quantitative study of comparative state politics within the discipline of political science (Citizens' Conference on State Legislatures 1971; ch. 5). And the Citizens' Conference (1972) has set up a process for monitoring the extent to which the state legislatures have moved to implement its recommendations.

Confidence in the ability of state legislatures to adapt has not been confined to this citizens' lobby. Alan Rosenthal's study of legislative performance, the most comprehensive of the academic analyses, also employs the doctor-patient analogy and concludes: "The patients have responded remarkably to the urgings for reform. Since the time of the reapportionment revolution, no state has been left wholly untouched by legislative improvement, and no recommendation has been completely disregarded. The past decade has been notable indeed" (1974a, p. 2). The Eagleton Institute of Politics at Rutgers University has become an active sponsor of reform efforts in several legislatures (Craft 1973; Ogle 1970; Ogle 1971; Smith 1970; Rosenthal 1968; Tantillo 1968; Chartock and Berking 1970). And graduate programs training students to be professional legislative staff members have been established at the Eagleton Institute and at the State University of New York—Albany.

PROPOSALS FOR LEGISLATIVE REFORM

That progress can be made, has been made, and will continue to be made is obvious. But what do we mean by "progress"? What have the Citizens' Conference and others done to state legislatures to make them more effective? To answer this question, we must consider what observers have believed to be the major factors in modernizing state legislative systems.

The Citizens' Conference (1971; pp. 12ff.) has proposed a set of criteria which they categorize by the acronym FAIIR: Functional, Accountable, Informed, Independent, Representative. A functional legislature has (1) adequate time to consider proposed legislation; (2) staff support for both leaders and individual members, with an emphasis on multipurpose staff; (3) office space for members, as well as desks on the floor of the legislature; (4) a manageable number of committees in the chamber, together with a "moderate" number of committee assignments for each member; (5) explicit procedures for originating and sponsoring bills, including the possibility of joint committees in bicameral legislatures; (6) continuity in leadership; and (7) decorum.

The accountable legislature is marked by (1) single-member districts; (2) explicit, published rules and procedures; (3) selection of leaders by either the full house or the majority caucus; (4) public access to the legislative process; and (5) individual members who have influence in normal legislative procedures, in contrast to control by "some small oligarchy."

The informed legislature has (1) standing and interim committees to handle information; (2) information-processing units supervised by legislative agencies; (3) presession opportunities for members to become acquainted with legislative procedures; (4) standing committees; (5) the indexing of bill documents; (6) a professional staff; and (7) fiscal information to enable the legislature to play an independent role in formulating the state's budget.

An independent legislature should have (1) autonomy in establishing criteria for holding sessions and determining the legislative budget; (2) access, independent of the executive branch, to information about state affairs; (3) autonomy from the lieutenant governor; (4) legislative oversight capabilities; (5) registration of lobbyists; and (6) explicit rules regarding conflicts of interest.

Finally, the representative legislature should be marked by (1) single-member districts, so that each member can identify with a particular constituency (and vice versa); (2) district offices for the members; (3) a diverse membership, unencumbered by overly stringent requirements of age, residence, and citizenship for membership, with adequate compensation so that members may be recruited from diverse groups within the state's population; (4) reasonable quorum requirements; (5) a moderate-sized chamber, so that individual effectiveness is not impeded; and (6) access by the member to technical resources and briefings on matters before the chamber.

The FAIIR criteria clearly overlap in many respects. They are also extremely comprehensive, so much so that no single reform effort can be expected to affect all areas of the legislature regardless of the degree of overlap. How strongly related are the five criteria? Since each is posited as a trait of an ideal legislative system, there is no clear-cut answer to this question. However, the Citizens' Conference has attempted to measure the extent to which each state has a functional, accountable, informed, independent, and representative legislature and has reported the rank-order correlations among the criteria (1971; pp. 77-79). All but two reach statistical significance at the .05 level, although there are indeed variations in the strength of these coefficients. The two which are not significant are the relationships between functionality-representativeness and independence-representativeness, suggesting that the last criterion may constitute a different dimension of legislative reform than the other four. The strongest relationships observed ($r_s \geq .60$) are those between (1) independence-informed legislature; (2) accountability-informed legislature; and (3) functionality-informed legislature. Thus the overlap we find in state legislative reform proposals seems to center around the problem of becoming informed. Indeed, two recent collections of articles on reform have stressed this dimension more than any other (Robinson 1973; Heaphy and Balutis 1975). And Rosenthal states that surveys he has conducted indicate that the most important improvement legislators mention is increased professional staff (1974a; p. 147). Does staffing actually improve legislative performance? To the extent that performance is measured in procedural terms, the studies that have been conducted indicate that the answer is indeed in the affirmative: in particular, centralizing staff in the party leadership has been shown to lead to more cohesive and ideologically distinct legislative parties (Rosenthal 1970; Rosenthal 1973; Gatlin 1973).

The central question that has dominated the academic literature is not whether procedures have been improved, but whether reforms have the potential to alter policy decisions in the American states. Such studies have not generally dealt with specific reforms, but rather with a more general concept of "legislative professionalism," as suggested by John G. Grumm (1971). Grumm created a factor-score index from the following raw objective indicators of professionalism for 1963-66: (1) average compensation per legislator; (2) number of bills introduced in a biennium; (3) legislative expenditures for services, including staff; (4) number of days in session; and (5) a legislative-services score developed by the Citizens' Conference. His analysis produced only a single dimension, suggesting that the indicators of professionalism he employed were strongly interrelated. While they do not contain the richness of the recommendations of the Citizens' Conference, the index based upon these components follows the most fundamental recommendations quite closely, and has the benefit of parsimony. It is not entirely fair to judge Grumm's analysis in terms of the recommendations of the Citizens' Conference since the latter group's suggested reforms were proposed after Grumm's index was constructed. In any event, the Grumm index has formed the basis for evaluating legislative professionalism in almost all of the academic literature on the topic. We find only two easily identifiable exceptions: studies in which we have been involved, in which four of Grumm's raw indicators were employed with the results of the factor analysis indicating a two-dimensional solution—in which session length was unrelated to an index of the "bureaucratization" of the legislature (Shaffer and Weber 1974; Uslaner and Weber 1975a);* and studies employing the FAIIR measures of the Citizens' Conference (1971; ch. 5; Ritt 1973; Le Loup 1976a).

The Grumm index (and others) has been widely employed not only because it seems theoretically related to changes in policies (although the direction is not always stated explicitly) but also because it has been such a good predictor of variation in policy outcomes in the states. One would be extremely hard-pressed to find another aggregate political or socioeconomic variable that has consistently had such high correlations with other variables in the entire literature on

---

*Because of the differing time periods for these analyses, we did not incorporate the Citizens' Conference on State Legislatures' services score. We doubt whether this altered the results of the analysis at all.

comparative state politics. What, however, is the impact of professionalism? Grumm posited that the more professionalized a state's
legislature was, the more liberal its policy outputs would be (1971;
pp. 318-19). He had expected that a more professionalized legislature would be more receptive to some types of demands, but he did
not specify exactly what these were. His approach was more induc-
tive; finding a strong positive correlation between professionalism
and more liberal welfare policies in the states. Therefore, Grumm
initiated a tradition in the literature that has led us to expect more
liberal policies from more professionalized legislatures. To be sure,
he also noted a substantial correlation (.65) between professionalism
and urbanization, providing further support for the liberalism hypothesis (p. 319). And most researchers have employed Grumm's initial
findings as the basis for their hypothesis.

We have done so ourselves, and have argued that there are
strong reasons to expect the professionalism-liberalism relationship
to hold. Our reasoning is that conservatives have generally opposed
the idea of a professional legislature on the basic ideological grounds
that the best government is the one that governs least. Liberals, on
the other hand, prefer a more activist government and would be more
likely to support increased facilities and salary scales for state legislators (Uslaner and Weber 1975a; p. 144). Indeed, as the Citizens'
Conference argued, "It has often been said that we get the kind of government we deserve. If our state legislatures are in sorry shape, it
is because we the people of the 50 states have simply sat back and
let them get that way" (Burns 1971; pp. 12-13).

We have also found that several factors, all pointing toward the
liberalism of a state's population, are related to legislative professionalism at the aggregate level. The most notable finding is a strong
relationship between professionalism and the extent to which a state
has an "attentive" public; other predictors of professionalism include
the extent to which a state's industrial base is heterogeneous rather
than homogeneous and Democratic party strength in the state. There
was a smaller, but noticeable, relationship between the proportion of
a state's electorate that considered itself to be ideologically liberal
and the professionalism index. Overall, these four predictors account-
ed for almost 60 percent of the variance in legislative professionalism
for the 46 contiguous states with partisan legislatures in 1960 (Uslaner
and Weber 1975a; pp. 151-54). Thus our findings are consistent with
those of Grumm: we expect that the more professionalized a state legislature is, the more liberal its policy outputs will be.

The aggregate research on comparative state policy formation
has employed the Grumm professionalism variable as a predictor for
various "liberal" policy outputs. The results have generally strongly
supported the proposition that more professionalized legislatures are

more progressive. In particular, Jack L. Walker's (1969) index of "innovation" among the states is correlated with professionalism and withstands controls for "socioeconomic" variables (except when four of the latter are controlled simultaneously). Ira Sharkansky and Richard I. Hofferbert (1969) constructed a more general index of "professionalism-local reliance" which was positively related to a "welfare-education" dimension of state policy (representing a liberal orientation) and negatively correlated with a "highways-Natural resources" factor (which we interpret as representing a more conservative measure of state policy outputs). These relationships are maintained, although they are reduced, when controlled for socioeconomic variables.

A more complex index of state fiscal policy, called the "redistribution" index by Brian R. Fry and Richard F. Winters (1970), was also highly correlated with professionalism (as measured by the Grumm index). While the correlations dropped significantly when controls for socioeconomic factors were entered into the analysis, the Grumm index had the highest zero-order relationships with the redistribution index both for the entire set of 48 contiguous states (r = .56) of 18 predictor variables analyzed for both groups of states. In a reexamination of the Fry-Winters data set, John L. Sullivan (1972) found that professionalism and a related concept—civil service coverage—were among the best "political" predictors of redistribution, arguing further that elite behavior does indeed seem to reflect the underlying socioeconomic forces in a state's demography. In another study, Bernard H. Booms and James R. Halldorson (1973) focused on the properties of the Fry-Winters redistribution index rather than on the predictors the latter employed. Their "reformulated" redistribution index had an even higher zero-order correlation with legislative professionalism than did the Fry-Winters index. The partial correlation, however, was lower and the regression coefficient, though positive, was not statistically significant. And this pattern of relationships was maintained for their analysis of the non-South as well.

Edward G. Carmines (1974) employed the Grumm legislative-professionalism index as a variable mediating the relationship between interparty competition and welfare policies in the states and found that the states with high levels of legislative professionalism displayed stronger correlations between interparty competition and welfare effort than did the states with low levels of legislative professionalism. In effect, professionalism worked to facilitate the linkage between interparty competition and liberal welfare policies.

We have also reanalyzed the "politics of redistribution," employing the original Fry-Winters data base, and found that our measure of legislative professionalism (almost completely analogous to that of Grumm, but based upon the 1958-59 biennium and excluding the Citizens' Conference services score as an indicator) is strongly related to redistribution (Uslaner and Weber 1975a; pp. 152, 154-55). This relationship is particularly pronounced for strongly Republican states (when we split our sample into states according to the degree of interparty competition), with professionalism having the highest beta weight (standardized regression coefficient) of any of the five variables we analyzed (pp. 158-60). Indeed, we argued that the impact of professionalism on liberal policy outputs is perhaps strongest in states dominated by the GOP: "Redistributive bills, which ordinarily might be passed over because they seem too controversial, might have a greater prospect of passing after members' detailed consideration. The fairly high beta for professionalism for the Republicans indicates that such an interpretation might be plausible, particularly given the relationship of the latter variable with liberalism" (p. 159).

These findings on the impact of legislative professionalism on liberal policy outputs have not gone unchallenged. In particular, Leonard Ritt posed the question, "Does legislative reform have an obvious and measurable impact on public policy, or does it simply result in a reshuffling of men and institutions with minimal impact on the allocation of public resources?" (1973, p. 500). The Citizens' Conference had attempted to resolve that question in the section of their study which related their indices to political, socioeconomic, and policy variables and met with some success in so doing it. Employing five measures of policy, the FAIIR criteria and an overall index of legislative capability all yielded positive rank-order correlations. Furthermore, except for the independence and representativeness measures, the Conference's correlations were significant at the .05 level or better in the majority of cases (1971; p. 78). Ritt was not convinced; he first noted that the Grumm index "had its limitations and [Grumm] labeled his findings only tentative" (1973; p. 500). What the limitations were Ritt did not say; however, the correlations between the Grumm index and the six Citizens' Conference (1971; p. 70) measures tended to be modest at best, with the highest correlations found for the independence and representativeness scales. However, these are precisely the indices we discussed above which did not strongly correlate with most of the "liberal policy output" measures in the Conference's own study!

Ritt then examined the correlations between the six measures of professionalism of the Citizens' Conference and various measures of expenditures in the following areas: general expenditures; education; welfare; highways; and health, hospitals, criminal justice, and natural resources. Examining these results, he concluded that the answer to this question, "State Legislative Reform: Does It Matter?" is "sometimes yes, but most of the time, no." Only 44 of the 180 zero-order correlations (24 percent) reached the magnitude of .20 or higher; when controls for income were added, the figure fell to only 22, or 12 percent of the relationships examined. Ritt concluded:

> . . . legislatures which are functional—that is, more ef-
> fecient in their organization—tend to spend more money
> overall, to give more direct aid to local governments,
> and to be more generous in the fields of education, old-
> age assistance, and natural-resource development. In
> the areas of welfare, highways, health, and hospitals,
> however, there is no such tendency. Representative leg-
> islatures—that is, those in which individual legislators
> are most able to press their constituents' demands—are
> generous in their welfare expenditures. But reforming
> a legislature so that it is more representative will not
> have a significant impact on public policy in any other
> areas. (1973, p. 505)

Ritt's arguments are interesting, not simply because his findings run so contrary to the other literature on professionalism, but
also because they draw our attention to measurement problems in
both the independent (professionalism) and dependent (liberal policy
outputs) variables in our analysis. He does not rely upon the Grumm
index, but instead uses the Citizens' Conference measures. One obvious reason for preferring the latter is that they are more comprehensive than the Grumm index in the range of services covered. However, the Grumm index, unlike the measures of the Citizens' Conference, is a unidimensional scale. The properties of overall FAIIR index are not discussed in the "technical section" of the Conference
(1971) book. Now, it does turn out that the overall scores do appear
to be strongly correlated with all five of the FAIIR criteria. The lowest correlation with the overall index (which we have computed) is .53
for the representative legislature; the highest is .87 for the informed
legislature. Yet since these five criteria do not form a unidimensional scale themselves (based upon examining the intercorrelations cited
above), it is not at all clear what the overall index does indeed measure.

The Ritt article, as well as the aggregate literature on policy
formation more generally, is beset by measurement problems. In the
first place, 16 of Ritt's 30 policy variables involve per capita spending measures (the article provides no information on how spending on
Aid to Families with Dependent Children or Old Age Assistance is
measured); but comparisons between total expenditures—or expenditures measured in units of $1,000—and per capita expenditures may
be totally meaningless (Uslaner 1976; Cortés and Przeworski 1977).
Second, of the several articles considered, only those of Ritt (1973),

Grumm (1971), and Sharkansky and Hofferbert (1969) employ as measures of "liberalism" indices directly based upon expenditures. Now, as Sharkansky (1968b) argues in the analysis of state spending patterns and as Richard F. Fenno, Jr. (1966) and Aaron Wildavsky (1964) have also argued in studies of congressional patterns, most expenditure levels are determined by a process of incremental increases and thus may not be subject to such intervening forces as a more professionalized legislature.

Particularly because the studies cited are cross-sectional in design rather than longitudinal, they cannot measure the effects of reform within legislative bodies (Uslaner and Weber 1975a; Uslaner forthcoming). But even if they could, the incremental nature of policy formation on spending levels would suggest that such factors as professionalism would at best be spurious predictors of given levels of expenditure at any particular time. Such factors may have had an effect once they were initiated, but, in particular, the more routinized (or bureaucratized) the legislature, the more incrementalism would seem to be the basic procedure followed in budgeting. It is thus not surprising to find that cross-sectional studies have found professionalism and nonfiscal variables to be highly correlated (in particular, see the study of innovation by Walker 1969). Other expenditure-based measures such as redistribution (an index based upon a complex interaction of spending and taxation rates for the most and least advantaged groups within a state's population) are not as readily affected by incrementalism, so that the moderate-to-high relationships found are more understandable.

Our most important objection, however, to the studies of state policy outputs which employ legislative professionalism as a predictor variable is that they are all based upon aggregate measures, both of policies and of the extent of professionalism. Thus, there is a danger of falling into the "ecological fallacy," that is, making assumptions about individual behavior (orientations of legislators) from aggregate data (Robinson 1950; Alker 1969). This approach has, of course, been dictated by the available data. We simply did not have data on legislator's orientations toward reform in previous studies.

Our 50-state legislator survey, however, did include several questions on attitudes toward reform and strengthening of the legislature, including many of the critical factors stressed by the Citizens' Conference. Thus, we shall examine the linkage between individual-level policy orientations (rather than aggregate legislative policy outputs) and attitudes toward legislative reform. We have derived scales measuring the legislators' attitudes toward reform of their institutions and shall discuss them below. We now turn to an examination of the policy variables we shall consider.

MEASUREMENT OF VARIABLES

As stated above, we maintain that if professionalism (or attitudes toward professionalism) is to have any impact on policy formation, this impact will be most apparent on nonfiscal policy areas. Our
survey asked respondents their opinions (measured on a five-point
Likert scale, from very favorable to very unfavorable) on the following issues: (1) legislating capital punishment for persons convicted of
murder; (2) legalizing abortion during the first three months of pregnancy; (3) requiring all new automobiles to be equipped with antipollution devices which would add approximately $100 to the price of a car;
(4) requiring a police permit before a person could purchase a handgun; (5) allowing public school teachers to join unions; (6) permitting
public school teachers to strike; (7) permitting policemen and firemen
to join unions; (8) permitting these public employees to strike; (9) legalizing marijuana use; (10) requiring automobile drivers who are
suspected of having consumed too much alcohol to take a breath or
blood test; (11) instituting a "no-fault" automobile insurance plan;
(12) permitting state aid for education to be dispersed to Catholic and
other private schools; and (13) allowing birth-control information to
be available to anyone who wants it.

We consider the more favorable responses as indicating liberal
policy orientations on the questions dealing with abortions, antipollution devices, permits for gun purchases, unions and strikes by the
public employee groups, legalized marijuana use, the test for sobriety,
the no-fault insurance plan, and the availability of birth-control information. The remaining questions (capital punishment and state aid to
private schools) were considered to elicit conservative responses if
the legislators appeared favorably disposed toward them. The sobriety question is perhaps the most difficult question to scale on a liberal-conservative continuum, and we would expect that there should be
a less clear-cut pattern between support for such a statute and orientations toward legislative reform than for the other 12 questions in
our survey. We have classified this question as eliciting a liberal response if a legislator favored the statute because conservatives have
often stressed the importance of maintaining individual rights to the
exclusion of government intervention in the lives of citizens. Now it
is clearly not the case that an inebriated driver is performing a private act in any way; however, we chose to view the question as one of
increasing the power of the state in general. "Libertarian" conservatives might also support the legalization of marijuana, abortion on de-
mand, and making birth-control information available. However, we
have classified favorable reactions to these questions as indicative of
liberalism because several recent studies have indicated that contemporary liberalism is marked by such social-issue questions to a great-

er degree than it is by the more traditional question of increasing the size and power of the federal government (Miller and Levitin 1976; ch. 7; Nie, Verba, and Petrocik 1976; pp. 133–35).

We should draw another distinction here between this study and those which have preceded it. Our policy questions deal with general orientations toward specific issues, rather than the policies actually adopted by the state legislators under examination (or their predecessors). We believe that subjective orientations toward general policy questions are the most appropriate way to consider whatever linkages might obtain with subjective responses to questions on professionalism. The policy-making process in the American states does not operate through such "hidden-hand" factors as per capita income, interparty competition, or even aggregate measures of legislative professionalism. Indeed, we found in our recent examination of redistributive politics that the best overall predictor of even an aggregate measure of redistribution was a variable measuring the extent to which individual legislators in a state were concerned with questions of social welfare policy—and that this finding was considerably enhanced in the strongly Democratic and the competitive two-party states (Uslaner and Weber 1975a). However, we found that it was extremely difficult to achieve even a modicum of predictive success in predicting the level of social welfare policy concern by the aggregate variables we examined. Thus, we firmly believe that the most appropriate way of studying how the policy process operates in the American states is through the perceptions of the legislators (and other actors) themselves.

Having made this argument, we must also realize some potential limitations of this approach. Many of the policy proposals (or "state issues," as we called them in our questionnaire) are actually policies in various states. Each state is represented in the sample and we have weighted our responses to account for under- or over-representation by some states. Yet it would not be surprising to expect stronger support for policy alternatives among legislators in states in which the policy is already in effect (for example, no-fault automobile insurance in states such as Massachusetts or Florida). Rather than attempting to devise some method of controlling for this problem, we also recognize that subjective orientations toward legislative reform are more likely to be positive in states with the more professionalized legislatures. Therefore, we would expect that liberal policy orientations and support for professionalism would be highly related, as many of the aggregate studies have suggested. Attempting to control for the level of professionalism already found in a state or for whether a state has or has not adopted a policy alternative before our survey is certainly important; however, it lies beyond the scope of our present study and it obscures the general hypothesis that we are advancing about the impact of orientations of professionalism on liberal policy attitudes at a more fundamental level. If we attempted to control for each of these confounding factors, we might, for example, wind up taking the liberalism out of states such as New York and Massachusetts or the conservatism out of Idaho and Arizona. At least at this stage of the analysis, it is far from clear to us that this would constitute a desirable research strategy.

Two independent variables are employed throughout this chapter—the FTLO and LSO scales, discussed in Chapter 1. The two-dimensional scheme we have generated to measure legislative professionalism does not differ drastically from the objective measures developed by Grumm (1971) and the Citizens' Conference (1971). Our factor-analytic solution does differ from that of Grumm in that we have found that support for the legislator's personal needs (such as income and the ability to serve as a full-time member of the chamber) is not part of the same subjective dimension as support for staff, despite the aggregate findings' contrary results. Our FTLO scale seems to be most similar to the Citizens' Conference concept of a "functional" legislature, while our LSO scale seems to have the most in common with the Conference's concept of an "informed" legislator. Three of the latter group's FAIIR criteria are absent in our analysis—the accountable legislature, the independent legislature, and the representative chamber. They seem difficult to measure according to the types of questions we posed to our sample of legislators, although we do not deny their importance.

District competitiveness and typicality are used again as control variables. Their construction was discussed in detail in Chapter 2 and needs no further elaboration here.

HYPOTHESES

We argue, as have Grumm (1971) and others—including at least implicitly the nonpartisan Citizens' Conference (1970)—that a more professionalized legislature will be more likely to produce more liberal policies. Or stated in terms of the professionalism and policy variables we have measured:

1. The greater the legislator's score on the FTLO scale, the more likely he will be to support the liberal position on the policy areas cited above.
2. The greater the legislator's score on the LSO scale, the more likely he will be to support the liberal position on the policy areas cited above.

After examining these hypotheses, we shall then reexamine them controlling for the perceived level of party competition in the legislator's district and the typicality of the district. Our expectation is that members from highly competitive districts may feel more compelled to take positions congruent with those of their constituents (or how they believe their constituents feel), while members from more typical districts should feel less constrained in their behavior. Indeed, while members from highly competitive districts may feel somewhat constrained in their support for some of the more controversial policy alternatives in our 13-issue set, those from more typical districts should find the correspondence between their perception of district competitiveness and their own status reinforcing in terms of fostering whatever views they already hold. Thus, we hypothesize:

3. Legislators from competitive districts will be less likely to take liberal positions than members from safe districts, relative to their scores on the two subjective orientation scales.

4. Legislators from typical districts will be more likely to support the liberal positions than will members from atypical districts, relative to their scores on the two subjective orientation scales.

These hypotheses need some further justification. It would seem that members from competitive districts (as perceived by the legislators themselves) would gravitate toward the center position rather than the liberal or conservative positions and that members from atypical districts would also tend to moderate their stands on such issues as we are considering. In the context of the present hypotheses, however, we are treating both the perceived level of competition and the typicality of the district as control variables for the more fundamental relationships between our policy alternatives and our professionalism scales. Therefore, we simply argue that the controls should either moderate or reinforce the effects of the subjective orientations toward professionalism on liberal policy attitudes—instead of predicting a direct link between competition, typicality, and policy orientations. The latter question would lead us beyond the scope of this chapter, which is concerned with the effects of professionalism rather than of party competition.

LEGISLATIVE PROFESSIONALISM AND POLICY LIBERALISM

Do "pro-legislative professionalism" orientations on our two scales also indicate a tendency for such legislators to take the liberal policy positions we have identified? Not surprisingly, we do not have a uniform set of findings across the 13 issues considered. However, as we shall discuss in detail below, there does seem to be an overall tendency for members who have high scores on the FTLO scale and the LSO scale to take the more liberal positions on these nonfiscal issues. Of the 13 issue areas we are considering, only two policy areas have correlations contrary to the direction we had predicted (the question of breath-tests for automobile drivers suspected of drunken driving and state aid to parochial and other private schools), and it was precisely these questions that we had the most difficulty in clearly classifying as liberal or conservative. For only one other policy area, abortion, did there appear to be no systematic relationship whatsoever with either scale. Overall, the relationships seem to be considerably stronger for our FTLO scale than for the legislator-staff orientations of the members. We shall discuss this result in greater detail below as well.

Before beginning our analysis, we should note that six of the thirteen issues are more consensual than others in that overwhelming majorities of our respondents either favored or did not favor the adoption of such policies. There were substantial majorities opposed to permitting strikes by public employees; the respective figures are more than 70 percent in the two unfavorable categories for teachers and more than 80 percent for firemen and policemen. Approximately 83 percent of our respondents opposed the legalization of marijuana. On the other hand, we found strong majorities favoring breath-tests (over 90 percent), no-fault insurance (75 percent), and making birth-control information readily available (about 90 percent). It is hardly surprising that these issue areas would be consensual, since one would expect to find similar patterns on most of these issues for the mass public as well. It is, indeed, somewhat surprising to find less consensus among our legislative respondents on questions such as gun permits and capital punishment, which tend to be consensual for the mass public.

In the tabular analyses below, we shall report both row and column marginals, the total sample sizes, the percentages down the columns; and values to tau-c and gamma. For the consensual policies, we should be cautious in evaluating the measures of association with our professionalism scales, particularly since gamma is extremely sensitive to skewed marginals. On the other hand, tau-c has a tendency to be "depressed" (that is, to have values smaller than the actual underlying correlation)—and this is particularly the case when making comparisons to the curvilinear measure, gamma. Thus, when attempting to assess the extent of the linkages between our measures of professionalism and policy attitudes, we should be particularly careful to consider both tau-c and gamma when the marginals are skewed. It does not necessarily follow that such unequal marginals will automatically yield high values of gamma; this will be confirmed in our analyses below. This coefficient can also attain very small values by a simple change in the values of the cells with very few cases. For example, if we had a sample of 800, 790 of whom supported a policy and 10 of whom opposed it, consider the following two situations: (1) Let half of the second group have high FTLO scores and half low scores; then, gamma will equal zero; (2) suppose that five members who oppose the policy and have high FTLO scores "change" their professionalism orientations toward low scores; then, the curvilinear measure will equal 1.000 (or -1.000 if the attitudinal changes were reversed). Thus, for such consensual policies, the value of gamma is not necessarily inflated, but rather is subject to great fluctuations given small changes in the marginals.

TABLE 5.1

Legislators' Position on the Capital-Punishment Issue by
the FTLO Scale
(in percent)

Position	High	Medium	Low	N
Strongly favorable	22.6	30.5	46.0	350
Favorable	28.4	39.1	35.6	401
Unfavorable	24.7	20.2	10 8	236
Strongly unfavorable	24.3	10.2	7.7	175
N	437	529	196	1,162

Note: tau-c = -.219; gamma = -.320.
In this and succeeding tables, respondents with no opinion (on either the dependent or independent variable) are omitted. Thus, the total number of responses will vary from table to table.

The results of our analyses are presented in Tables 5.1 to 5.26 below. We first present a table showing the distribution of opinions and professionalism orientation scores for the FTLO scale and then for the LSO scale for each policy area. This procedure allows us to make comparisons first across different measures of professionalism for our issue areas. The former scale measures the extent to which members believe that the chambers should meet all year long, compensation for members should be sufficient to ensure that members need not work at another job, and legislators should feel like professionals in their jobs. The LSO dimension, on the other hand, is a

measure of the members' support for individual staff and offices for
all members and for standing committees, as well as for district offices. We would expect stronger relationships to obtain with the FTLO
scale since it clearly measures the professionalism aspect of legislative service; the LSO dimension, on the other hand, is more closely
associated with members' perceptions of themselves as needing further staff, often to communicate more effectively with their constituents. This orientation seems closer to that of providing service rather
than policies to constituents (Mayhew 1974; Fiorina forthcoming).
Hence we expect (as shall be demonstrated to be the case) the former
index to have stronger relationships to our policy areas.

Tables 5.1 and 5.2 present the distribution of support for capital punishment by our two subjective professionalism scales. We con-
ceptualize such support as indicating a conservative position and thus
hypothesized a negative relationship between support for this policy
and professionalism. We find that this is the case for both of our indices. The higher the score on the FTLO scale, the lower the support

TABLE 5.2

Legislators' Position on the Capital-Punishment Issue by
the LSO Scale
(in percent)

Position	High	Medium	Low	N
Strongly favorable	23.0	30.7	35.9	351
Favorable	20.3	37.4	40.8	398
Unfavorable	27.7	19.3	15.3	234
Strongly unfavorable	29.0	12.6	8.0	175
N	261	608	289	1,158

Note: tau-c = -.182; gamma = -.270.

for capital punishment (tau-c = -.219 and gamma = -.320). For the
LSO scale, both relationships are somewhat weaker (tau-c = -.182,
gamma = -.270). None of the relationships is overwhelming, but the
direction is clear. In particular, the values of tau-c are not as small
as their absolute magnitude would suggest, given the tendency for this
coefficient to be depressed and the large sample size. It is hardly a
universal truth that members who support the ideas behind both dimensions of legislative professionalism oppose capital punishment,
but there is certainly a tendency in that direction. The relationship

appears to be basically linear, comparing the relative values of tau-c and gamma. There is also support for our argument that policy preferences should display stronger relationships with the FTLO scale than with the legislative-staff orientation dimension. Yet, even members with high scores on the latter scale show a tendency to oppose the death penalty.

Our first predictive failure (taking the issues in the order in which they were discussed initially, the same order in which they were posed to our respondents) is on abortion. For both scales, we do find positive correlations between support for abortion and professionalism orientations, but the measures of association are very small (Tables 5.3, 5.4), particularly for the LSO scale, where tau-c = .056 and gamma = .082 (Table 5.4). A member's attitude toward professionalism does not appear to have any relationship to his propensity

TABLE 5.3

Legislators' Position on the Abortion Issue by the
FTLO Scale
(in percent)

Position	High	Medium	Low	N
Strongly favorable	25.2	19.3	17.3	237
Favorable	30.5	34.0	25.4	350
Unfavorable	23.3	28.9	27.3	297
Strongly unfavorable	21.0	17.8	29.9	235
N	417	517	185	1,119

Note: tau-c = .075; gamma = .109.

to support or oppose legislation which would allow a woman to end a pregnancy during its first three months. There are of course several alternative explanations for the failure of the professionalism-policy linkage to hold, including the argument that we cannot establish a clear-cut dichotomy on an issue which has strong moral and religious dimensions. Indeed, the passage of abortion reform bills has been attributed to the defeat of members from heavily Catholic districts who took positions contrary to their constituents'. Yet we do find a stronger relationship below with aid to parochial schools, a similar issue which is differentiated by its lower salience and broader base of support among constituency groups.

On the question of requiring all new automobiles to be equipped with antipollution devices, we find once more moderate support for

TABLE 5.4

Legislators' Position on the Abortion Issue by the
LSO Scale
(in percent)

Position	High	Medium	Low	N
Strongly favorable	30.5	20.2	15.4	238
Favorable	25.4	32.8	33.2	348
Unfavorable	20.5	26.7	31.5	295
Strongly unfavorable	23.6	20.3	19.9	234
N	252	589	274	1,115

Note: tau-c = .056; gamma = .082.

our liberalism-professionalism linkage (see Tables 5.5 and 5.6). And, for both professionalism indices, the relationship appears to be linear (tau-c is approximately .200, gamma somewhat above .300 for each index). The relationship is far from being conclusive, but it is at least moderate. Furthermore, we are somewhat surprised that both the linear and curvilinear relationships are higher for the LSO than for the FTLO scale. There is nothing in the nature of the issue which suggests that it should have a stronger relationship to the staff-orientation index—there does not seem to be any particular relationship to questions of office space or staffing. It thus appears that both indices seem to tap liberal orientations of the respondents.

For the policy proposal which would require a permit before an individual could purchase a handgun, we find considerable support for the professionalism-liberalism hypothesis (Tables 5.7 and 5.8). As expected, the relationship is stronger with the FTLO scale, although it is at least respectable for the LSO index (tau-c = .208; gamma = .301). There is also evidence of a curvilinear relationship for both scales, although the value of tau-c (.286) is among the highest we observe for the FTLO scale. Gamma is a strong .404. These findings appear to indicate that on issues which are more clearly defined in liberal-conservative terms, the patterns of correlation with the professionalism indices are the strongest. We shall see that this is the case with respect to the next four policy areas we consider.

We consider together the related issues of teacher unionization and strikes and unionization and strike authorization for police and

TABLE 5.5

Legislators' Position on the Antipollution–Device Issue
by the FTLO Scale
(in percent)

Position	High	Medium	Low	N
Strongly favorable	13.9	10.8	8.6	128
Favorable	48.8	34.2	20.7	411
Unfavorable	27.5	38.2	39.4	380
Strongly unfavorable	9.8	16.8	31.3	184
N	409	504	190	1,103

Note: tau–c = .211; gamma = .316.

firemen. These four questions all deal with labor relations with public employees (Tables 5.9 to 5.16). The four questions all involve

TABLE 5.6

Legislators' Position on the Antipollution–Device Issue
by the LSO Scale
(in percent)

Position	High	Medium	Low	N
Strongly favorable	21.0	9.3	7.9	128
Favorable	47.7	38.8	24.2	409
Unfavorable	20.6	37.4	41.0	379
Strongly unfavorable	10.7	14.5	26.9	184
N	252	570	276	1,099

Note: tau–c = .226; gamma = .344.

issues that have become increasingly salient over the past several years. There appear to be two basic dimensions involved in the four questions: public–employee unionization and situations involving the potential withholding of public services by groups which can (police-men and firemen) and cannot (teachers) affect the basic security of the citizens. A substantially larger percentage of our legislator respondents opposed strikes by policemen and firemen than by teachers;

TABLE 5.7

Legislators' Position on the Gun-Permit Issue by the
FTLO Scale
(in percent)

Position	High	Medium	Low	N
Strongly favorable	30.2	16.7	7.6	233
Favorable	37.2	29.5	17.6	350
Unfavorable	19.3	30.6	29.3	300
Strongly unfavorable	13.4	23.3	45.5	268
N	434	522	195	1,151

Note: tau-c = .286; gamma = .404.

the security issue undoubtedly was influential here. The more funda-mental distinction, however, is on the unionization/permission to strike issue. While many states permit public employees to form unions, none allows them to engage in strikes. The withholding of such employees' services directly affects the constituents of our re-

TABLE 5.8

Legislators' Position on the Gun-Permit Issue by the
LSO Scale
(in percent)

Position	High	Medium	Low	N
Strongly favorable	39.1	15.5	13.5	233
Favorable	27.7	33.9	24.2	345
Unfavorable	17.7	28.5	29.0	301
Strongly unfavorable	15.4	22.0	33.4	268
N	257	604	287	1,147

Note: tau-c = .208; gamma = .301.

spondents; it is therefore not surprising to note that the strike questions for both employee groups is not even moderately related to the

TABLE 5.9

Legislators' Position on the Teacher-Unionization Issue
by the FTLO Scale
(in percent)

Position	High	Medium	Low	N
Strongly favorable	29.9	9.0	7.0	190
Favorable	47.3	41.5	28.5	475
Unfavorable	13.6	26.6	21.9	239
Strongly unfavorable	9.2	22.9	42.6	239
N	433	521	188	1,143

Note: tau-c = .326; gamma = .479.

LSO scale. The values of both tau-c and gamma are quite low for the two strike questions and the LSO index (Tables 5.12 and 5.16). The

TABLE 5.10

Legislators' Position on the Teacher-Unionization Issue
by the LSO Scale
(in percent)

Position	High	Medium	Low	N
Strongly favorable	38.2	11.5	7.9	191
Favorable	48.2	44.2	34.4	472
Unfavorable	7.8	21.7	31.0	237
Strongly unfavorable	11.2	22.6	26.7	239
N	263	594	284	1,139

Note: tau-c = .262; gamma = .391.

small values of the latter coefficient can easily be explained by the skewed marginals, but the values of tau-c are not as subject to this problem, particularly when one compares them to: (1) the same dependent variables related to the FTLO scale; and (2) the overall pattern of relationships with both scales, particularly on the unionization questions.

TABLE 5.11

Legislators' Position on the Teachers' Strike Issue by the
FTLO Scale
(in percent)

Position	High	Medium	Low	N
Strongly favorable	15.1	4.7	2.6	94
Favorable	27.5	14.4	7.7	208
Unfavorable	30.9	40.4	22.7	387
Strongly unfavorable	26.6	40.5	67.0	455
N	429	522	192	1,144

Note: tau-c = .285; gamma = .438.

The teacher–unionization question (Table 5.9) provides the strongest link between liberalism on policy questions and support for

TABLE 5.12

Legislators' Position on the Teachers' Strike Issue by the
LSO Scale
(in percent)

Position	High	Medium	Low	N
Strongly favorable	19.9	4.9	5.2	95
Favorable	23.9	17.8	14.0	208
Unfavorable	22.9	37.2	35.7	384
Strongly unfavorable	33.3	40.0	45.1	454
N	255	602	283	1,141

Note: tau-c = .135; gamma = .212.

legislative professionalism in the set of 13 issues. This relationship holds up for both professionalism scales. The FTLO index has what might be considered a good linear fit (tau-c = .326) with teacher un-ionization, but the curvilinear hypothesis is even more strongly sup-ported (gamma = .479). Similarly, the LSO measure has a linear re-lationship of .262 with teacher unionization, but again the curvilinear measure is considerably stronger (gamma = .391), as Table 5.11 in-dicates. The relationships are almost as strong for the unionization

TABLE 5.13

Legislators' Position on the Policemen- and
Firemen-Unionization Issue by the FTLO Scale
(in percent)

Position	High	Medium	Low	N
Strongly favorable	24.4	9.0	6.6	163
Favorable	54.3	42.2	31.8	510
Unfavorable	11.8	29.0	25.7	248
Strongly unfavorable	9.5	19.8	36.0	210
N	428	515	188	1,131

Note: tau-c = .297; gamma = .448.

of policemen and firemen. For both scales, the measures of associa-tion rank second in terms of overall strength (although the LSO index relationship is tied with that for antipollution devices). We find mod-erate support for the linear hypotheses, stronger for the FTLO scale (Table 5.13) where tau-c is .297; but, again, there is even stronger evidence for the curvilinear hypothesis (gamma = .448 for FTLO and .344 for LSO). Thus, at least the unionization issue varies system-atically with the two components of professionalism in our analysis. We find quite respectable values of tau-c for both strike questions: .285 for teachers and .250 for police and firemen (see Tables 5.11 and 5.15, respectively, for the FTLO scale). As noted above, we do not find any systematic pattern of variation with the LSO scale for either strike question.

What we have seen, then, is that questions traditionally asso-ciated with liberalism—general government power and the support for organized labor that has constituted the "lib-lab" (liberal-labor) policy and electoral coalition—are strongly related to attitudes on legislative reform. These are the questions of gun control and the four unioniza-tion questions. When there is a potential cleavage between the policies espoused by the leaders of the political coalitions which have supported

liberal candidates (in particular, labor leaders) and the constituents
who might oppose certain policies, the two subjective professionalism

TABLE 5.14

Legislators' Position on the Policemen- and
Firemen-Unionization Issue by the LSO Scale
(in percent)

Position	High	Medium	Low	N
Strongly favorable	33.0	9.7	7.4	164
Favorable	45.3	48.0	37.8	506
Unfavorable	9.3	22.4	32.7	247
Strongly unfavorable	12.4	19.9	22.0	210
N	262	588	277	1,127

Note: tau-c = .224; gamma = .344.

scales discriminate well between general reform attitudes about both
policies and legislative structure and those professionalism attitudes
more closely linked to a member's constituency. Thus, we find considerably weaker linkages between the LSO and the two strike questions than we do for the FTLO scale. The latter index thus seems to
be a more general reform orientation: pro-big government, full-time
legislatures, and the liberalism that Grumm also posited to go hand
in hand with such attitudes. The LSO scale, which also advocates
greater spending on government functions, is nevertheless a less
ideological construct. If a legislator had his own office with greater
staff support, this might well lead to increased potential for the independence of the understaffed minority party in the legislature.
    We also find (Tables 5.17 and 5.18) some support for the argu-
ment that professionalism is also related to a component of the "new
liberalism" (Nie, Verba, and Petrocik 1976; Miller and Levitin 1976)
dealing with the legalization of marijuana. While the marginals are
greatly skewed toward disapproval of the proposal (almost 85 percent
of our respondents were either unfavorably disposed or very unfavorable to this policy alternative), the tau-c coefficient does indicate
some support for the linkage we have posited (tau-c = .233), at least
for the FTLO scale. There is a much more restrained relationship
with the LSO scale.
    Our most confusing predictions occurred on the troublesome
question of the sobriety-test proposal. We argued that this should be

considered more of a liberal policy alternative, since it involves the overall power of the government. On the other hand, there are funda-

TABLE 5. 15

Legislators' Position on Policemen- and Firemen-Strike
Issue by the FTLO Scale
(in percent)

Position	High	Medium	Low	N
Strongly favorable	9.0	2.5	1.5	54
Favorable	16.9	8.2	3.5	122
Unfavorable	41.7	45.7	21.9	457
Strongly unfavorable	32.3	43.6	73.1	504
N	426	519	192	1,137

Note: tau-c = . 250; gamma = . 420.

mental civil-liberties questions that arise from this proposal which might give many liberals pause in supporting it. Is this, then, a lib-

TABLE 5. 16

Legislators' Position on the Policemen- and Firemen-
Strike Issue by the LSO Scale
(in percent)

Position	High	Medium	Low	N
Strongly favorable	12.8	2.4	3.1	55
Favorable	14.3	9.9	9.4	122
Unfavorable	32.5	42.6	41.3	454
Strongly unfavorable	40.4	45.1	46.2	502
N	250	602	281	1,133

Note: tau-c = . 072; gamma = . 124.

eral or a conservative proposal? If we examine the pattern of correlations with the subjective professionalism scales, we can answer:
(1) liberal; (2) conservative; or (3) none of the above. There are posi-

tive relationships with the LSO scale (liberalism), and negative ones with the FTLO index (conservatism), as Tables 5.19 and 5.20 indicate. However, the pattern of support for the policies is so pervasive and

TABLE 5.17

Legislators' Position on the Marijuana-Legalization
Issue by the FTLO Scale
(in percent)

Position	High	Medium	Low	N
Strongly favorable	7.2	2.3	0.8	42
Favorable	20.1	11.0	5.3	147
Unfavorable	40.2	40.7	25.1	416
Strongly unfavorable	32.4	46.0	68.7	494
N	401	508	189	1,098

Note: tau-c = .233; gamma = .389.

uniform that neither table indicates that the professionalism scales predict the distribution of support (or opposition) at all. The correla-

TABLE 5.18

Legislators' Position on the Marijuana-Legalization
Issue by the LSO Scale
(in percent)

Position	High	Medium	Low	N
Strongly favorable	9.7	1.8	3.2	42
Favorable	19.2	13.3	8.5	147
Unfavorable	36.7	42.1	29.7	414
Strongly unfavorable	34.4	42.8	58.6	493
N	238	581	277	1,097

Note: tau-c = .163; gamma = .278.

tions are miniscule. Here, we find a second issue area (the first being abortion) which is clearly not associated with professionalism. In this case, however, there is such overwhelming support among all groups for the policy that it would be too rash to reject a more general hypothesis on the basis of a question such as this one.

TABLE 5.19

Legislators' Position on the Breath-Test Issue by the
FTLO Scale
(in percent)

Position	High	Medium	Low	N
Strongly favorable	35.2	35.1	48.8	435
Favorable	52.5	56.8	44.5	618
Unfavorable	10.1	6.3	3.8	85
Strongly unfavorable	2.3	1.8	2.9	25
N	438	532	194	1,164

Note: tau-c = -.073; gamma = -.136.

TABLE 5.20

Legislators' Position on the Breath-Test Issue by the
LSO Scale
(in percent)

Position	High	Medium	Low	N
Strongly favorable	45.8	34.3	36.2	434
Favorable	41.2	56.0	57.8	617
Unfavorable	9.9	7.3	5.1	85
Strongly unfavorable	3.1	2.4	.9	25
N	262	613	286	1,161

Note: tau-c = .021; gamma = .039.

Finally, we consider three issues, two of which have skewed marginals (no-fault automobile insurance and birth-control information) and produce modest support for the professionalism-liberalism linkage on questions of public policy. No-fault insurance (Tables 5.21 and 5.22) is supported by about 75 percent of our legislative respondents. The professionalism variables, particularly the LSO scale, do not do a very good job in predicting what variations in support there are for this type of automobile insurance. There are weak tendencies at best for support for no-fault insurance to be associated with the LSO scale. An interesting control (which we did not employ) for this question would be the occupation of the respondent. We would expect that members who stated that their major occupation was attorney

TABLE 5. 21

Legislators' Position on the No-Fault Insurance Issue
by the FTLO Scale
(in percent)

Position	High	Medium	Low	N
Strongly favorable	33. 5	20. 1	20. 4	272
Favorable	46. 7	55. 2	47. 6	549
Unfavorable	13. 1	18. 3	18. 7	178
Strongly unfavorable	6. 7	6. 3	13. 3	82
N	406	496	180	1, 081

Note: tau-c = . 122; gamma = . 200.

TABLE 5. 22

Legislators' Position on the No-Fault Insurance Issue
by the LSO Scale
(in percent)

Position	High	Medium	Low	N
Strongly favorable	36. 8	22. 7	20. 3	274
Favorable	44. 4	52. 5	52. 7	548
Unfavorable	9. 8	17. 7	19. 6	177
Strongly unfavorable	8. 9	7. 2	7. 4	82
N	244	569	268	1, 081

Note: tau-c = . 094; gamma = . 157.

(other than legislator) would tend to oppose no-fault proposals regardless of their attitude toward professionalism (Dyer 1976).

For parochial-school aid, we found moderate positive coefficients, indicating that if support for this policy is liberal in orientation, there is some degree of confirmation of our hypothesis. If, on the other hand, we consider such responses conservative, then we

TABLE 5.23

Legislators' Position on the School-Aid Issue by the
FTLO Scale
(in percent)

Position	High	Medium	Low	N
Strongly favorable	16.2	6.4	10.9	122
Favorable	42.0	32.0	25.1	387
Unfavorable	24.1	40.8	29.8	364
Strongly unfavorable	17.8	20.8	34.2	245
N	424	505	189	1,118

Note: tau-c = .169; gamma = .249.

have the first—and the only one in this analysis—instance in which there are findings which consistently go against our hypotheses. Note, however, that the relationships can at best be described as moderate: tau-c = .169 for the first index, .143 for the second, while gamma = .249 for the FTLO scale and .216 for the LSO scale.

We believe that there are two factors that account for the sign of the coefficients, on the one hand, and their magnitude, on the other hand. First, if, as occurs in most states, the dichotomy is between state support in contrast to locally raised revenue for education, we would expect to find positive relationships. This would indicate a liberal response. However, because the issue of state aid to education has been a traditional liberal-conservative one in American politics, we would expect much stronger relationships than we have found. As is the case with abortion, however, we find (not surprisingly) a strongly religious dimension to this issue which is not consistent with the ideological "left-right" arguments on educational aid. Support for aid to private schools (including, but not limited to parochial schools) has tended to come from conservatives who may not have been opposed to education aid or who believed that, if the government were to support education, private schools should get their share. The question of aid to parochial schools has been particularly troublesome. Most support, but not all, has come from Catholic groups. Yet orthodox Jews have favored such proposals, as have many Lutherans and upwardly mobile blacks. Indeed, the Elementary and Secondary Education Act of 1965 was delayed in becoming law because of inability of pro-parochial-school aid legislators and opponents of such provisions to resolve this basic difficulty, even when aggreement on the most comprehensive parts of the bill had long been obtained. Thus, we would expect that the positive correlations, if these are our assumptions, would be reduced by this set of potential cross-pressures.

Finally, the skewed pattern of support for permitting birth-control information to be available to anyone who wants it is marked by

TABLE 5.24

Legislators' Position on the School-Aid Issue by the
LSO Scale
(in percent)

Position	High	Medium	Low	N
Strongly favorable	19.6	10.4	3.9	122
Favorable	36.7	35.8	30.5	387
Unfavorable	24.2	33.2	38.8	363
Strongly unfavorable	19.5	20.6	26.8	244
N	257	578	281	1,116

Note: tau-c = .143; gamma = .216.

rather low values of the correlation coefficients (although in the posited direction). This time the coefficient for LSO is greater than that for FTLO. We hypothesize that the general question of birth-control information (at the least) is so widely accepted by the mass public that legislators might even view the provision of birth-control information as a potential constituency-service function.

What, then, can we conclude about the relationship between our two subjective professionalism scales and support for liberal policy alternatives? We certainly do not maintain that professionalism, at either the level of individual or aggregate data analysis, is the best predictor for explaining these policy variables (see Weber and Shaffer 1972; Shaffer and Weber 1974; Hopkins 1974a, 1974b). Nor do we want to be too optimistic or pessimistic about the findings we have presented in this paper. It is even more tempting, but also more frustrating, to sum up with the evaluation "it all depends," or, as Charles O. Jones (1973) so aptly described the results of aggregate-level state policy analysis, "Lots of things are related to lots of things, other things being equal." To aid the reader in reaching some evaluation, we summarize the simple relationships we have found so far in Table 5.27; the policy areas underlined are those we have called consensual, that is, those having large majorities either supporting or opposing them.

TABLE 5.25

Legislators' Position on the Birth-Control Information
Issue by the FTLO Scale
(in percent)

Position	High	Medium	Low	N
Strongly favorable	46.0	32.1	36.9	438
Favorable	45.6	57.0	44.7	581
Unfavorable	6.8	8.9	8.8	93
Strongly unfavorable	1.6	1.9	9.6	36
N	432	522	195	1,149

Note: tau-c = .102; gamma = .182.

Our summary judgment is that attitudes favoring legislative professionalism are generally associated with liberal attitudes on questions of public policy. There are exceptions, of course, such as abortion and breath-tests, where no systematic relations were established; such as parochial-school aid where the relationship was opposite to that hypothesized; and other questions such as no-fault insurance and the provision of birth-control information, on which the linkages were in the posited direction but not very strong. It is on the more traditionally liberal policy alternatives, particularly those dealing with labor and gun control, on which there appears to be a reform-policy congruence. And, furthermore, this pattern is strongest for the FTLO scale, the more general professionalism dimension. The two issues that were more strongly related to the LSO scale were antipollution devices and the provision of birth-control information. For the latter there might be some evidence of a constituency connection. For antipollution devices, it may simply be that sampling variations account for the small differences in the magnitudes of the FTLO and LSO correlations. Thus, even accepting the argument that there is a general professionalism-liberal policy linkage, we should keep in mind the eternal truth that every social-science generalization is couched in "more or less" terminology.

TABLE 5.26

Legislators' Position on the Birth-Control Information
Issue by the LSO Scale
(in percent)

Position	High	Medium	Low	N
Strongly favorable	51.1	36.0	30.8	437
Favorable	39.7	53.9	53.6	580
Unfavorable	6.7	8.0	9.8	93
Strongly unfavorable	2.5	2.1	5.8	36
N	260	601	286	1,147

Note: tau-c = .120; gamma = .218.

What we do find most interesting, however, is that only one of our policies had correlations which were (across both professionalism scales) contrary to our hypotheses—and, indeed, only one other policy had mixed coefficients. Even if one finds our interpretation of the data presented so far in this chapter and summarized in Table 5.27 too strong, one cannot make the inference that support for legislative reform is associated with conservatism. We believe that this analysis has shown that the early studies which employed aggregate measures of professionalism were moving in the proper direction. Unlike Ritt, we are not ready to dismiss the impact of professionalism on liberal policy orientations (although he was specifically concerned with liberal outputs and outcomes). On the other hand, the preceding analysis has made us somewhat less optimistic about the ability of professionalism to correlate strongly with virtually every aggregate policy measure. The impact of professionalism is, from this perspective, certainly multidimensional and likely to vary from one issue area to another.

THE PROFESSIONALISM-POLICY LINKAGE AND
PARTY COMPETITION

Our third general hypothesis, stated earlier in this chapter, is that the impact of party competition should moderate the linkage be-

TABLE 5.27

Summary Table of Measures of Association between
Professionalism Scale and Policy-Support Variables

Policy Area	Measure	FTLO	LSO
Capital punishment	tau-c	-.219	-.182
	gamma	-.320	-.270
Abortion	tau-c	.075	.056
	gamma	.109	.082
Antipollution devices	tau-c	.211	.226
	gamma	.316	.344
Gun permits	tau-c	.286	.208
	gamma	.404	.301
Teacher unionization	tau-c	.326	.262
	gamma	.479	.391
Teacher strikes	tau-c	.285	.135
	gamma	.438	.212
Police/fire unions	tau-c	.297	.224
	gamma	.448	.344
Police/fire strikes	tau-c	.250	.072
	gamma	.420	.124
Marijuana legalization	tau-c	.233	.163
	gamma	.389	.278
Breath-test	tau-c	-.073	.021
	gamma	-.136	.039
No-fault insurance	tau-c	.122	.094
	gamma	.200	.157
Parochial-school aid	tau-c	.169	.143
	gamma	.249	.216
Birth-control information	tau-c	.102	.120
	gamma	.182	.218

Note: Underlined policies are consensual, as defined in text.

tween support for professionalism and a member's liberal policy orientations. We argued, similarly to Wilder Crane and Meredith Watts (1968; p. 87), that members from the most competitive districts should be less party-oriented and more concerned with constituency interests. We extend this thesis here to the professionalism-policy linkage posited here, maintaining that members from more competitive districts should have weaker relationships with respect to the linkage hypothesis than members from safe or mostly one-party districts. The competition control was derived from a simple question posed to each respondent as to whether he considered his district safe Democratic (Republican), mostly Democratic (Republican), or competitive. Since we are not concerned with a particular party in this analysis, we have derived a threefold classification of safe, mostly one-party, and competitive districts.

Tables 5.28 and 5.29 present the results of our analysis with the controls for perceived party competition included for the FTLO and LSO scales respectively. We shall not discuss each control in

TABLE 5.28

Legislators' Policy Positions with the FTLO Scale by
Perceived Competitiveness of the Legislative District

Policy Area	Measure	Safe	Mostly One-Party	Competitive
Capital punishment	tau-c	-.222	-.240	-.176
	gamma	-.324	-.353	-.253
Abortion	tau-c	.119	.046	.069
	gamma	.174	.066	.099
Antipollution devices	tau-c	.244	.222	.131
	gamma	.370	.331	.199
Gun permits	tau-c	.265	.314	.233
	gamma	.386	.441	.330
Teacher unionization	tau-c	.326	.331	.303
	gamma	.484	.487	.442
Teacher strikes	tau-c	.275	.294	.273
	gamma	.425	.454	.418
Police/fire unions	tau-c	.265	.319	.288
	gamma	.403	.474	.442
Police/fire strikes	tau-c	.211	.287	.220
	gamma	.353	.481	.379
Marijuana legalization	tau-c	.179	.307	.157
	gamma	.291	.514	.271
Breath-test	tau-c	-.160	-.055	-.015
	gamma	-.282	-.107	-.028
No-fault insurance	tau-c	.096	.099	.190
	gamma	.157	.161	.325
Parochial-school aid	tau-c	.113	.219	.142
	gamma	.168	.320	.216
Birth-control information	tau-c	.147	.072	.084
	gamma	.268	.127	.153

detail; to do so would take us far beyond the scope of this study (and of reason as well). Instead, we shall consider the more general patterns in the tables below. The hypothesis we have offered is largely

TABLE 5.29

Legislators' Policy Positions with the LSO Scale by
Perceived Competitiveness of the Legislative District

Policy Area	Measure	Safe	Mostly One-Party	Competitive
Capital punishment	tau-c	-.210	-.156	-.195
	gamma	-.298	-.236	-.294
Abortion	tau-c	.091	.022	.063
	gamma	.130	.033	.094
Antipollution devices	tau-c	.280	.214	.174
	gamma	.405	.330	.275
Gun permits	tau-c	.294	.221	.087
	gamma	.415	.324	.129
Teacher unionization	tau-c	.294	.219	.295
	gamma	.420	.336	.449
Teacher strikes	tau-c	.168	.099	.157
	gamma	.249	.159	.254
Police/fire unions	tau-c	.218	.213	.243
	gamma	.318	.332	.388
Police/fire strikes	tau-c	.088	.068	.064
	gamma	.141	.119	.115
Marijuana legalization	tau-c	.133	.197	.134
	gamma	.207	.347	.240
Breath-test	tau-c	-.060	.044	.067
	gamma	-.107	.087	.129
No-fault insurance	tau-c	.092	.073	.129
	gamma	.145	.125	.234
Parochial-school aid	tau-c	.093	.233	.048
	gamma	.135	.354	.077
Birth-control information	tau-c	.142	.108	.101
	gamma	.260	.195	.190

unsupported. We find support for a monotonically decreasing level of professionalism-policy linkage for our two scales for only one issue: antipollution devices. The linkage is somewhat stronger for both the FTLO and LSO scales for abortion, birth-control information, and gun permits than it is for the other policies we are considering. The relationship for birth-control information is monotonically decreasing for the LSO scale, but not for the FTLO index. In that situation, we find, as we do for abortion and gun permits on both indices of professionalism, stronger relationships in the safe constituencies than in either alternative category. In the case of abortion, however, the relationship even in the safe districts is weak. Finally, there is a reverse tendency on no-fault automobile insurance: for this policy area, the most competitive districts display the strongest linkages between policy liberalism and professionalism attitudes.

The remaining relationships we find are either virtually nil, indicating that the effects of professionalism upon policy attitudes discussed above are not affected by the perceived level of interparty competition in a district, or follow a different pattern than we had posited. For capital punishment and parochial-school aid on both scales, gun permits, police and fire strikes, and marijuana legalization (for the FTLO scale), and the two questions on teachers in public schools (on the FTLO scale), and the two questions on teachers in public schools (on the LSO index), we find that the relationships are strongest or weakest in the mostly one-party districts, that is, the strongest and weakest correlations are observed for the middle category. For the variables with highly skewed marginals, such as the strike questions and marijuana legalization, the effects of the controls cannot be adequately assessed. The capital punishment and parochial-school aid questions both find the strongest linkages in the mostly one-party districts. These findings support neither the view of Crane and Watts on the direct relationship between competition and policy moderation or the alternative concept offered by Warren E. Miller (1964) that the least secure members are often the least moderate. Instead, we find members from the middle category with the strongest professionalism-policy linkages. This finding is similar to that of Francis that policy success is greatest in his "one-party competitive" states, as opposed to situations involving divided control of the legislative and executive branches and those in which a single party is dominant (1967, p. 55).

How do we explain such findings? It appears that members from competitive districts may indeed be more moderate in their policies (relative to others with similar scores on the two professionalism indices), but so are legislators from safe seats. The former members may pay more attention to their constituents; the latter will, by virtue of their electoral security, be more insulated from their constituents. This does not, however, mean that they will be concerned with policy innovation. Such members may seek an alternative route, to affect policy making, that is, seeking positions of institutional power within the legislature (Fenno 1973; chs. 2 and 3). Their chief concerns may not be in the area of policy innovation at all. The members from mostly one-party districts, perhaps with their eyes on higher office, will be more interested in policy innovation. They have enough electoral security to engage in policy initiation; but they are not so removed from their constituents as to be unwilling to seize the initiative on a major policy question that might be of salience to their present (or future, if they are oriented toward higher office) constituents.

This interpretation seems to apply to a few areas that we have considered. Overall, the impact of the perceived level of competition does not seem to be great. The controlled levels of support for such policies, using the professionalism scales as the predictors, are not very different from the simple relationships. Thus, at least with respect to this control, we maintain that the linkages we have found (and those that are absent) are not dramatically affected by the level of party competition in the member's district except on the antipollution-device issue. We turn now to an examination of another control, the typicality of a member's district.

THE PROFESSIONALISM-POLICY LINKAGE AND DISTRICT TYPICALITY

Another potential intervening factor in the professionalism-policy linkage is the extent to which a member's district is typical of his party. Here we posit that members who are from the most typical districts will have relatively stronger professionalism-policy linkages than members from atypical districts. A member from a typical district will, according to the same logic underlying the competitiveness hypothesis, be less constrained by constituency opinions. In contrast, a member from a very atypical district would be expected to moderate his policy positions, to be less innovative relative to other members with similar orientations toward legislative professionalism. There are too few members from the least typical districts (a constituency represented by a Democrat which the member considers to be "safe Republican" or vice versa); but the columns for these districts in Tables 5.30 and 5.31 below (for the FTLO and LSO scales respectively) report the observed correlations for the sake of completeness. The comparisons will be made from the second least typical district (referred to as "not very typical") to the most typical. The median category will be called "somewhat typical," while the second most typical districts will be designated as "quite typical."

The control for typicality for the FTLO scale (Table 5.30) reveals only one instance of monotonically increasing professionalism-policy relationships as we move from the not very typical to the most typical districts. This is the case for the antipollution-device issue, which also was affected by the perceived level of competition control.

TABLE 5.30

Legislators' Policy Positions with the FTLO Scale by Typicality of the Legislative District

Policy Area	Measure	Least Typical*	Not Very Typical	Somewhat Typical	Quite Typical	Most Typical
Capital punishment	tau-c	-.328	-.102	-.181	-.283	-.218
	gamma	-.410	-.152	-.259	-.414	-.322
Abortion	tau-c	-.107	-.030	.074	.060	.119
	gamma	.160	-.046	.106	.085	.175
Antipollution devices	tau-c	.040	.100	.132	.257	.253
	gamma	.055	.150	.201	.382	.386
Gun permits	tau-c	.215	.219	.245	.340	.266
	gamma	.299	.319	.347	.472	.391
Teacher unionization	tau-c	.317	.239	.306	.346	.333
	gamma	.511	.381	.446	.500	.495
Teacher strikes	tau-c	.506	.155	.278	.332	.261
	gamma	.623	.251	.421	.502	.408
Police/fire unions	tau-c	.268	.205	.291	.344	.265
	gamma	.487	.326	.446	.501	.403
Police/fire strikes	tau-c	.438	.089	.228	.346	.198
	gamma	.588	.155	.389	.568	.334
Marijuana legalization	tau-c	.263	.222	.161	.327	.175
	gamma	.445	.380	.276	.545	.287
Breath-test	tau-c	-.197	-.061	-.019	-.052	-.164
	gamma	-.313	-.122	-.034	-.100	-.294
No-fault insurance	tau-c	.183	.161	.190	.090	.086
	gamma	.276	.278	.329	.144	.143
Parochial-school aid	tau-c	-.129	.224	.147	.212	.130
	gamma	-.182	.335	.222	.308	.193
Birth-control information	tau-c	.001	.007	.081	.097	.153
	gamma	.002	-.012	.146	.171	.283

TABLE 5.31

Legislators' Policy Positions with the LSO Scale by Typicality of the Legislative District

Policy Area	Measure	Least Typical*	Not Very Typical	Somewhat Typical	Quite Typical	Most Typical
Capital punishment	tau-c	-.424	-.069	-.210	-.181	-.198
	gamma	-.589	-.096	-.315	-.281	-.283
Abortion	tau-c	.378	-.034	.080	.035	.067
	gamma	.530	-.047	.121	.054	.097
Antipollution devices	tau-c	.097	.292	.186	.183	.289
	gamma	.140	.412	.296	.293	.419
Gun permits	tau-c	.426	.217	.106	.221	.282
	gamma	.553	.299	.157	.332	.400
Teacher unionization	tau-c	.477	.188	.308	.224	.281
	gamma	.755	.203	.468	.354	.400
Teacher strikes	tau-c	.455	-.020	.172	.134	.146
	gamma	.652	-.029	.277	.222	.216
Police/fire unions	tau-c	.361	.131	.244	.238	.208
	gamma	.587	.199	.391	.378	.303
Police/fire strikes	tau-c	.334	-.079	.077	.115	.067
	gamma	.496	-.127	.137	.208	.108
Marijuana legalization	tau-c	.495	.250	.150	.173	.109
	gamma	.711	.401	.267	.318	.171
Breath-test	tau-c	-.198	.116	.068	.019	-.046
	gamma	-.332	.219	.131	.038	-.082
No-fault insurance	tau-c	.078	.059	.142	.084	.090
	gamma	.117	.096	.261	.147	.143
Parochial-school aid	tau-c	-.425	.334	.050	.200	.117
	gamma	-.518	.455	.080	.317	.170
Birth-control information	tau-c	.373	.151	.104	.094	.119
	gamma	.646	.255	.196	.176	.221

Examining the pattern of correlations (both tau-c and gamma coefficients) for those policy areas in which the marginals were not very skewed, we find that four other policy alternatives appear to have general trends regarding the typicality control, even if such relationships are not completely monotonic for the FTLO scales. Capital punishment, gun permits, and teacher unionization each peak in the quite typical districts—only to drop again (although by very little for teacher unionization) for the most typical constituencies. In each case, there does seem to be a unidirectional increase in the level of the correlations up to the most typical districts. We view this set of results as indicating a threshold effect for at least several of the policy areas we are considering—and the critical point for the threshold is the most typical districts. A somewhat analogous process is at work for the abortion question: the not very typical districts form a threshold (one in which the correlation is negative). This category is different from the others; once we move to the somewhat typical districts, there is no clear-cut pattern of relationships.

The LSO scale (Table 5.31) does not display any systematic pattern of covariation between the professionalism-policy linkage and the control for typicality. Capital punishment, for example, displays its strongest relationship in the somewhat typical districts. Antipollution devices have strong relationships in the not very typical districts, on the one hand, and the most typical ones, on the other hand. Gun permits decrease from the not very typical districts to the somewhat typical ones, after which the relationships monotonically increase. For the LSO scale, then, it simply does not appear that there is any consistent set of controls which serve to differentiate districts according to their level of professionalism-policy linkages.

CONCLUSION

We have found in this chapter that members' subjective orientations toward legislative professionalism are generally associated with more liberal policy attitudes. Thus, contrary to the arguments of Ritt (1973), it does appear that state legislative reform matters. On the other hand, we did not find the effects of legislative professionalism to be quite as pervasive as some of the aggregate studies have indicated they might be. This is not an unexpected finding, since studies based upon aggregate data tend to produce higher correlations than those based upon individuals. Sample size obviously plays a major role here, and we have thus been somewhat generous in reporting the values of our coefficients as "moderate" and "high" when the relationships might not always appear to be that striking. Even without this problem, the state-by-state analyses would be expected to produce higher coefficients simply because of a statistical property called "aggregation bias" (Thiel 1971; pp. 181 and 556ff.).

We do believe that this study has indicated that there is a substantial linkage between policy liberalism, at least on selected policies which are most clearly identified on a left-right continuum, and support for legislative professionalism. Here we mean by "professionalism" the concept in its broadest sense. Both the FTLO scale and the LSO scale displayed the posited relationships with liberal attitudes on most of the public-policy questions we examined. There was only one linkage between support for professionalism and a conservative position on the 13 issues considered. Again, we note variations in our results. The linkages appeared to be stronger for the FTLO scale than for the LSO scale because the former scale appears to us to be more programmatic in its orientation than the latter.

Any discussion of reform must end on a caveat, however. Our study is cross-sectional in nature and thus cannot answer the most fundamental question: what will changes in a particular legislative system produce in terms of altered patterns of decision making and different policy decisions? Our cross-sectional analysis has indicated that there is a general relationship between members' attitudes toward professionalism and policy liberalism. Unfortunately, such analyses tell us little about the potential for change within a legislature or the likely consequences of changes in a given political culture. This area has not been systematically explored; but the answers to these questions will ultimately answer the larger question: "State Legislative Reform: Does It Matter?"

6

CONCLUSIONS AND
DIRECTIONS FOR FUTURE RESEARCH

WHERE WE HAVE GONE

We begin this concluding chapter by an examination of what we have learned, or failed to learn, about patterns of decision making in state legislatures. We shall then discuss a research agenda for future studies of state legislative politics and comparative state politics and policy formation in general, including some topics that we are either currently examining or intend to pursue further. Not every unresolved question is part of our research agenda, so we encourage other researchers to pursue these problems—or even to improve upon our own analyses in the preceding chapters.

In discussing the results of our analyses, we shall not simply reiterate every finding. Rather, we shall stress the major themes and hypotheses presented in Chapters 2 through 5, the linkages between them, and the extent to which we were successful in our analyses. These themes will also form the basis for questions which we believe need further attention. Throughout Chapters 2, 3, and 4 we were concerned with the sources of information and perceptions of decision loci in American state legislatures. In the fifth chapter, we changed our emphasis to a more specific concern with the impact of subjective orientations about the decision-making environment upon questions of public policy. Throughout our analysis, we have concentrated on the individual legislator. We have not analyzed the institutional framework in which the legislators work on a day-to-day basis. (This is clearly on our future research agenda.) Rather, we have analyzed responses to our 50-state survey by individual legislators in an attempt to achieve a better understanding of how the subjective orientations of this elite group affect their behavior and policy preferences as a group. We have attempted to consider institutional factors where possible and theoretically relevant. But basically we have tried to understand factors affecting information seeking and perceptions of decision loci, as well as policy positions, rather than predicting which policies will be adopted by specific states or in which chambers the parties, committees, or executives are most powerful.

Thus, our study might be called The American State Legislator, although we do not claim that its implications are as widespread as those of The American Voter (Campbell et al. 1960). We felt the need to investigate the patterns of behavior of this elite group before moving on to studies which aggregate these variables to the state level. Data on state legislatures has generally been sketchy; many studies have either been idiographic analyses, comparisons among a "sample" of states (with the justification the selection of states often not stated), or aggregate analyses such as those we have criticized in the previous chapter. We do not condemn aggregate analyses; indeed, we believe that they will be necessary to establish more complex models of the state policy-making processes. We strongly believe that most of the theoretically important questions in the study of state policy formation require data on the preference structures and general attitudes of the people who are involved in the decision-making process. This is our major source of disagreement with the many studies of comparative state politics in which aggregate measures of the supposed "determinants" of public policy, such as party competition, malapportionment, economic variables, and so on are presumed to have identifiable impacts on the process of policy formation (see Uslaner and Weber 1975a). Many of these analyses are based upon misreadings of the original causal factors in state politics or upon an inadequate conceptualization of these factors in building statistical models (see Uslaner forthcoming) or fail to consider critical intervening variables (see Uslaner and Weber 1973). Aggregate variables based upon survey responses are preferable in the study of policy formation in the states. They may well prove to be the strongest predictors we can obtain (Uslaner and Weber 1975a). The only other study in which legislators from all 50 states were surveyed (Francis 1967) employed only data aggregated to the state level. A comparison of the individual-level data for several policy areas between this study and the earlier one (see Weber and Francis 1975, and Chapter 4 of this book) revealed substantial change over time in members' perceptions of the importance of policy alternatives. This research strategy suggested to us that a vital first step involves the analysis of the attitudes of the individual members.

Recent analyses of legislative decision making at the national level (Kingdon 1973; Matthews and Stimson 1975) have suggested the importance of cues—information resources—in the decisional calculus of legislators. Thus, we assumed that state legislators are even more

dependent upon cues than members of Congress, because of the greater "information gap" in the states and the lesser status of subnational
legislatures in comparison with the U.S. House and the U.S. Senate.
The major sources of cues in the legislature were (1) personal friends;
(2) legislative specialists in particular policy areas; and (3) interest
groups. Yet none of these groups has been discussed in great depth
by scholars of the national legislature. Committee leaders, legislative party leaders, and the chief executive have been analyzed to a
greater extent by students of Congress and thus provided a theoretical
framework which has been more thoroughly developed than any aspect
of comparative state politics. It also allowed for comparisons between
the national and state legislatures, clearly a question of critical importance.

       We asked our respondents to rank in order the top 5 cue givers
from a list of 13 provided them (expanded to 14, when we also consider
the respondents who cited constituency cues). Information is clearly
a vital resource in legislative decision making, but information is not
equivalent to power. Therefore, we also asked our respondents to
select the major source of power in state legislatures. Regular committee meetings were the most frequently mentioned, response constituting 35.7 percent of all responses; the party caucus ranked second, cited by 24.7 percent of those surveyed; finally, 11.4 percent
mentioned the governor's office, the only other decision locus to obtain more than 10 percent of the mentions in our study. We then
sought to determine the extent to which members' subjective orientations toward the party system, the committee system, and legislative-
executive relations affected sources of cue-seeking behavior and perceptions of the most powerful decision loci by our respondents.

SUMMARY OF FINDINGS

       We found that our weighted percentages of cue sources in the
states generally conformed to the findings of Kingdon (1973; p. 19),
although party leaders were of greater importance in the states. Given
the differences in our questions, we were somewhat surprised at the
close correspondence in results. We were even more fascinated by
the greater similarity in our findings with Kingdon than with Matthews
and Stimson (1975), who employed questions very similar to ours.
Yet, all three studies developed their survey instruments independent-
ly of each other. We found a modest correlation between party-related sources of cues and partisan decision loci, a finding that we also
obtained for gubernatorial power and influence. For committees, on
the other hand, there was virtually no relationship between the pro-

pensity to seek out cues and the perception of such bodies as the major decision loci in the legislature.

In our analysis of legislative party systems in the states, we found considerable support for our hypothesis that members' orientations toward the party system are related to their propensity to seek out party-related cues. This was particularly the case for legislative party leaders as cue givers (as opposed to all party-related information sources) and support for strong legislative parties (as opposed to a more diffuse measure of support for the party system). These relationships were generally reinforced when we controlled for the level of competition in the district, as perceived by the member, and the typicality of a district. Members from safe districts were even more likely to take their cues from legislative party leaders, given that they were supportive of strong legislative parties. Similarly, members from the more typical districts were, given their support for strong legislative parties, the most likely in our sample to seek out information from party leaders. For the party-orientation scales, the relationships with perceived partisan decision loci were not as strong as we found for our cue variables, but they were nevertheless generally at the "moderate" level. Our controls for competition and typicality were less helpful in determining systematic relations between the party-orientation scales and partisan decision loci than was the case for the party-related cues.

Using a rather crude measure of support for the committee system, we found very little support for the proposition that subjective orientations toward committees produced cues from these sources. Nor did it appear that party orientations were related to cue taking with respect to committee leaders. Our competitiveness and typicality controls did not add to our understanding of committee cue taking. And the hypothesized negative relationships between our committee orientation scale and either party-orientation measure; or between committee cue taking versus party-oriented information seeking, did not receive support. We concluded that the variations in cue taking from committee leaders is probably attributable to different structural characteristics of committee systems in the states, which obscured our attempt to analyze all respondents on a single dimension. We also met with predictive failure for perceived decision locus, although the control variables were in the predicted direction. We did find some support for the argument which has been emphasized in studies of parties and committees in legislative bodies since the first publication of Woodrow Wilson's Congressional Government (1885): strong legislative parties are inconsistent with strong legislative committees. We found that both party-orientation scales, but particularly the LPO scale, were moderately and negatively related to the propensity to perceive committee meetings as the major decision loci in the legislature.

Finally, with respect to our analysis of the impact of subjective orientations toward cue seeking and perceived arenas of power, we examined these questions for sources of executive influence within the legislative branch. We were initially surprised at the relatively low standing that our respondents gave to state chief executives as cue givers and sources of power. Therefore, we hypothesized that the linkage between support for a strong role for the executive in state politics and cue seeking from the executive branch would be affected by the political party of the respondent. Respondents from the governor's party were predicted to be more receptive to gubernatorial cues and to be more likely to see the executive branch as the major decision locus. We found little overall variation in the cue-seeking behavior of the executive-oriented cues with our GO scale. There was only a weak effect, at best, of the party-match variable either as a control or as a direct predictor of the propensity to seek executive-oriented cues or to perceive the executive branch as being the major center of power within the legislature. We did, however, find that the moderate relationship between executive cue seeking and perception of decision locus within the legislature was reinforced for members of the governor's party and was attenuated for members of the opposition party.

Neither subjective orientations toward the executive nor those about the committees were even moderately related to how members behaved (that is, which cues they sought out) or how they view the decision-making process (their perception of the major decision loci). On the other hand, we did find that attitudes toward the legislative party system did have strong or moderate impacts on cue seeking, in particular on perceptions of decision loci. What this may suggest is that policy changes in the legislature arena may be more realizable if members develop stronger attitudes toward the party system. Of course, this is a speculation since the analysis we have conducted is cross-sectional rather than longitudinal. There is some evidence that parties in Wisconsin did indeed become more cohesive after a set of reforms designed to strengthen the legislative party leadership (Rosenthal 1970).

Our analysis of public-policy alternatives began in Chapter 4, where we considered 22 policy areas cited by our respondents as the most important problems facing their states. We found that there was considerable stability in the salience of policy areas from the Francis survey (1967; pp. 76-78) and our analysis. However, for both years, there was only a modest relationship between the frequency of mentions of the various policy areas and attribution of gubernatorial activity in the states. We found that gubernatorial activity was concentrated in those policy areas in which there is the greatest need for state action and also the least potential for negative reaction on the part of voters. The weakest areas of gubernatorial activity were those policies on which there is little conflict (liquor and gambling), which are primarily within the confines of the legislature (apportionment), or which have become the predominant domain of the federal government (labor, health, civil rights, and social welfare).

What is the potential for changes in policy outputs, at least to the extent that such a cross-sectional analysis can answer such questions? To investigate this problem, we examined the linkages between subjective support for legislative professionalism and legislative-reform proposals and 13 nonfiscal policy areas. With only a few exceptions, we found support for a positive relationship between our two measures of legislative professionalism and the more liberal policy alternatives, particularly those which are associated with the liberal-labor coalition (such as unionization and the right to strike by public employees, and gun control). Thus, we found support for these liberal positions on most issues regardless of the level of perceived competition in a member's district or the typicality of the district. We have found that there is at least the basis for a liberal-conservative continuum on both substantive and procedural issues within the legislatures. Furthermore, our data also indicate that support for procedural reform is strongly related to the party of the respondent (with Democrats favoring such reforms) and somewhat less strongly related to region (with heaviest support coming from the Northeast). These findings, along with the linkage of legislative party orientation to legislative decision making (for parties with respect to both cues and decision loci and for committees on decision loci), of party to procedural reform, and of procedural reform to policy positions, suggests that party is a potential linkage mechanism. Indeed, this somewhat intricate linkage pattern is consistent with a more direct one we have proposed for an aggregate data analysis of comparative state policy formation (Uslaner and Weber 1975a). We report there that Democratic party success in the electoral arena and especially the subjective orientations of members toward social welfare concern affect the level of redistribution policies in the American states.

Our analyses have thus suggested that to a certain extent, the subjective orientations of members of state legislatures do play a major role in the behavior of the legislators and also in shaping policy alternatives. On the other hand, the domains of the committee system and the executive branch do not appear as susceptible to the subjective orientations of state legislators with respect to cue taking and perceptions of decision loci. The task ahead is to link the processes of cue taking to policy making, of perceived decision loci to the dynamics of the decision-making process. What do we believe are the critical questions in the analysis of state politics and policy formation and how can they be handled?

THE RESEARCH AGENDA

The most important aspect of the research agenda is to develop a general model of the policy-making process in the American states. This, of course, is so ambitious that we cannot realistically hope to reach that goal. However, we shall sketch at least the outlines of how we would approach the formulation of such a model. We have already suggested many research questions above, in the preceding pages of this chapter and throughout the earlier chapters. With respect to the study of state legislatures, our survey includes many items dealing with the specific mechanisms of internal politics. To what extent does gubernatorial activity in various policy areas lead to the success or failure of proposals in these areas? To what extent can the behavioral phenomena which subjective orientations fail to explain be predicted by institutional considerations, such as the nature of standing committees in the states, the formal powers of such committees and of the governor, and the partisan balance of power in the state legislature? What are the policy implications of divided control of the legislative and executive branch of state government in comparison to single-party control of the state institutions? What does the aggregate analysis of these subjective orientations for the 50 states suggest?

Broad as these questions are, our plan of study is even more ambitious. Our study includes survey responses on questions of subjective orientations toward institutions, behavior and attitudes, and the policy preferences of both the members themselves and their constituents. These are broad areas and their importance should be obvious. Our study is unique in that it is only the second study of the attitudes of all 50 states and has been specifically designed to permit direct comparisons with the earlier one (Francis 1967); moreover, we have completed companion surveys, identical in many questions, based upon national surveys of county party chairmen and of state bureaucrats, both covering all 50 states with response rates of over 60 percent. We thus have attitudinal data for three elite groups. The county party chairmen often play major roles in the selection or recruitment of legislative candidates, followed by frequent help in the ensuing election. The legislators are assumed to "make the laws," whereas the bureaucrats "administer" them, with varying degrees of discretion. How do these groups perceive their own roles, the roles of each other, and the views of their respective constituents? To what extent does each group perceive itself to be the dominant factor in the policy-making process? How much power do members of one group attribute to the others?

We can answer some of these questions by comparative survey analysis, and others by aggregating responses to the state level for comparison. But perhaps the most important comparisons we can make, particularly in establishing linkages as the basis for a preliminary model of the state policy-making process, are between the positions of each group and public opinion on matters of public policy. To examine this question, we intend to derive estimates of statewide opinions on the public-policy questions from national surveys by a computer-simulation technique (see Weber 1971; Weber et al. 1972). The 13 nonfiscal policy questions examined in the previous chapter were selected according to three criteria: (1) the importance of these issues to contemporary problems in state policy formation; (2) the availability of longitudinal survey responses which can yield simulated estimates of public opinion (see Shaffer and Weber 1974) on most of the questions; and (3) the availability of recent survey responses, close enough in time to each of our elite surveys to make comparisons feasible of attitudes across elite groups and between such groups and public opinion.

We are currently investigating the extent to which each elite group (with preferences aggregated to the state level) is more in accord with public opinion on these 13 issues. As elected representatives, we would hypothesize that state legislators should be closest to public opinion overall. Yet county party chairmen, who have (or are reputed to have) a keen sense of what constitutes "electability," might be closer to public opinion. The bureaucrats should have the least degree of correspondence with such opinion, largely because they have no organized mass constituency. We shall also examine the perceived policy preferences that each elite group believes is favored by public opinion (see Miller and Stokes 1963; Miller 1964) in comparison with the group's own policy positions and our estimates of public opinion on these questions. For example, how insulated are the bureaucrats from public opinion? Joel D. Aberbach and Bert A. Rockman (1976a; 1976b) have been examining the backgrounds and ideological positions of federal bureaucrats and members of Congress, finding that the former are disproportionately liberals and Democrats with respect to the overall population—and, therefore, quite insulated from both public opinion and the policies of a Republican administration when one is in power. The Aberbach-Rockman study suggests that another fruitful line of inquiry would be in the area of the personal background of the various elite groups, as well as the ways in which they were recruited into political careers.

The issues which we analyzed in Chapter 5 can also be compared with the most important issues facing a state, as our salience measures for broad policy categories in Chapter 4 indicated. Have we in fact tapped the more salient issues, according to any of our elite groups? Furthermore, we can examine the policies individually or as clusters of related issues. In the previous chapter, the similar findings for teacher unionization, teachers' strikes, police and fire

unionization, policemen and firemen strikes, and gun control suggest
that these issues might form some type of unidimensional scale representing the traditional liberalism of the 1960s. Abortion and marijuana
legalization, however, may clearly distinguish the "New Liberals"
from the "Silent Minority" (Miller and Levitin 1976), while such issues
as capital punishment and parochial-school aid all involve cross-cut-
ting cleavages between and within various ethnic groups. Is one elite
group overall more supportive of either the "new issues" or the ones
which involve overlapping cleavages? What are the effects of the age
of the elite respondents, their level of education, and the decisional
arena in which they operate upon support for various policies?

Clearly, a linkage model of the policy-making and political processes in the American states must consider questions such as these.
Our attempt in the present study has been more modest. We have presented the results of analyses of our survey data with the individual
legislator as the unit of analysis. We chose to concentrate on party
leaders, committee leaders, and chief executives because of their
prominence in the research on legislative behavior. Drawing upon diverse bodies of literature, we have tested alternative hypotheses rather than presented an overall picture of the American state legislator.
Some were supported by the data analysis (particularly those in Chapters 2 and 5); others were not. In some cases, we simply could not
account for the variations in behavior and attitudes at all. The importance of other sources of information in the legislature—particularly personal friends, specialists in policy areas, and interest groups—
cannot be downplayed. Our specific omissions suggest almost as many
areas for future research as the questions of comparability of responses across mass and elite groups at both the individual and aggregate levels of analysis.

Finally, we believe that one of the more pressing tasks involved
in studies of policy formation and decision making is the development
of a theoretical framework that not only assumes that the attitudes of
decision makers are the key variables but also attempts to link these
attitudes with the decision-making environment under examination.
We have concentrated on two major questions in Chapters 2 through 4:
the determinants of cue seeking and of perceptions of decision loci.
The research on Congress, as stated in Chapter 2, has clearly indicated the importance of cue taking in the legislator's decision calculus.
But there is a linkage process in this literature (Kingdon 1973; Matthews and Stimson 1975) which assumes that cues lead directly to voting decisions and thus to policy alternatives. Cues are related to votes
and votes mean "power." Aage R. Clausen maintained that the cue-
seeking approach ". . . clearly places the individual legislator in a
state of high dependence upon the cue-giver. However, it does not explain how the cue-giver arrives at his vote decision . . . the cue-taking

theory permits the cue-givers to be group majorities, including the majority of the whole house. Furthermore, in known tests to date it is the group cue-givers that are far and away the most important. Thus, the failure of the theory to explain the decisions of the cue-givers is no small matter" (1973, p. 35).

We find this statement to be quite important, although we do not completely agree with Clausen. At least in the case of party leaders (groups or individuals?), we have found that orientations toward the party system do indeed account for the decisions of the cue seekers. The more important question, from our perspective, is the establishment of an interconnection between information seeking and the outcome of the decision on a policy or set of related policies. The predominance of individual cue givers in our sample, most notably personal friends in the legislature and legislator-specialists in a policy area, does not cause us to worry about group cue givers.

We are somewhat disturbed by the lack of a linkage between sources of information and perceived decision loci. Indeed, examining the two principal studies of cue taking in Congress, we find one (Kingdon 1973) in which the questions were more similar to our decision-locus item and another (Matthews and Stimson 1975) which was more oriented toward sources of information. Yet information is not, according to our findings in the three chapters cited, equivalent to power. The two do not seem to be related as strongly as we would expect. We have suggested that cue seeking probably describes a pattern of power that members might prefer, while our decision-locus variable is a measure of how power is actually distributed in the legislature.

Even if members might prefer an alternative distribution of power, it is not at all clear that this latter decisional structure would conform to the members' ideal pattern of decision making (given the poor predictive power of our attitudinal scales for cue taking for committee leaders and governors). Power and information may be more interrelated in the Congress. This appears likely, although we have no direct evidence on the hypothesis. In the states, however, the still-prevalent part-time legislatures may have more complex and diverse decision-making processes. We have found that our respondents were not at all reluctant to admit that they both sought out cues and had quite distinct perceptions of the major arena of power in the legislature. Yet they did not equate the two. This suggests that the development of a linkage model will indeed be difficult. We must examine not only the patterns of covariation between perceptions, behavior, and subjective orientations but also how each of these key elements in the decision-making process is structured within its context, as well as within the domain of existing theory.

APPENDIX A

STATE LEGISLATOR OPINION STUDY

1. What do you consider to be the most important problem facing your state today?

_____

2. What is your opinion on the following state issues:

Are you favorable or unfavorable toward:	Very Favorable	Favorable	Unfavorable	Very Unfavorable	No Opinion
a) the death penalty for persons convicted of murder?	( )	( )	( )	( )	( )
b) a law which would permit a woman to go to a doctor to end a pregnancy anytime during the first three months?	( )	( )	( )	( )	( )
c) having all new automobiles equipped with an anti-pollution device which would add approximately $100 to the price of an automobile?	( )	( )	( )	( )	( )
d) a law which would require a person to obtain a police permit before he or she could buy a gun?	( )	( )	( )	( )	( )
e) permitting public school teachers to join unions?	( )	( )	( )	( )	( )
f) permitting public school teachers to strike?	( )	( )	( )	( )	( )
g) permitting policemen and firemen to join unions?	( )	( )	( )	( )	( )
h) permitting policemen and firemen to strike?	( )	( )	( )	( )	( )
i) making the use of marijuana legal?	( )	( )	( )	( )	( )
j) a law requiring automobile drivers suspected of having consumed too much alcohol to take a breath test or a blood test?	( )	( )	( )	( )	( )
k) the "no fault" plan dealing with auto insurance?	( )	( )	( )	( )	( )
l) state aid for education going to Catholic and other private schools?	( )	( )	( )	( )	( )
m) birth control information being available to anyone who wants it?	( )	( )	( )	( )	( )

3. How would you classify your legislative district (please check one)?
____Safe Dem. ____Mostly Dem. ____Competitive ____Mostly Rep. ____Safe Rep.

4. How competitive was the primary for your legislative seat at the last election?
____None ____Little ____Moderate ____Quite a bit ____Very Competitive

5. How strong are the local (county, ward, etc.) party organizations in your district?
____Very Weak ____Weak ____About Average ____Strong ____Very Strong

189

6. How important are the party organizations in determining who will win a seat from your legislative district, considering both the primary and the general election?
___Very Unimportant ___Unimportant ___Important ___Very Important

7. How active were the county party organizations from your party in your last election?
___Very Active ___Active ___Somewhat Active ___Not Very Active ___Not Active At All

8. How active were the precinct or ward party organizations from your party in your last election?
___Very Active ___Active ___Somewhat Active ___Not Very Active ___Not Active At All

9. How important are interest groups in determining who will win a seat from your legislative district, considering both the primary and the general election?
___Very Unimportant ___Unimportant ___Important ___Very Important

10. Do you think the average voters in your district have specific preferences concerning the more important bills you vote on in the legislature, that is, do most have preferences, some, or only a few?
___Only a few do ___Some do ___Most do ___Don't Know

11. Do you think you generally know how the rank-and-file voters in your district feel about issues that concern them, that is, do you almost always feel you know, sometimes feel you know, or hardly ever feel you know?
___Almost always ___Sometimes ___Hardly ever ___Don't Know

12. One hears a lot these days about the activities of interest groups and lobbies. Which would you weigh as the most powerful organizations of this kind in your state?
1._____ 2._____ 3._____
4._____ 5._____ 6._____

13. Which of the above groups would you estimate is the most effective in making its case before the legislature? _____

14. Are there any particular subjects or fields of legislation in which you think of yourself as particularly expert? ___Yes ___No
If "Yes," which area(s)? 1._____ 2._____

15. We are trying to get an idea of how a legislator goes about making up his mind when he is uncertain about whether he will support or oppose a bill. Who do you usually consult when making such a decision? Please rank the top five sources of information you consult with in deciding how to vote. Write "1" beside the source you consult most often, "2" beside the source next most important, "3" beside the source next most important, "4" beside the source next most important, and "5" beside the source least important.
___Committee chairman
___Governor
___Ranking minority member of committee
___Party leaders in the legislature
___Interest group representatives
___Personal friends in legislature
___State Party Chairman
___Precinct Committeemen in my district
___Legislators of my party from my district or adjacent districts
___Administrator-specialist in policy
___Legislator-specialist in policy
___Legislators of both parties from my district or adjacent districts
___County Chairman in my district

16. During the past legislative session, how many times per week on the average were you contacted about legislation by the following:

	Zero	1-5	6-10	11-25	Over 25
County party leaders from your district	( )	( )	( )	( )	( )
Interest group representatives	( )	( )	( )	( )	( )
Members of the Governor's Staff	( )	( )	( )	( )	( )
Leaders of your party caucus	( )	( )	( )	( )	( )
Representatives of Executive Agencies	( )	( )	( )	( )	( )
State Chairman of your party	( )	( )	( )	( )	( )
Precinct or ward leaders from your party	( )	( )	( )	( )	( )
Other legislators	( )	( )	( )	( )	( )

17. What do you think is the general opinion of the people in your district on the following state issues? Are they favorable or unfavorable toward:

	Very Favorable	Favorable	Unfavorable	Very Unfavorable	No Opinion
a) the death penalty for persons convicted of murder?	( )	( )	( )	( )	( )
b) a law which would permit a woman to go to a doctor to end a pregnancy anytime during the first three months?	( )	( )	( )	( )	( )
c) having all new automobiles equipped with an anti-pollution device which would add approximately $100 to the price of an automobile?	( )	( )	( )	( )	( )
d) a law which would require a person to obtain a police permit before he or she could buy a gun?	( )	( )	( )	( )	( )
e) permitting public school teachers to join unions?	( )	( )	( )	( )	( )
f) permitting public school teachers to strike?	( )	( )	( )	( )	( )
g) permitting policemen and firemen to join unions?	( )	( )	( )	( )	( )
h) permitting policemen and firemen to strike?	( )	( )	( )	( )	( )
i) making the use of marijuana legal?	( )	( )	( )	( )	( )
j) a law requiring automobile drivers suspected of having consumed too much alcohol to take a breath test or a blood test?	( )	( )	( )	( )	( )
k) the "no fault" plan dealing with auto insurance?	( )	( )	( )	( )	( )
l) state aid for education going to Catholic and other private schools?	( )	( )	( )	( )	( )
m) birth control information being available to anyone who wants it?	( )	( )	( )	( )	( )

18. In the last year how often have you contacted the following on such party matters as political appointments, fund raising and campaign activities?

	Often	Sometimes	Hardly Ever	Never
Your County Party Chairman	( )	( )	( )	( )
The Governor's Staff	( )	( )	( )	( )
State Party Chairman	( )	( )	( )	( )
Other Local Party Leaders	( )	( )	( )	( )
Other State Party Leaders	( )	( )	( )	( )
Precinct Committeemen or Ward Chairmen	( )	( )	( )	( )

19. In your legislature, where would you say the most significant decisions are made (check one)?

____ Party Caucus   ____ Regular Committee Meetings   ____ Prelegislative Session
____ On the floor   ____ In the Governor's Office   ____ In policy committee
____ Other _____

20. We are very interested in obtaining a more accurate picture of the kinds of issues which characterize our state legislatures. What would you estimate to be the most important matters of policy to come before the most recent regular session of your legislature (for example, sales tax increase, mental health appropriation, reapportionment, right-to-work bill, etc.)?

1._____ 2._____
3._____ 4._____

Taking one matter of policy at a time, as you have listed them, please consider the following statements and check-mark the appropriate box when the statement helps describe the matter of policy.

	Matters of Policy Above			
	1	2	3	4
The Governor was pressing hard for legislation in this area.	( )	( )	( )	( )
The newspapers and/or broadcasters gave a great deal of publicity to the matter.	( )	( )	( )	( )
At least one or two fairly important pressure groups made it known that they had a vital interest at stake.	( )	( )	( )	( )
From all appearances, a substantial majority of legislators were personally interested in the matter.	( )	( )	( )	( )
The average citizen, it seemed, was expressing an unusual amount of concern over the matter.	( )	( )	( )	( )
There was a heated partisan fight, Democrats versus Republicans.	( )	( )	( )	( )
There was a substantial amount of conflict within my own party.	( )	( )	( )	( )
There were at least two major interest groups who were at odds with one another over this matter.	( )	( )	( )	( )
There was a substantial amount of regional conflict (Urban-rural, upstate-downstate, urban-suburban, etc.)	( )	( )	( )	( )
There was very little conflict--almost everyone agreed.	( )	( )	( )	( )
The proposed legislation involved a large amount of money.	( )	( )	( )	( )
Proposed legislation involved many levels or branches of government.	( )	( )	( )	( )
Proposed legislation meant a long-term government commitment, if passed.	( )	( )	( )	( )
I felt the proposed legislation would have a direct impact upon a large number of people in this state.	( )	( )	( )	( )
I felt the proposed legislation would represent or result in a marked departure from present practices.	( )	( )	( )	( )
I felt that if this matter were delayed, more radical legislation might be necessary in the future.	( )	( )	( )	( )
I felt the proposed legislation would lead to more radical legislation in the future.	( )	( )	( )	( )
Strong legislation was passed in this area.	( )	( )	( )	( )
Legislation was passed, but in a considerably modified form.	( )	( )	( )	( )
Legislation was defeated, but then passed in a special session called by the Governor.	( )	( )	( )	( )
Legislation was defeated either in the legislature or by a veto.	( )	( )	( )	( )

21. As of today, how willing are you to consider serving three or more terms in the legislature in the future?
__Very Willing __Somewhat Willing __Somewhat Unwilling __Quite Unwilling __Undecided

22. Would you like to run for some higher political office at some point in the future?
____Yes ____Maybe ____No ____Undecided

23. Now, let's consider some statements that legislators and others have made about the nature of legislative life. You may very well find some of these to be quite over-simplified, particularly since they deal with complex subjects. But we would like your general reaction to each one. These are all matters of opinion so there are no correct or incorrect answers. Would you please read each statement and then check the response which best indicates your agreement or disagreement with the statement.

	Strongly Agree	Agree	Disagree	Strongly Disagree	No Opinion
a) The legislature should play the major role in the making of public policy in this state.	( )	( )	( )	( )	( )
b) Legislators should be paid enough so that they do not need to work at any other job.	( )	( )	( )	( )	( )
c) The leadership in my party in the legislature makes a concerted effort to hold the party together on roll call votes.	( )	( )	( )	( )	( )
d) The business of state government is simple enough that legislators can afford to spend a lot of time consulting with their constituents.	( )	( )	( )	( )	( )
e) The legislature should be in session all year long to conduct the state's business.	( )	( )	( )	( )	( )
f) If a bill is important for his party's record, a member should vote with his party, even if it costs him some support in his district.	( )	( )	( )	( )	( )
g) The legislature and the governor should be equal partners in the making of public policy in this state.	( )	( )	( )	( )	( )
h) The party helped him to get elected to the legislature. Even if he disagrees with its stand, he has an obligation to vote with his party.	( )	( )	( )	( )	( )
i) Every legislator should be provided a sum of money with which to establish a district office to handle constituent matters.	( )	( )	( )	( )	( )
j) The business of state government is so complex that legislators must spend a lot of time in the state capital developing expertise on various policy matters.	( )	( )	( )	( )	( )
k) Every legislator should have an individual office for personal and staff use.	( )	( )	( )	( )	( )
l) Legislators should never be paid so much that they might begin to feel like professional legislators.	( )	( )	( )	( )	( )
m) A legislator's first loyalty should be to his party's legislative leaders rather than to the governor, if they are in disagreement.	( )	( )	( )	( )	( )
n) No legislator except those in leadership positions should be provided with full-time staff aids.	( )	( )	( )	( )	( )
o) Standing committees of the legislature should be staffed on a permanent year-round basis.	( )	( )	( )	( )	( )
p) The governor should play the major role in the making of policy in this state.	( )	( )	( )	( )	( )
q) The best interests of the people would be better served if legislators were elected without party labels.	( )	( )	( )	( )	( )

24. What percentage of the jobs in state agencies as a whole are patronage jobs?_____

25. What is the effect of having patronage jobs on the performance of state agencies?
___Increases turnover ___Inexperienced workers ___Little motivation
___Eliminates stagnation ___Increases public responsiveness ___No effect
Other_____

26. What is the effect of having patronage jobs on the party organization?
___Provides campaign workers ___Provides funds ___Creates hard feelings
___Increases policy power ___No effect Other_____

193

27. What positive or negative effects does patronage have on your job as a legislator?
    ___Provides campaign workers   ___Provides funds   ___Creates hard feelings
    ___Increases policy power   ___No effect   Other_____

28. In determining the following kinds of policies, in general how much influence would these people be able to have in determining the decision?

    Policy A. Level of budget for a state agency.   Policy C. Priorities among programs
    Policy B. Who is hired in a state agency.   or activities of a state agency.

	A — Level of budget for an agency					B — Who is hired in an agency					C — Program priorities for the agency				
	Much Influence	Some Influence	A Little Influence	No Influence		Much Influence	Some Influence	A Little Influence	No Influence		Much Influence	Some Influence	A Little Influence	No Influence	
State legislator from majority party	( )	( )	( )	( )	( )	( )	( )	( )	( )	( )	( )	( )	( )	( )	( )
State legislator from minority party	( )	( )	( )	( )	( )	( )	( )	( )	( )	( )	( )	( )	( )	( )	( )
Governor	( )	( )	( )	( )	( )	( )	( )	( )	( )	( )	( )	( )	( )	( )	( )
State party chairman-majority party	( )	( )	( )	( )	( )	( )	( )	( )	( )	( )	( )	( )	( )	( )	( )
State party chairman-minority party	( )	( )	( )	( )	( )	( )	( )	( )	( )	( )	( )	( )	( )	( )	( )
County party chairman-majority party	( )	( )	( )	( )	( )	( )	( )	( )	( )	( )	( )	( )	( )	( )	( )
County party chairman-minority party	( )	( )	( )	( )	( )	( )	( )	( )	( )	( )	( )	( )	( )	( )	( )
Personnel Agency	( )	( )	( )	( )	( )	( )	( )	( )	( )	( )	( )	( )	( )	( )	( )
Budget Agency	( )	( )	( )	( )	( )	( )	( )	( )	( )	( )	( )	( )	( )	( )	( )

29. Did you initially decide to run for the legislature because of the urgings of others (such as a political party, interest groups or community leaders), or would you classify yourself as pretty much of a self-starter?
    ___Self-starter   ___Recruited by party   ___Recruited by interest groups
    ___Rectuited by community leaders not associated with party or interest group

30. a.   ___ Male   ___Female   b. What is your age?___

    c. What is your party affiliation?   ___Dem.   ___Rep.   ___Ind.

    d. What is your major occupation (other than legislator)?_____

    e. Check the highest level of education completed.

None	Some Grade School	Finished Grade School	Some High School	Graduated From High School	Some College	Graduated From College	Post-Graduate Work
___	___	___	___	___	___	___	___

    f. Race: ___White   ___Black   ___Latino   ___Oriental   ___Other

    g. How long have you served in the state legislature?_____

    h. What political positions both within government and within your party have you held prior to your election to the legislature, beginning with the position most recent in time and working your way back?

        1._____   2._____
        3._____   4._____

    If you would like to have the results of this survey, check here. ( )

REFERENCES

Aberbach, Joel D., and Bert A. Rockman. 1976a. "The Overlapping Worlds of American Federal Executives and Congressmen." Paper delivered at the Annual Meeting of the Midwest Political Science Association, April 29- May 1, Chicago.

____. 1976b. "Clashing Beliefs within the Executive Branch: The Nixon Administration." American Political Science Review 70 (June): 456-68.

Achen, Christopher H. 1975. "Mass Political Attitudes and the Survey Response." American Political Science Review 69 (December): 1218-32.

Alker, Hayward R., Jr. 1969. "A Typology of Ecological Fallacies." In Quantitative Ecological Analysis in the Social Sciences, ed. Mattei Dogan and Stein Rokken, pp. 69-86. Cambridge; Mass.: MIT Press.

American Political Science Association Committee on Political Parties. 1950. Toward a More Responsible Two-Party System. New York: Reinhart.

Asher, Herbert B. 1973. Freshman Representatives and the Learning of Voting Cues. Sage Professional Papers in American Politics, 1 (04-003). Beverly Hills; Calif: Sage Publications.

Barber, James D. 1965. The Lawmakers. New Haven: Yale University Press.

Beyle, Thad, and J. Oliver Williams. 1972. "Views of the Governor's Role." In The American Governor in Behavioral Perspective, ed. Thad Beyle and J. Oliver Williams, pp. 257-58. New York: Harper and Row.

Booms, Bernard H., and James R. Halldorson. 1973. "The Politics of Redistribution: A Reformulation." American Political Science Review 67 (September): 924-33.

Broach, Glen T. 1972. "A Comparative Dimensional Analysis of Partisan and Urban-Rural Voting in State Legislature." Journal of Politics 34 (August): 905-21.

Burns, John. 1971. The Sometime Government. New York: Bantam.

Campbell, Angus, Philip E. Converse, Warren E. Miller, and Donald E. Stokes. 1960. The American Voter. New York: Wiley.

Carmines, Edward G. 1974. "The Mediating Influence of State Legislatures on the Linkage Between Inter-party Competition and Welfare Policies." American Political Science Review 68 (September): 1118-24.

Chaffey, Douglas C. 1970. "The Institutionalization of State Legislatures: A Comparative Study." Western Political Quarterly 23 (March): 180-96.

Chartock. Alan S., and Max Berking. 1970. Strengthening the Wisconsin Legislature. New Brunswick, N.J.: Rutgers University Press.

Cherryholmes, Cleo, and Michael Shapiro. 1969. Representative and Roll Calls. Indianapolis: Bobbs-Merrill.

Citizens' Conference on State Legislatures. 1971. State Legislatures: An Evaluation of their Effectiveness. New York: Praeger.

Clausen, Aage R. 1973. How Congressmen Decide. New York: St. Martins.

Converse, Philip E. 1964. "The Nature of Belief Systems in Mass Publics." In Ideology and Discontent, ed. David E. Apter, pp. 206-61. New York: Free Press.

Cortés, Fernando, and Adam Przeworski. 1977. "Comparing Partial and Ratio Regression Models." Political Methodology.

Council of State Governments. 1972. Selected Bibliography on State Government. Lexington, Ky.

_____. 1973. State Elective Officials and the Legislature. Lexington, Ky.

Craft, Ralph. 1973. Strengthening the Arkansas Legislature. New Brunswick, N.J.: Rutgers University Press.

Crane, Wilder, Jr. 1960. "A Caveat on Roll Call Studies of Party
    Voting." Midwest Journal of Political Science 4 (August):
    237-49.

Crane, Wilder, Jr., and Meredith Watts. 1968. State Legislative
    Systems: Englewood Cliffs, N.J.: Prentice-Hall.

Davidson, Roger, David Kovenock, and Michael O'Leary. 1966.
    Congress in Crisis: Politics and Congressional Reform.
    Belmont, Calif.: Wadsworth.

Dawson, Richard E., and James A. Robinson. 1963. "Inter-party
    Competition. Economic Variables, and Welfare Policies in
    the American States." Journal of Politics 25 (May): 265-89.

Dennis, Jack. 1966. "Support for the Party System by the Mass
    Public." American Political Science Review 60 (September):
    600-615.

____. 1975. "Trends in Public Support for the American Political
    Party System." British Journal of Political Science 5 (April):
    187-230.

Derge, David R. 1958. "Metropolitan and Outside Alignments in
    Illinois and Missouri Legislative Delegation." American
    Political Science Review 52 (December): 1051-65.

Dye, Thomas R. 1969. "Executive Power and Public Policy in the
    States." Western Political Quarterly 27 (December): 926-39.

____. 1971. "State Legislative Politics." In Politics in the American
    States: A Comparative Analysis, 2d ed., ed. Herbert Jacob
    and Kenneth N. Vines, pp. 163-209. Boston: Little, Brown.

Dyer, James A. 1976. "Do Lawyers Vote Differently? A Study of
    Voting on No-Fault Insurance." Journal of Politics 38 (May):
    450-56.

Edwards, Allen L. 1957. Techniques of Attitude Scale Construction.
    New York: Appleton-Century-Crofts.

Fenno, Richard F. Jr. 1966. The Power of the Purse. Boston:
    Little, Brown.

____. 1973. Congressmen in Committees. Boston: Little, Brown.

Fiorina, Morris P. 1977. "The Case of the Vanishing Marginals: The Bureaucracy Did It." American Political Science Review.

Francis, Wayne L. 1967. Legislative Issues in the Fifty States. Chicago: Rand McNally.

Fry, Brian R., and Richard F. Winters. 1970. "The Politics of Redistribution." American Political Science Review 64 (June): 508-22.

Fulbright, J. William. 1966. The Arrogance of Power. New York: Random House.

Garceau, Oliver. 1966. "Research in State Politics." In American State Politics: Readings for Comparative Analysis, ed. Frank Munger, pp. 2-16. New York: Crowell.

Gatlin, Douglas S. 1973. "The Development of a Responsible Party System in the Florida Legislature." In State Legislative Innovation, ed. James A. Robinson, pp. 1-45. New York: Praeger.

Gilbert, Jane. 1973. Constituent Preferences and Roll Call Behavior. Mimeograph, Swarthmore College.

Grant, Lawrence V. 1973. "Specialization as a Strategy in Legislative Decision-Making." American Journal of Political Science 17 (February): 123-47.

Gray, Virginia. 1976. "Models of Comparative State Politics: A Comparison of Cross-Sectional and Time-Series Analysis." American Journal of Political Science 20 (May): 235-56.

Greenstein, Fred I., and Elton F. Jackson. 1963. "A Second Look at the Validity of Roll Call Analysis." Midwest Journal of Political Science 7 (May): 156-66.

Grumm, John G. 1971. "The Effects of Legislative Structure on Legislative Performance." In State and Urban Politics, ed. Richard I. Hofferbert and Ira Sharkansky, pp. 298-322. Boston: Little Brown.

Heaphy, James J., and Alan P. Balutis, eds. 1975. Legislative Staffing. New York: Halstead-Wiley.

Heard, Alexander. 1966. "Introduction—Old Problems, New Context."
    In State Legislatures in American Politics, ed. Alexander
    Heard, pp. 1-4. Englewood Cliffs, N.J.: Prentice-Hall.

Hedlund, Ronald, and Keith E. Hamm. 1976. "Conflict and Perceived
    Group Benefits from Legislative Rule Changes." Legislative
    Studies Quarterly 1 (May): 181-200.

Henkel, Ramon E. 1976. Tests of Significance. Sage University
    Papers on Quantitative Applications in the Social Sciences,
    07-004. Beverly Hills; Calif.: Sage Publications.

Hildebrand, David, James Laing, and Howard Rosenthal. 1977.
    Analysis of Ordinal Data. Sage University Papers on Quantitative
    Application in the Social Sciences. Beverly Hills; Calif: Sage
    Publications. 07-008.

Hofferbert, Richard I. 1972. "State and Community Policy Studies:
    A Review of Comparative Input-Output Analyses." In Political
    Science Annual, ed. James A. Robinson, 3: 3-72. Indianapolis:
    Bobbs-Merrill.

Hopkins, Anne H. 1974a. "Opinion Publics and Support for Public
    Policy in the American States." American Journal of Political
    Science 18 (February): 167-77.

____. 1974b. "Right-to-Work Legislation in the States: A Causal
    Analysis." In Quantitative Analysis of Political Data, ed.
    Samuel A. Kirkpatrick, pp. 181-202. Columbus, Ohio: Charles
    E. Merrill.

Huitt, Ralph K. 1961. "Democratic Party Leadership in the Senate."
    American Political Science Review 55 (June): 331-44.

Huntington, Samuel P. 1973. "Congressional Responses to the
    Twentieth Century." In The Congress and America's Future,
    2d ed., ed. David B. Truman, pp. 5-31. Englewood Cliffs,
    N.J.: Prentice-Hall.

Jennings, M. Kent, and Harmon Zeigler. 1970. "The Salience of
    American State Politics." American Political Science Review
    64 (June): 523-35.

Jewell, Malcolm E. 1955. "Party Voting in American State Legis-
    latures." American Political Science Review 49 (September):
    773-91.

____. 1969. The State Legislature. 2d ed. New York: Random House.

Jewell, Malcolm E., and Samuel C. Patterson. 1972. The Legislative Process in the United States. 2d ed. New York: Random House.

Jones Charles O. 1970. The Minority Party in Congress. Boston: Little, Brown.

____. 1973. "State and Local Public Policy Analysis: A Review of Progress." In Political Science and State and Local Government, pp. 27-54. Washington: American Political Science Association.

____. 1974. "Speculative Argumentation in Federal Air Pollution Policy-Making." Journal of Politics 36 (May): 438-64.

Key, V.O., Jr. 1949. Southern Politics in State and Nation. New York: Knopf.

____. 1956. American State Politics: An Introduction. New York: Knopf.

____. 1964. Politics, Parties, and Pressure Groups. 5th ed. New York: Crowell.

Kingdon, John W. 1973. Congressmen's Voting Decisions. New York: Harper and Row.

Kovenock, David. 1973. "Influence in the U.S. House of Representatives: A Statistical Analysis of Communications." American Politics Quarterly 4 (October): 407-64.

Le Blanc, Hugh. 1969. "Voting in State Senates: Party and Constituency Influences." Midwest Journal of Political Science 13 (February): 33-57.

Lehner, Robert G. 1972. "Public Views of the Governor." In The American Governor in Behavioral Perspective, ed. Thad Beyle and J. Oliver Williams, pp. 258-69. New York: Harper and Row.

Le Loup, Lance J. 1976a. "The Policy Consequences of State Legislative Reform." Paper delivered at the Annual Meeting of the Midwest Political Science Association, April 29-May 1, Chicago.

_____. 1976b. "Policy, Party, and Voting in U.S. State Legislatures:
    A Test of the Content-Process Linkage." Legislative Studies
    Quarterly 1 (May): 213-30.

Lockard, Duane. 1959. New England State Politics. Princeton, N.J.:
    Princeton University Press.

Manley, John F. 1970. The Politics of Finance. Boston: Little, Brown.

Maranell, Gary M., ed. 1974. Scaling: A Source-book for Behavioral
    Scientists. Chicago: Aldine.

Markus, Gregory B. 1974. "Electoral Coalition and Senate Roll Call
    Behavior: An Ecological Analysis." American Journal of
    Political Science 18 (August): 595-607.

Masters, Nicholas A. 1961. "Congressional Committee Assignments."
    American Political Science Review 55 (June): 345-57.

Matthews, Donald R. 1960. U.S. Senators and Their World. Chapel
    Hill: University of North Carolina Press.

Matthews, Donald R., and James A. Stimson. 1970. "Decision-
    Making by U.S. Representatives: A Preliminary Model."
    In Political Decision-Making, ed. S. Sidney Ulmer, pp. 14-43.
    New York: Van Nostrand Reinhold.

_____. 1975. Yeas and Nays: Normal Decision-Making in the U.S.
    House of Representatives. New York: Wiley.

Mayhew, David R. 1974. Congress: The Electoral Connection. New
    Haven: Yale University Press.

McCally, Sarah P. 1966. "The Governor and His Legislative Party."
    American Political Science Review 60 (December): 923-42.

Miller, Warren E. 1964. "Majority Rule and the Representative
    System of Government." In Cleavages, Ideologies, and Party
    Systems, ed. Erik Allardt and Y. Littunen, pp. 343-76. Helsinki;
    Finland: Transactions of the Westermarck Society.

Miller, Warren E., and Teresa E. Levitin. 1976. Leadership and
    Change. Cambridge: Winthrop.

Miller, Warren E., and Donald E. Stokes. 1963. "Constituency
Influence in Congress." American Political Science Review
57 (March): 45-56.

Mishler, William, James Lee, and Alan Thorpe. 1973. "Determi-
nants of Institutional Continuity: Freshman Cue-Taking in the
U.S. House of Representatives." In Legislators in Comparative
Perspective, ed. Allan Kornberg, pp. 363-97. New York:
David McKay.

Morehouse, Sarah McCally. 1973. "The State Political Party and the
Policy-Making Process." American Political Science Review
67 (March): 55-72.

Morrison, Denton E., and Ramon E. Henkel. 1970. The Significance
Test Controversy. Chicago: Aldine.

Neustadt, Richard E. 1964. Presidential Power. New York: Mentor.

Nie, Norman H., with Kristi Anderson. 1974. "Mass Belief Systems
Revisited: Political Change and Attitude Structure." Journal of
Politics 36 (August): 540-91.

Nie, Norman H., Sidney Verba, and John R. Petrocik. 1976. The
Changing American Voter. Cambridge; Mass.: Harvard University Press.

Ogle, David B. 1970. Strengthening the Connecticut Legislature.
New Brunswick, N.J.: Rutgers University Press.

_____. 1971. Strengthening the Mississippi Legislature. New Brunswick,
N.J.: Rutgers University Press.

Patterson, Samuel C. 1959. "Patterns of Interpersonal Relations in
a State Legislative Group: The Wisconsin Assembly." Public
Opinion Quarterly 23 (Spring): 101-09.

Patterson, Samuel C, Ronald D. Hedlund, and G. Robert Boynton.
1975. Representatives and Represented: Bases of Public Support
for the American Legislatures. New York: Wiley.

Peroff, Kathleen, and Eric M. Uslaner. 1976. "Longitudinal and
Cross-Sectional Models of State Politics Revisited: or, 'Keep
on Tracking'." Mimeo. University of Maryland.

Polsby, Nelson W. 1968. "The Institutionalization of the U.S. House of Representatives." American Political Science Review 62 (March): 144-68.

Porter, H. Owen. 1974. "Legislative Experts and Outsiders: The Two-Step Flow of Communication." Journal of Politics 36 (August): 703-30.

Price, David. 1972. Who Makes the Laws? Morristown, N.J.: General Learning Press.

Ranney, Austin. 1962. The Doctrine of Responsible Party Government. Urbana: University of Illinois Press.

Ransone, Coleman B., Jr. 1956. The Office of Governor in the United States. University: University of Alabama Press.

Rao, Potluri, and Roger L. Miller. 1971. Applied Econometrics. Belmont, Calif.: Wadsworth.

Rieselbach, Leroy N. 1977. Congressional Reform in the Seventies. Morristown, N.J.: General Learning Press.

Ritt, Leonard G. 1973. "State Legislative Reform: Does It Matter?" American Politics Quarterly 1 (October): 499-510.

Robinson, James A., ed. 1973. State Legislative Innovation: Case Studies of Washington, Ohio, Florida, Illinois, Wisconsin, and California. New York: Praeger.

Robinson, W.S. 1950. "Ecological Correlations and the Behavior of Individuals." American Sociological Review 15 (June): 351-57.

Rosenthal, Alan. 1968. Strengthening the Maryland Legislature. New Brunswick, N.J.: Rutgers University Press.

_____. 1970. "An Analysis of Institutional Effects: Staffing Legislative Parties in Wisconsin." Journal of Politics 32 (August): 531-62.

_____. 1973a. "Contemporary Research on State Legislatures: From Individual Cases to Comparative Analysis." In Political Science and State and Local Government, pp. 55-85. Washington: American Political Science Association.

_____. 1973b. "Legislative Committee Systems: An Exploratory Analysis." Western Political Quarterly 26 (June): 252-62.

_____. 1973c. "Professional Staff and Legislative Influence in Wisconsin." In State Legislative Innovation, ed. James A. Robinson, pp. 183-225. New York: Praeger.

_____. 1974a. Legislative Performance in the States. New York: Free Press.

_____. 1974b. "Turnover in State Legislatures." American Journal of Political Science 18 (August): 609-16.

Schlesinger, Arthur M., Jr. 1973. The Imperial Presidency. Boston: Houghton Mifflin.

Schlesinger, Joseph A. 1965. "The Politics of the Executive." In Politics in the American States: A Comparative Analysis, ed. Herbert Jacob and Kenneth N. Vines, pp. 207-37. Boston: Little Brown.

Shaffer, William R., and Ronald E. Weber. 1974. Policy Responsiveness in the American States. Sage Professional Papers in Administrative and Policy Studies, 2 (03-021). Beverly Hills; Calif.: Sage Publications.

Sharkansky, Ira. 1968a. "Agency Requests, Gubernatorial Support, and Budget Success in State Legislatures." American Political Science Review 62 (December): 1220-31.

_____. 1968b. Spending in the American States. Chicago: Rand McNally.

Sharkansky, Ira, and Richard I. Hofferbert. 1969. "Dimensions of State Politics, Economics, and Public Policy." American Political Science Review 63 (September): 867-79.

Smith, C. Lynwood, Jr. 1970. Strengthening the Florida Legislature. New Brunswick, N.J.: Rutgers University Press.

Stimson, James A. 1975. "Five Propositions About Congressional Decision-Making." Political Methodology 2 (Fall): 415-36.

Sullivan, John L. 1972. "A Note on Redistributive Politics." American Political Science Review 66 (December): 1301-05.

Tantillo, Charles. 1968. Strengthening the Rhode Island Legislature. New Brunswick, N.J.: Rutgers University Press.

Theil, Henri. 1971. Principles of Econometrics. New York: Wiley.

Uslaner, Eric M. 1974. Congressional Committee Assignments: Alternative Models for Behavior. Sage Professional Papers in American Politics, 2 (04-019). Beverly Hills; Calif.: Sage Publications.

_____. 1976. "The Pitfalls of Per Capita." American Journal of Political Science 20 (February): 125-33.

_____. Forthcoming. "Comparative State Policy Formation, Inter-Party Competition, and Malapportionment: A New Look at 'V. O. Key's Hypotheses.'"

Uslaner, Eric M., and Ronald E. Weber. 1973. "The Electoral Impact of Reapportionment." Paper delivered at the Annual Meeting of the Southern Political Science Association, Nov. 1-3, Atlanta.

_____. 1975a. "The 'Politics' of Redistribution: Towards a Model of the Policy-Making Process in the American States." American Politics Quarterly 3 (April): 130-70.

_____. 1975b. "Partisan Cues and Legislative Decision-Making in the American States." Paper delivered at Annual Meeting of the Midwest Political Science Association, May 1-3, Chicago.

Wahlke, John, Heinz Eulau, William Buchanan, and Leroy C. Ferguson. 1962. The Legislative System. New York: Wiley.

Walker, Jack L. 1969. "The Diffusion of Innovations Among the American States." American Political Science Review 63 (September): 880-99.

Weber, Ronald E. 1971. Public Policy Preferences in the States. Bloomington: Indiana University Institute of Public Administration.

Weber, Ronald E., and Wayne L. Francis. 1975. "Legislative Issues in the States: 1963-1973." Paper delivered at Annual Meeting of the Western Political Science Association, March 20-22.

Weber, Ronald E., Anne H. Hopkins, Michael L. Mezey, and Frank
    J. Munger. 1972. "Computer Simulation of State Electorates."
    Public Opinion Quarterly 36 (Winter): 549-65.

Weber, Ronald E., and William R. Shaffer. 1972. "Public Opinion
    and American State Policy-Making." Midwest Journal of
    Political Science 16 (November): 683-99.

Weisberg, Herbert F. 1976. "The Inherent Predictability of Legis-
    lative Votes." Paper delivered at Annual Meeting of the Mid-
    west Political Science Association, April 29-May 1, Chicago.

Wildavsky, Aaron. 1964. The Politics of the Budgetary Process.
    Boston: Little, Brown.

Wilson, Woodrow. 1885. Congressional Government, A Study in
    American Politics. Boston: Houghton Mifflin.

Winters, Richard F. 1976. "Party Control and Policy Change."
    American Journal of Political Science 20 (November):
    597-636.

Wissel, Peter, Robert O'Conner, and Michael King. 1976. "The
    Hunting of the Legislative Snark: Inofrmation Searches and
    Reforms in U.S. State Legislatures." Legislative Studies
    Quarterly 1 (May): 251-68.

Wright, Deil S. 1967. "Executive Leadership in State Administration."
    Midwest Journal of Political Science 11 (February): 1-26.

Young, James Sterling. 1966. The Washington Community 1800-1828.
    New York: Harcourt, Brace, and World.

Zeller, Belle, ed. 1954. American State Legislatures. New York:
    Crowell.

Aberbach, Joel D., 187
Achen, Christopher, 127
Alabama, 5, 107
Alaska, 5
Alker, Howard R., Jr., 146
Anderson, Kristi, 127
Arizona, 149
Asher, Herbert B., 21

Balutis, Alan P., 140
Barber, James David, 137
Berking, Max, 139
Beyle, Thad, 107
Boynton, G. Robert, 3
Broach, Glen T., 2
Buchanan, William, 3
Burns, John, 24, 136-37, 138, 142

California, 5
Carmines, Edward G., 143
Campbell, Angus, 180
Carnegie Foundation, 1
Chaffey, Douglas C., 2
Chartock, Alan S., 139
Cherryholmes, Cleo, 21, 22
Citizens' Conference on State
    Legislatures, 15, 24, 80,
    138, 139-40, 141, 143, 144,
    146, 149
Citizenship Clearing House, 1
Clausen, Aage R., 187
Committee on American Legis-
    lature, 74
Committee on Political Behavior
    of the Social Science Research
    Council, 1
Committee on Political Parties
    of the APSA, 25-26

Converse, Philip E., 127
Cortes, Fernando, 145
Council of State Governments, 4,
    78
Craft, Ralph, 139
Crane, Wilder, Jr., 2, 168-73

Davidson, Roger, 15
Dawson, Richard E., 2
Dennis, Jack, 13, 26
Derge, David R., 2
district competitiveness: parties,
    50-54, 55-64, 71, 72; commit-
    tees, 83-84, 88, 90-92, 94-97;
    gubernatorial, 111; legislative
    reform, 170-74
district typicality: parties, 31, 46,
    50-53, 54-64, 71, 182; commit-
    tees, 83-84, 89-92, 94-95, 96-
    97; gubernatorial, 111; legisla-
    tive reform, 174-77
Dye, Thomas R., 78, 81, 101,
    108
Dyer, James A., 165

Edwards, Allen L., 11
Eulau, Heinz, 3
executive dominance, 9, 37, 40,
    41, 106

FAIR, 139-40, 149
Fenno, Richard F., Jr., 75, 78,
    102, 105, 146, 173
Ferguson, Leroy C., 3
Fiorina, Morris P., 80-153
Florida, 43, 81, 148
Francis, Wayne L., 3, 10, 28,
    111, 127-30, 131, 133, 173,
    180, 183, 185

friendship groups, 9, 35, 39, 181
Fry, Brian R., 108, 143
Fulbright, J. William, 106

Garceau, Oliver, 1
Gatlin, Douglas S., 141
Georgia, 134
Gilbert, Jane, 31
Grant, Lawrence V., 22
Gray, Virginia, 2
Green, Mark J., 138
Greenstein, Fred J., 2, 13
Grumm, John G., 15, 24, 141,
    142, 143, 144, 146, 149

Halldorson, James R., 143
Hamm, Keith E., 3
Hawaii, 5
Heaphy, James J., 140
Heard, Alexander, 137
Hedlund, Ronald D., 3
Henkel, Ramon E., 16
Hildebrand, David, 17, 18, 19
Hofferbert, Richard I., 2, 143,
    146
Hopkins, Anne H., 167
Huitt, Ralph K., 76, 101
Hyneman, Charles S., 2
hypotheses: overall, 10; sources
    of information and parties, 32-
    33, 39; committees, 82-83;
    gubernatorial, 110-11, 130;
    reform, 150

Idaho, 149
Illinois, 5
Indiana, 2
Iowa, 97

Jackson, Elton F., 2, 13
Jennings, M. Kent, 107
Jewell, Malcolm E., 1, 2, 25,
    79, 81, 84, 106-07, 109
Jones, Charles O., 2, 120, 130,
    167

Keefe, William J., 2
Kentucky, 4
Key, V. O., Jr. 1, 76, 107, 109,
    136-37
King, Michael, 3
Kingdon, John W., 7, 21, 22, 23,
    25, 28, 35, 36, 37, 40, 41, 52,
    180, 181, 187, 188
Kovenock, David, 15, 21

Laing, James, 17, 18
Le Blanc, Hugh, 2
Le Loup, Lance J., 2, 141
Lee, James, 21
legislative professionalism, 8, 10,
    15, 79-81, 136, 184
legislative sample, 3-7
legislator specialists, 38, 41, 115,
    181
legislator surveys, 3-4, 8, 22
Lehnen, Robert G., 108
Levitin, Teresa, 148, 161, 187
linkages, 186, 187, 188
Lockard, Duane, 1

Manley, John F., 78
Maranell, Gary M., 11
Markus, Gregory, B., 84
Massachusetts, 5, 107, 148, 149
Masters, Nicholas A., 80
Matthews, Donald R., 7, 21, 22,
    23, 25, 28, 37, 38, 39, 40, 74,
    180, 181, 187, 188
Mayhew, David R., 31, 78, 153
McCally, Sarah P., 24, 36
measures of association, 16-19
Michigan, 5
Miller, Roger L., 130
Miller, Warren E., 148, 161,
    173, 186, 187
Minnesota, 2
Mishler, William, 21
Montana, 5
Morehouse, Sarah McCally, 108,
    111, 134

Morrison, Denton E., 16

Nebraska, 2, 4, 5, 25
Neustadt, Richard, 107
New Hampshire, 5
New Jersey, 4, 97, 107
New York, 80-149
Nie, Norman H., 127, 148, 161

O'Conner, Robert, 3
O'Leary, Michael, 15
Ogle, David B., 139

party caucus, 43, 44, 69, 74, 85
party match, 110-11, 112, 117-28
party voting, 1-2
Patterson, Samuel C., 3, 35, 106
Peroff, Kathleen, 3
Petrocik, John R., 148, 161
policy preferences, 153-70, 171-78
Polsby, Nelson W., 24, 38
Porter, H. Owen, 24
Price, David, 78
Przeworski, Adam, 145

Ranney, Austin, 26
Ransone, Coleman B., Jr., 108, 128
Rao, Potluri, 130
reapportionment, 81
Report of the Committee on American Legislatures, 1
responsible party government, 26
Rieselbach, Leroy N., 78
Ritt, Leonard G., 140, 144, 145, 169, 177
Robinson, James A., 2, 140
Robinson, W. S., 146
Rockman, Bert A., 186
roll call voting, 1-2, 21
Rosenthal, Alan, 3, 25, 76, 77-78, 80, 81, 101, 136, 138, 139, 141, 182
Rosenthal, Howard, 17, 18, 19

scales: general party orientation, 13, 30, 46, 47, 48-64, 65-68, 69-73, 99-102, 103; legislative party orientation, 13, 30, 47-64, 65-68, 69-73, 95, 101-02, 103, 182; full-time legislator orientation, 14, 149, 150-66, 170-73, 174-78; legislator staff orientation, 15, 84, 85, 87-92, 93-94, 95-97, 98, 99-102, 103 149, 150-70, 171-73, 174-78; legislative expertise orientation, 15; gubernatorial orientation, 16, 112, 114-17, 119, 120-25
Schlesinger, Arthur M., Jr., 106
Schlesinger, Joseph A., 108
Shaffer, William R., 142, 167, 186
Shapiro, Michael, 21, 22
Sharkansky, Ira, 24, 36, 108, 133-34, 143, 146
Smith, C. Lynwood, Jr., 139
Stimson, James A., 7, 21, 22, 23, 25, 28, 37, 38, 39, 40, 41, 74, 180, 181-82, 187, 188
Stokes, Donald E., 186
Sullivan, John L., 143
survey: county party chairmen, 185-86; state bureaucrats, 185-86

Tantillo, Charles, 139
Texas, 5
Theil, Henri, 178
Thorpe, Alan, 21

Uslaner, Eric M., 3, 8, 77, 115, 141, 142, 144, 148, 180, 184

Verba, Sidney, 148, 161
Virginia, 4, 107

Wahlke, John, 3
Walker, Jack L., 10, 143, 146
Watts, Meredith, 170, 173

Weber, Ronald E. , 3, 115, 130, 141, 142, 144, 146, 148, 167, 180, 184, 186
Weisberg, Herbert F. , 22
West Virginia, 81
Wildavsky, Aaron, 146
Williams, J. Oliver, 107
Wilson, Woodrow, 74–77, 78, 79, 80, 84, 101, 182

Winters, Richard F. , 2, 108, 143
Wisconsin, 81, 182
Wissel, Peter, 3
Wright, Deil S. , 108–09, 133

Young, James Sterling, 39

Zeller, Belle, 1, 75
Ziegler, Harmon, 107

ERIC M. USLANER is Assistant Professor of Government and Politics at the University of Maryland—College Park. From 1972 to 1975, he was Assistant Professor of Political Science at the University of Florida. He received his B.A. from Brandeis University in 1968 and his M.A. and Ph.D. in political science from Indiana University in 1970 and 1973. His major research interests, in addition to comparative state politics, are in the areas of Congress and American political parties, research methodology, and mathematical models of political behavior. He is the coauthor of How American Foreign Policy Is Made (Praeger, 1974; second edition forthcoming, 1978) and is editor of Sage University Papers on Quantitative Applications in the Social Sciences. His articles have appeared in the American Political Science Review, American Journal of Political Science, Political Methodology, Behavioral Science, American Behavioral Scientist, American Politics Quarterly, Sage Professional Papers in American Politics, and other journals and collections of articles.

RONALD E. WEBER is an Associate Professor of Political Science and Director of the Political Science Laboratory and Data Archive. The holder of a Ph.D. from Syracuse University, he is the author of several articles and monographs on public policy making in the American states. Currently, he is conducting research on the policy preferences of American state elites.

LEGISLATIVE POLITICS IN NEW YORK STATE:
A Comparative Analysis

Alan G. Hevesi

LEGISLATIVE REVIEW OF GOVERNMENT PROGRAMS:
Tools for Accountability

Edgar G. Crane, Jr.

STATE CONSTITUTIONAL CONVENTIONS: The Politics
of the Revision Process in Seven States

Elmer E. Cornwell, Jr.
Jay S. Goodman
Wayne R. Swanson

STATE GOVERNMENT PRODUCTIVITY: The
Environment for Improvement

Edgar G. Crane
Bernard F. Lentz
Jay M. Shafritz